Press and Speech Freedoms in the World, from Antiquity until 1998

PRESS AND SPEECH FREEDOMS IN THE WORLD, FROM ANTIQUITY UNTIL 1998

A Chronology

Compiled by
Louis Edward Ingelhart

Greenwood Press
Westport, Connecticut • London

Library of Congress Cataloging-in-Publication Data

Ingelhart, Louis E. (Louis Edward)
  Press and speech freedoms in the world, from antiquity until 1998
  : a chronology / compiled by Louis Edward Ingelhart.
    p.   cm.
  Includes bibliographical references and indexes.
  ISBN 0–313–30851–9 (alk. paper)
    1. Censorship—History—Chronology.   2. Freedom of the press—
  History—Chronology.   3. Freedom of speech—History—Chronology.
  I. Title.
  Z657.I525   1998
  363.3′1′09—dc21   98–21823

British Library Cataloguing in Publication Data is available.

Library of Congress Catalog Card Number: 98–21823
ISBN: 0–313–30851–9

First published in 1998

Greenwood Press, 88 Post Road West, Westport, CT 06881
An imprint of Greenwood Publishing Group, Inc.

Printed in the United States of America

The paper used in this book complies with the
Permanent Paper Standard issued by the National
Information Standards Organization (Z39.48–1984).

10 9 8 7 6 5 4 3 2 1

CONTENTS

PREFACE

When articulate speech became recordable, it became possible to trace the history of expression and efforts to achieve freedom for that expression. That journey has been fraught with dangers and repression. How free expression has fared as the twenty-first century begins is demonstrated by this chronology. *Press and Speech Freedoms in the World, from Antiquity until 1998* attempts to record many of the human endeavors to establish an atmosphere of freedom and free expression throughout the world in nations other than the United States. It presents episodes and viewpoints year by year and, whenever possible, in alphabetical order within each year reported. The book is a companion volume to *Press and Speech Freedoms in America, 1619-1995* published by Greenwood Press in 1997.

Since we have inherited many ideas about freedom from England and other nations, this book grew as a logical companion to the first. Our heritage has been somewhat complex and confused, however. In order to understand it, this book presents viewpoints and actions of persons or agencies either very much pro-freedom or partially or completely opposed to such freedom. The quotations, viewpoints, episodes, and actions presented herein demonstrate the slow journey toward freedom and the disappointments of backward steps.

Although more items could have been included, it was necessary to keep the book of a manageable length. The author used his sense of significance in selecting the items and some of the longer quotations were edited for length. In no instance, however, was there an alteration of what was said or what actually happened. Fortunately, there was considerable material available about England, the country that had the greatest impact upon our present situation; data from other nations was also voluminous.

Chapters 2, 4, 5, 6, 8, and 9 report on England; Chapters 1, 3, 7, and 10 cover other nations. Both England and other nations appear in Chapters 11, 12, 13, 14, and 15. In Chapter 16, the emphasis of the book changes from the nature of free expression in individual nations to international agencies. The new chronology covers international agencies from around 1927, when they entered the discussion, until today, primarily through the functions of United Nations agencies.

The author's concerns and interests in the history of free expression were greatly heightened by Frank Luther Mott, dean of the journalism school at the University of Missouri, where the author earned his Ph.D. in journalism in 1953.

Chapter 1

FROM ANTIQUITY TO PRINTING

30,000 B.C. to 1499

Humankind attained its present stature a little more than 100,000 years ago. It took another 50,000 years to develop regularized and articulate speech. First evidence of recorded ideas was found in extensive drawings discovered in 1995 in a cave in France. These drawings pre-date the pictograph discoveries in Italy dating back to 15,000 B.C.[1]

4000 to 2550 B.C.

Words could be written in 4000 B.C. in Mesopotamia. By 2550 B.C. Mesopotamians were using carved cylinder wheels as a quick way of printing clay tablets.[2]

3500 B.C.

The Armeoid Sumarians invented their writing in 3500 B.C. Sumarians used pictorial signs and signals for things, numbering, and even abstract ideas and terms; they established schools and the cylinder seal which might be considered the first form of printing. Cuneiform writing developed in Babylon.

3400 B.C. to 400 B.C.

The Egyptians developed their hieroglyphic picture language. By 2500 B.C. they were manufacturing papyrus paper. In 2400 B.C. Ptahhgote, governor of Egypt, said, "Do not repeat slander; you should not hear it, for it is the result of hot temper."[3]

2050 B.C.

Urakagina, king of Lagash, used the word "freedom" for the first time in history and he restored many of the rights of the people.[4]

2000 B.C.

The Minoans had a script language in Crete in 2000 B.C.

1900 B.C.

In 1900, the Egyptians developed an alphabet which they would use until 400 B.C.[5]

1800 B.C.

A phonetic alphabet and lettering existed in Canaan in 1800 B.C.[6]

1765 B.C. to 1100 B.C.

Books existed during the Chang dynasty in China in 1765 B.C. An 1100 B.C. Chinese proverb of the twelfth century said, "Remember always to tell the truth, for the tongue is ever at the bottom of calamity."[7]

1600 B.C.

Syrians began using a purely phonetic alphabet in 1600 B.C.

1000 B.C. to 500 B.C.

According to the Rabbinical Talmud a person who can protest and does not, is an accomplice in the act. "First learn, then form opinions."[8]

Other statements concerning freedom of expression appear frequently in the Old Testament, among these are the following:

The Preacher said,
"Of making many books there is no end, and much study is a weariness of the flesh." (Ecclesiastes 12:12)

Isaiah 35:5-6 said, "The eyes of the blind will be opened, and the ears of the deaf unstopped; Then the lame shall leap like a deer, and the tongue of the speechless sing for joy."

Isaiah reported that God said,"Woe to those who decree iniquitous decrees, and the writers who keep writing oppression to turn aside the needy from justice and to rob the poor of my people of their right, that widows may be their spoil, and that they may make the fatherless their prey!" (Isaiah 10:1-2)

"Then Jeremiah took another scroll and gave it to Baruch, the scribe, who wrote on it at the dictation of Jeremiah all the words of the scroll which Jehoiakim, king of Judah, had burned in the fire; and many similar words were added to them." (Jehudi, the king, had burned the original scrolls, piece by piece, cut off by a pen knife because he did not like the prophecy of Jeremiah.) Jeremiah 36:19-32

Job said, "How forcible are right words!" (Job 6:25)

Eliphaz the Temanite said, "For your iniquity teaches your mouth, and you choose the tongue of the crafty. Your own mouth condemns you, and not I; your own lips testify against you." (Job 15:5-6)

Job said, "Oh, that my words were written! Oh, that they were inscribed in a book! Oh, that with an iron pen and lead they were graven in the rock forever! (Job 19:23-24)

Proverbs said, "He that uttereth a slander is a fool." (Proverbs 10:18)

Proverbs 17:28 said, "Even a fool, when he holdeth his peace, is counted wise."

Proverbs said, "A fool uttereth all of his mind." (Proverbs 29:11)

900 B.C.

The earliest known Greek inscription was found on a stone in Thera.[9]

850 B.C.

Homer said, "Speak out, hide not thy thoughts."[10]

800 B.C.

The Phoenicians developed the first modern type alphabet and introduced it into Rome by 800 B.C.

600 B.C.

Confucius said, "They who know the truth are not equal to those who love it, and they who love it are not equal to those who delight in it."[11]

Confucius also said, "Of what value is smartness of speech? Opposing a man with the mouth excites anger."[12]

The 600 B.C. royal library at Ninevah was one of several established by the Babylonians and the Assyrians.

594 B.C.

Solon outlawed evil speaking about the living and the dead.

550 B.C.

Lao-Tze, Chinese philosopher, said, "Be sparing of speech, and things will come right of themselves."[13]

450 B.C.

The books of Amaxagoras, a Greek philosopher, were burned because his research was considered derogatory to the gods. He was exiled.[14]

451 B.C.

Ancient Rome had libel laws in its *Twelve Tables* in 451 B.C.

442 B.C.

Sophocles, Greek playwright, said, "Nobody likes the bringers of bad news."[15]

440 B.C.

Herodotus, Greek historian, said, "It is my duty to report all that is said, but I am not obliged to believe it all alike.[16]

431 B.C.

Pericles extolled freedom of speech when he praised Athenian soldiers of the Pelopennesian War.[17]

409 B.C.

Dionysus the Elder, a Greek military leader, said in the fourth century B.C., "Let thy speech be better than silence, or be silent."[18]

Euripides wrote, "This is true liberty when free born men, having to advise the public, may speak free; which he who can and will, deserves high praise; who neither can nor will, may hold his peace; what can be juster in a state than this?"

His characters in his play *Ion* said:
Jocasta: Where for exiles lies its sting?
Polyneices: This most of all — a curb is on the tongue.
Jocasta: This is the slave's lot, not to speak one's thought!
Polyneices: The unwisdom of his rulers must one bear. Of Athen's daughters may my mother be, that by my mother may free speech be

mine. The alien who entereth a burg of pure blood, burger through he be in name, hath not free speech, he bears a bondman's tongue.[19]

408 B.C.

Plato said, "As to the people, they have no understanding, and only repeat what their rulers are pleased to tell them.[20]

400 B.C.

Plato wrote, "The poet shall compose nothing contrary to the ideas of the lawful, or just, or beautiful, or good which are allowed in the state; nor shall he be permitted to show his composition to any private individual, until he shall have given them to the appointed censors and the guardians of the law, and they are satisfied with them.[21]

399 B.C.

Socrates was executed in 399 B.C. by Athens authorities. His unrelenting questions of popular ideas were believed to encourage young men to disrespect traditional values. The jury asked Socrates to moderate his method; when he refused he was sentenced to drink poison.

Socrates said:
"In me you have a stimulating critic, persistently urging you with persuasion and reproaches, persistently testing your opinion and trying to show you that you are really ignorant of what you suppose you know. Daily discussions of the matters about which you hear me conversing is the highest good for me. Life that is not tested by such discussion is not worth living.

"Men of Athens, I honor and love you; but I shall obey the god rather than you, and while I have life and strength I shall never cease from the practice and teaching of philosophy, exhorting anyone whom I meet, after my manner, and convincing him.

"I tell you that virtue is not obtained by money, but that from virtue come money and every other good of man, public as well as private. This is my teaching, and if this is the doctrine which corrupts the youth, my influence is ruinous indeed.

"For if you kill me you will not easily find another like me, who, if I may use such a ludicrous figure of speech, am sort of gadfly, given to the state by the god; and the state is like a great and noble steed, who is tardy in his motions owing to his very size, and requires to be stirred into life. I am that gadfly which the god has given the state, and all day long and in all places am always fastening upon you, arousing and persuading and reproaching you.

"Some one will say: 'Yes, Socrates, but cannot you hold your tongue; and then you may go into a foreign city and no one will influence with you?' If I tell you that this would be disobedience to a divine command, and therefore that I am serious; and If I say again that the greatest good of man is daily to converse about virtue and all that concerning which you hear me examining myself and others, and that the life that is unexamined is not worth living—that you are still less likely to believe.

"If you say to me, Socrates, this time we will let you off, but upon one condition, that you are not to inquire and speculate in this way any more, and if you are caught doing this again you shall die: If this was the condition on which you let me go, I should reply: my friend, why do you, who are a citizens of the great and mighty and wise city of Athens, care so much about laying up the greatest amount of money and honor and reputation, and so little about wisdom and truth and the greatest improvement of the soul, which you never regard or heed at all? Are you not condemning me?

"And now, Athenians, I am not going to argue for my own sake, as you may think, but for yours, that you may not sin against the god, or lightly reject his benefits by condemning me.

"And as you will not easily find another like me; I would advise you to spare me.

"Do not be angry with me if I tell you the truth."[22]

268 B.C.

Zeno, leader of the Greek Stoic concept of philosophy, said that natural law is based on a strong belief in an over-riding power of a divine providence. Stoicism proclaimed a universal, unchangeable standard of right and just thought and action. Since it recognized that customs varied from place to place, it contended that two legal systems existed simultaneously. One was the customary law and the other was the natural law. The concept of natural law appeared in many ages and civilizations thereafter.

250 B.C.

The ruler of China burned books pertaining to Confucius and had hundreds of the philosophers' disciples buried alive. This persecution of Confusicianism continued for many years. The *Analects* written by Confucius were burned. Since Emperor Shih Huang Ti's purpose was to destroy the traditional culture of China, he also burned all other books except those about medicine, agriculture, science, and divinations, which he put in his imperial library.

210 B.C.

Callimachus, an Alexandrian poet and librarian, warned symbolically that "a big book is a big evil."[23]

The office of the Censors was one of the noblest institutions of the ancient Roman Commonwealth; their chief province was to direct and preserve the public discipline and manners, to preside at the Tribunal of Fame, to reward the brave and virtuous with masks of honour and distinction and to brand the degenerate and corrupt with dishonour and ignominy. This institution was of admirable use in maintaining the morals and virtues of the people; and at the same time highly contributed to support the vigor of the laws, and to preserve or restore the Roman Constitution to its first principles. [24]

168 B.C.

When Antiochus sought to unify religion by forbidding the ancient Jewish worship, resistance developed and non-conformists were executed.[25]

Publius Syrus, a first century Latin writer, said, "Speech is the mirror of the soul; as a man speaks, so he is."[26]

58 B.C. to 44 B.C.

Cicero, Roman orator, said, "We must make a personal attack when there is no argumentative basis for our speech."[27]

"Actually he believed in 50 B.C. in a constant, eternal law of right reasons in agreement with natural law." In 44 B C. he said, "Freedom suppressed and again regained bites with keener fangs than freedom never endangered."[28]

43 B.C.

Publius Syrus, Latin writer, said, "Where liberty has fallen, no one dares speak freely."[29]

42 B.C. to 40 B.C.

Roman Emperor Tiberius had reformers report on Romans uttering objectionable comments. Julius Caesar in 40 B.C. produced his Acta Diurna as a report to the public of the Roman Senator's actions.[30]

8 B.C.

Horace, Roman poet, said, "Painters and poets have always had licence to dare anything. We know that, and we both claim and allow to others in their turn, this indulgence."[31]

12 A.D. to 50 A.D.

During his lifetime Jesus Christ discussed news and communications from time to time. In 12 A.D., when he was only a 12-year-old child, he astounded his listeners with philosophy and law when he spoke in the temple in Jerusalem. Later he said: "And ye shall know the truth, and the truth shall make you free."[32]

[The Lord has sent me] "to preach good news to the poor, he has sent me to proclaim release to the captives and recovering of sight to the blind, to set at liberty those who are oppressed." (Luke 4:18)

"I must preach the good news of the kingdom of God to the other cities also; for I was sent for this purpose." (Luke 4:43)

"...many prophets and kings desired to see what you see, and did not see it, and to hear what you hear, and did not hear it." (Luke 10:24)

"Do you think that I have come to give peace on earth? No, I tell you, but rather division." (Luke 12:51)

His followers also commented in 50 A.D.
Colossians says, "Let your speech be always with grace, seasoned with salt." (Colossians 1:6)

Paul reported in Acts 19:19 that "a number of those who practiced magic acts brought their books together and burned them in the sight of all; and they counted the value of them and found it came to fifty thousand pieces of silver."

65 A.D.

Seneca, Roman dramatist, said, "Let us say what we feel what we say; let speech harmonize with life."[33]

In the first century, Seneca also said that freedom cannot be bought for nothing. "If you hold her precious, you must hold all else of little worth."
"When I think over what I have said, I envy dumb people."[34]

100 A.D.

A Burmese proverb said, "Too much talk will include errors."[35]

Use of the codex system of binding flat and uniform size pages into a volume replaced the old scroll system.[36]

Plutarch, a Greek historian, said, "It is a thing of great difficulty to raise objections against another man's oration,—nay, it is a very easy matter, but to produce a better one in its place is a work extremely troublesome."

110 A.D.

Tacitus, a Roman historian, said, "It is the felicity of the times that you may think as you wish and speak as you think."[37]

170 A.D.

Lucian of Samosata, Greek satirist and artist, said, "It is better to guard speech than to guard wealth."[38]

200 A.D.

Epictetus, a Greek philosopher said, "First learn the meaning of what you say and then speak."[39]

Juvenal, a Roman satirist, said, "Many suffer from the incurable disease of writing, and it becomes chronic in their sick minds."[40]

300 to 380 A.D.

The Roman Church forbade Christians in Carthage to own or circulate the writings of pagans or unbelievers, or of other anti-religious works. However, the Roman Empire permitted religious freedom until Emperor Constantine made Christianity the state religion.

In that same year, Arius, the presbyter of Alexandria, was condemned by the Council of Nicea for his *Thaleia.* Constantine ordered its destruction. This was among the first writings banned by the Catholic Church.

In 380, Rome made blasphemy and heresy state crimes.[41]

642 A.D.

More than 700,000 manuscripts in the library at Alexandria were burned in various attacks by Romans, Christians, and Arabs. In 642, Omar, the Arabian leader, used the burning books to heat bath water. He said, "These books are either in accordance with the teaching of the Koran or they are opposed to it. If in accord, then they are useless since the Koran itself is sufficient, and if in opposition, they are pernicious and must be destroyed."[42]

496 A.D.

A catalog of prohibited books called *The Descretum Gelascanium* was issued in Rome in 496 by Papal authorities.

960 A.D.

As the Sung dynasty unfolded, book printing from wood blocks became very wide-spread in China. That's why the works of Confucius and other scholars became widely distributed.[43]

1090 A.D.

Sue Che reported to the Che T'sung emperor that "people of this dynasty make blocks for printing. Many of the books thus produced are circulating there. Ignorant, common people have been printing even obscene literature in order to make a profit. If books were allowed to spread freely to the north, they might, either reveal national secrets or arouse the barbarians' contempt and disgust. Either would be bad." The Board of Rites set up censorship procedures and punishments in 1090.

1100 A.D.

Marie de France, a French poet, said in the twelfth century that the fool shouts loudly, thinking to impress the world.[44]

A Japanese proverb said, "The tongue is more to be feared then the sword."[45]

A series of rulings to suppress rumors affecting local governments was issued in 1100 as the *Medieval Scandalum Magnatum*. Its concepts included provisions that a prosecutor had to prove the falsity of any writings that were objected to and that dissemination of any information against the government was a crime. Inventing such information was an even graver criminal offense. "From henceforth none be so hardy to tell or publish any false news or tales, whereby discord or occasion of discord or slander may grow between the King and his people or the Great Men of the Realm."

1184 A.D. to 1252 A.D.

Pope Lucius III ordered the inquisitions of heretics in 1884; by 1215, Pope Innocent III told members of the Roman Church to exterminate heretics. One million persons were subsequently executed. Pope Gregory IX set up a tribunal of inquisition in Rome in 1231. Pope Innocent IV forbade translating the Bible into vernacular languages in 1252.

1253 A.D.

Hangzhou, capital of the Song Dynasty in China and probably the largest city in the world, had an extensive book printing industry.[46]

1258 A.D.

Sadi, a Persian author, said, "In the faculty of speech man excels the brute; but if thou utterest what is improper, the brute is thy superior."[47]

1273 A.D.

Thomas Aquinas produced his *Summa Theologica*. It presented the philosophy of scholasticism which believed knowledge came from the truths of the Christian faith and the truths of human reason, but the revelation which comes from faith is the greatest and consists of mysteries to be believed rather than understood. Natural law as conceived by Aquinas provided that "man has a right to live as a human person, to perfect his moral nature and to live as a free, intelligent individual. These rights do not depend upon the authority of human government. Laws that are destructive of the natural rights of man or that are destructive of the common good deny natural justice, and therefore are not laws at all."

1275 A.D.

The *Scandalum Magnatum* forbade continuous discussions and provided "from henceforth none be so hardy or occasion of discord of slander may grow between the king and his people or the great men of the realm. A person could defend himself by pointing out that he was merely repeating something and if he would identify its source." By 1388, inventing false information was a greater crime than merely repeating it.[48]

1300 A.D.

Dante Alighieri in his *Divine Comedy* described Hell as a stageless amphitheater and Paradise as a step-pyramid. He was a champion of strong Imperial power. The 14th Century saw the spread of secular literature in the vulgar or common language.[49]

1350 A.D.

Giovanni Boccaccio, an Italian writer, said, "Stories, whatever their nature, may be harmful or useful, depending upon the listeners."[50]

1366 A.D.

De Republica was published in 1366 as the scholastic natural law manual and contained the elements of the natural law of Rome, (*Ius Gentium* and *Ius Naturale*) stemming from stoic philosophers. *Ius Gentium* imposed on every man the duty to play his allowed part in society, whatever it might be.

1381 A.D.

The peasants' revolt was partly inspired by the writings of John Wycliffe, a heretic and Church critic. He called the Pope the Antichrist.[51]

1403 A.D. to 1409 A.D.

King Sejong of Korea said, "To govern, it is necessary to spread knowledge of the laws and the books so as to satisfy reason and to reform men's evil nature; in this way, peace and order may be maintained. Our country is in the East beyond the sea and books from China are scarce. Wood blocks wear out easily and, besides, it is difficult to engrave all the books in the world. I want letters to be made from copper to be used for printing so that more books may be made available. This would produce benefits too extensive to measure." The first book printed from movable type probably was the *Sun-tzu-shi-chu*, published in Korea in 1409.

1446 A.D.

Lawrence Coster developed printing from movable type in 1446 in Harlem, Holland, but its invention languished and was soon forgotten. At least fifteen European cities claim to be the birthplace of printing.[52]

1450 A.D.

Johann Gutenberg perfected and operated a printing press using movable type in Mainz, Germany, in 1450. One of the first items he printed was a Catholic Church indulgence.[53]

1451 A.D.

The first book Gutenberg printed was *The Donatus Latin Grammar.*

1454 A.D.

Gutenberg's second printed book was *Appeal of Christianity Against the Turks* in 1454.

1455 A.D.

After the development of printing few controls existed until Pope Leo X issued his bull, *Contra Errores,* to condemn Martin Luther's teaching. Luther retaliated by burning a copy of the bull.[54]

1456 A.D.

Johann Gutenberg printed his famous Bible in 1456, which demonstrated fully the practicality of printing even major works. E.P. Goldschmidt in 1967 reported this legend: When Gutenberg and Schoeffer had finished the last sheet of their monumental Bible, the financier of the firm, John Fust, took a dozen copies to the University of Paris where 10,000 or more students were studying at the Sorbonne. A powerful guild of the book-trade, the Confrerie des Libraries, Relieurs, Enbimineurs, Ecrivains, et Parcheminiers, became alarmed by such a treasure of books. They called the police because they said only the devil could have provided them, and Fust had to run for his life to save the Bibles from a bonfire.[55]

1457 A.D.

Peter Schoeffer, a son-in-law of John Fust (the banker who foreclosed on a loan to Gutenberg to gain the printing shop) was the first person to print in colored inks. But all the printers had to flee from Mainz with what equipment they could carry because of a military invasion. They then set up printing shops in several German cities. [56]

1482 A.D. to 1496 A.D.

The Spanish Inquisition was used to regulate the press. The archbishop of Treviso set up a legal code demanding church authorization of any book concerning religion in 1482. The archbishop of Mainz set up a committee in 1485 to examine all books. In 1487 the Roman Church required all books had to be approved before publications. In 1496, the archbishop of Mainz threatened to excommunicate persons publishing unauthorized books.

1491 A.D.

The first printed advertisement with an illustration appeared. It advertised *The Lovely Melusina*, and the illustration showed the heroine in her bath. The Antwerp printer started the cheesecake that still engulfs the world.

1493 A.D.

An anonymous German writer in *Burning Books of the Alexandrian Library* reported a historical tradition saying the Great Library at Alexandria which had become the Greco-Roman greatest library repository was destroyed by forces of Julius Caesar. [57]

Chapter 2

ENGLAND STUGGLES INTO THE COMMUNICATIONS AGE
9 A.D. Through 1599

9 to 460

A fiercely independent tribe in northwestern Germany defeated the Roman army commanded by Varus in the Battle of Teutoburg forest in 9 A.D. These Saxons had developed a society of freedom and equality for each person and fought vigorously to maintain that society. In 209, they and neighboring Germanic tribes formed a nation based on the fierce tradition of freedom and independence. At a Saxon convention in 460, a major emigration to England was planned since so many Saxons had gone earlier to England to answer a request of the English King to help resist the Scot and Pict invaders from the north. The Saxons soon took over the government, slaughtering many of the natives, and set up a government similar to the tribal one of Saxony with its traditions of freedom and equality.

597

When Augustine began christianizing the English people, he installed rules against heresy and blasphemy.

735

Alcuin, Anglo-Saxon scholar, said, "The voice of the people is the voice of God."[1]

1066

Before the Norman conquest of 1066, a spreader of false rumors amongst the people had his tongue cut out. The Salisbury Oath, imposed on the English by William the Conqueror, demanded allegiance to him, and vested absolute sovereignty in the

Norman King. English peasants became serfs.

1213-1689

The first proposal for securing an English charter of liberties from King John was made by several nobles in 1213. The Magna Carta was issued at Runnymede in June 1215 by King John under military and political pressure by English nobles. It is the primary source of English civil and political liberties. Henry III, successor to King John, promptly reissued the Magna Carta in 1216 with several alterations. The Magna Carta was reissued with additional changes in 1217. The final revision of the Magna Carta was completed in 1225. Edward I confirmed the Magna Carta in 1297, which was afterward placed on the great roll of English statutes.

William Pitt, Earl of Chatham, said the Magna Carta, and the 1629 Petition of Right, and the 1689 Bill of Rights were the Bible to the English Constitution.[2]

1257

Roger Bacon was suspected by religious authorities of dealing in the black arts in 1257. He was ordered not to write anything for publication for ten years.

1275

Punishing libel began in the statute of Westminister I of 1275. King Edward I ruled that a person arrested for distributing discordant or slanderous stories would have to identify the originator or go to jail. Parliament outlawed "any false news or tales whereby discord or occasion of discord or slander may grow between the king and his people or the great men of the realm."

1298

King Edward I, in attempting to obliterate Scotland, burned the famous library of Restennoth which contained the books King Fergus II brought with him from Rome in 400 A.D. He also burned Scottish registers.[3]

1378

The list of persons who should not be slandered in England grew longer. Rules indicated that slanderous matter must be false and had to be disseminated. Parliament outlawed false speech which would destroy the realm by subversion.

1381 to 1428

John Wycliffe, England cleric, said, "I believe in the end the truth will conquer." (Wycliffe translated the Bible into English in 1384.)[4]

The Synad of Pisa condemned Wycliffe's works which were burned at Oxford in 1412.

More than 200 works of Wycliffe were burned in the courtyard of a Prague palace.

The bones of Wycliffe were dug up in 1428 and burned to punish him for the heresy of translating the Bible, and for denying transubstatiation.[5]

John Ball, a revolutionary priest, demanded that England eliminate class distinctions. He was convicted of treason, drawn, hanged, and quartered.[6]

1408

English Catholic church leaders prohibited translating the Bible into English in 1408 unless the proposed translation was examined and approved by church authorities. The Provincial Council took this action because of the Wycliffe heresies in 1382. The synod of Canterbury forbade translating scriptures from one tongue to another.[7]

1457

Reginald Pecock, a bishop of St. Asaph and of Chichester, was condemned by the King and the Lords for his theological views and writings, but quickly recanted those views and turned over 14 volumes as a forced choice to avoid execution; even so he was imprisoned.[8]

1476

The king was entitled to regulate printing because he was the one who brought it to England, strict control was necessary to assure stability and peace, and that it was established when the first press was set up, by Caxton at Westminister, probably on his own initiative.[9]

1481

One of the earliest books printed by Caxton in 1481, *Mirrour of the World*, contained the prophetic adage *Vox Audita perdit, littera scripta manet*: (The spoken word passes away, the written word remains).

An English law prohibited use of William Tyndale's translation or any other annotated Bible in English.[10]

1486

Henry VII issued a warning against "forged tydings and tales."[11]

1487

England established its Court of Star Chamber in 1487 which used the oath ex-officio to obtain quick convictions. The Star Chamber supplemented the *de Scandalum Magnatum* law with the Roman laws of *injuria* and *libellous famosis*, which treated verbal insults as crimes.[12]

1510

The first English copyright was issued.[13]

1514 to 1535

Thomas More wrote Utopia as a tract to rub in the lessons of Erasmus, leader of the new enlightenment. It condemned all-powerful autocracy, the new economics of large, private farms, and the destruction of the old common-field agriculture. It pled for religious tolerance and universal education.

Thomas More wrote:
> For oh, it was nuts to the Father of Lies
> As this wily fiend is named in the Bible
> To find its settled, by laws so wise,
> That the greater the truth, the worse the Libel.

Thomas More was knighted and became speaker of the House of Commons, High Stewart of Cambridge and Lord Chancellor in 1521. In 1523, he repeated his claim that all the members of Commons had the right to freedom of speech.

Sir Thomas More and Bishop John Fisher were executed for pro-Catholic views by Henry VIII. More refused to subscribe to the Oath of Succession. He protested that the indictment brought against him:
> was grounded upon an Act of Parliament, directly repugnant to the laws
> of God and his Holy Church, the supreme government of which, or any
> part thereof, no temporal person may by any law presume to take upon
> him. It is therefore, among Catholic Christians, insufficient in law, to
> charge any Christian to obey it.

His head was exhibited on London Bridge after his death sentence by decapitation was carried out.[14]

1519

"Seven godly martyrs" were burned at Coventry for teaching their children "The Lord's Prayer" and "The Ten Commandments" in English, according to John Foxe.[15]

1520

Martin Luther's writings reached England within three years. They were soon burned by the English Catholic King. They were forbidden in Scotland in 1525.[16]

1521

The English clergy staged a demonstration against heretical books at St. Paul's in London. Luther's books were burned, and Henry VIII was named "Defender of the Faith" by Pope Leo X in appreciation of a book he submitted.[17]

Assertio septum sacramentorum was usually attributed to Henry VIII while he was still a Catholic. The Pope gave him the title "Defender of the Faith" for it but John Fisher, bishop of Rochester, actually wrote it.[18]

1525

The first protest of the Crown's control of the press followed the printing of the first English New Testament. Bishops abolished the Scriptures and other books in English. John Gough, a London printer, was jailed in Fleet prison for such books; all Lutheran books were banned and burned.[19]

Printing did not became a sound and practical force in England even though it had been introduced back in 1476.[20]

William Tyndale's translation of the New Testament was the first to be printed in English. He fussed with the clergy in Gloucestershire and found London just as antagonistic to his idea to make the Bible so understandable that even a plough boy would know more scripture than most clergymen. He went to the continent, finished his translation, was driven from Cologne, but finally had it printed in Worms.[21]

Ecclesiastical authorities burned many copies of Tyndale's English translation of the Bible, which set the pattern for later translations, which in many cases used much of his work word-for-word.

1526

Thomas Berthelet was arrested by church authorities for publishing three harmless works because he had not submitted them for censorship before printing.[22]

Under the most comprehensive order yet issued, the Bishop of London and the Archbishop of Canterbury became the sole licensers of all books.[23]

1526

Henry VIII issued a list of 18 prohibited books. Three years later the list grew to 85 books.[24]

1527

Henry VIII helped circulate Reformation books to set up a ploy in which he would later stamp them out. This was supposed to please the Pope and trick him into granting Henry a divorce from Queen Catherine.[25]

1527

The English vicar-general prosecuted printer Robert Wyer.[26]

1528

Henry VIII regulated the activities of foreign printers to set up new shops. This effected the first royal control of the press.[27]

Henry VIII issued a list of prohibited books. Ecclesiastical officials were authorized to fine persons guilty of possessing these books but the fines collected were turned over to Henry and the police officials were authorized to punish them.[28]

1530

Henry VIII established the first licensing of printing and the granting of printing monopolies.[29]

Thomas Hutton was executed for publishing a book by William Tyndale; Richard Bayfield and John Teuksburg and Jamey Bainham were burned at the stake for heresy. In 1534, King Henry VIII turned on the Catholics and had Thomas More executed.[30]

1531

The Supplication of Beggars by Simon Fish was suppressed. [31]

Thomas Bilney and James Bainham, English booksellers, were burned in 1532 for reading a prayer book in English and for having English scripture books hidden under floor boards.[32]

1533

King Henry VIII ordered Thomas Cromwell to act against Edward Thwaites' *The Nun's Book* which told of miraculous cures by Sister Elizabeth Barton. The book criticized Henry's divorce and marriage to Ann Boleyn. Seven hundred copies of the book were destroyed and Sister Elizabeth and five clerics were executed.[33]

1534

The Anabaptists, the radical elements of the English Reformed Church, including Mennonites, Hutterites, and other sects, were condemned and censored by Protestants and Catholics.[34]

Henry VIII declared in the Act of Supremacy that the English church was established. Laws recognized that writing could endanger the throne.[35]

Henry VIII ordered that foreign books could not be sold in England. This move was partly motivated to protect local printers from foreign competition.[36]

1536

Richard Grafton sought a patent to have the exclusive right to print Bibles. He applied to Thomas Cromwell, Lord Privy Seal; but Cromwell had the monopoly issued to himself instead.[37]

1538

Thomas Cromwell produced a new translation of the Bible which was heavily edited to eliminate protestant theology. It was known as the "Great Bible," but its democratic and socialistic tone finally lead to Cromwell's execution.[38]

Henry VIII set up comprehensive regulations of the press with licensing, privilege, and censorship. A proclamation made publishers and possessors of some religious works having "divers heresies and erroneous opinions" liable to punishment.[39]

1541

Thomas Somers was convicted of owning books by Luther. He was required to ride from the Tower to Cheapside and be decked in these and other forbidden books when they were burned. But Somers managed to save his copy of the New Testament. He was then jailed in the Tower wherein he died soon thereafter.[40]

1542

Parliament gave legal power to the Crown to regulate the press and public discussions with absolute authority. Records of the Privy Council show proceedings against individuals for "unfitting words" or seditious utterances using or publishing to incorporate under Henry VIII to obtain civic honors, as well as to control scandalous, malicious, schismatical, and heretical printing.[41]

The Privy Council reported there were many seditious words, unfitting words, unseemly words, and evil opinions being printed. They included ballads against Richard Cromwell; Grafton and Richard Barker were accused of printing them, Grafton was imprisoned the second time in 1543. Printing the Bible was restricted.[42]

1539

Parliament made Henry VIII's press control rules official English law in 1539.

The "privilege" designation gave way to a patent or monopoly right for printed materials. They could be manipulated by the crown as a control of printing.[43]

Henry VIII declared William Tyndale's translation of the Bible to be the Great Bible of Henry VIII to be used by the newly reformed Church of England. The printing was supposed to be done in France, but the English had to smuggle printed sheets to England in hats so the printing could be finished. Every church had a copy before long and the king said each man should interpret scriptures for himself. Ultimately, the Catholics burned Tyndale for his translation of the Bible.[44]

1543

Henry VIII personally inspected and approved his official primer book used in school and ordered it the only one permitted.[45]

Six printers were finally released from prison where they had been jailed by the Privy Council for printing unlawful books. The council forced 25 printers to pay a bond to assure they would not print forbidden material. The use of the bonds to assure compliance was heavily used thereafter. Printers were imprisoned frequently.[46]

1544

Henry VIII prohibited books about his war against Scotland to keep scavengers away from the battlefields, even though people were eager for news.[47]

1546

Henry VIII had broken with the Catholic Church and issued a new list of forbidden books but this list condemned schismatic views written in England by Frith, Tyndale, Wickcliffe, Joy, Roy, Basil, Bale, Barnes, Coverdale, Turner, or Tracy.[48]

Three persons were executed under church rules for erroneous opinions.[49]

1547

The press control law based upon the Henry VIII proclamation of 1538 was repealed by Edward VI. The repeal had little effect on the king's control of the press. A May proclamation against seditious rumors was the first of several issued by Edward VI. The Treason Act included the words "by printing." English licensing was aimed primarily against papistical books.[50]

1547

King Edward VI issued a proclamation against seditious rumors.
An order provided taletellers should be punished as vagrants, other control rules said rude or seditious persons should be galley slaves and twenty crown rewards were to be given for turning in taletellers.[51]

Under Edward VI, the press was free to publish Reformation literature.[52]

1551

The Scottish estates forbade all printing "Unto the Tyme the Samin be sene, vewit and examit by sum wyse and discreet persons." The licensing system provided that no printer print or sell any matter in the English language, nor sell abroad any matter in foreign languages unless approved in advance by the crown, upon pain of imprisonment or fine.[53]

King Edward revived the press licensing system.[54]

1553

When the coinage was debased proclamations to stop rumors threatened the pillory and the loss of ears. An effort to revive the licensing system was attempted.[55]

Queen Mary issued a proclamation against seditious rumors. Her attitude toward religion was rational and tolerant.[56]

1554

The revision of *De Scandalus Magnatum* added seditious words; even vague or general words could support a common law action if spoken of a magistrate, and truth could not be used as a defense. The statute was administered by the Court of Star Chamber.[57]

William Thomas was executed for conspiracies against Queen Mary and for treason. He was hanged and quartered and his head set upon London Bridge for his writings about the conduct of the clergy in Italy.[58]

A proclamation by Queen Mary commanded "no books, paper, etc., in the name of Martin Luther, John Calvin, Miles Coverdale, Desiderius Erasmus, William Tyndale, etc., or any books containing doctrines against the Catholic faith" be brought to England.[59]

The Stationers Company was incorporated by Queen Mary to provide supervision and regulations of the press. This agency controlled the printing industry by making it a monopoly. The directors of the company were responsible for any abuses contained in printed materials. Printers organized the company, which was granted a charter by the Crown, but having special royal patents made it possible to ignore the company's rules, as did, the universities who claimed they were outside the company's control. Part of the Charter's motivation was to control the spread of heresy, as indicated thus:

> Know ye that we, considering and manifestly perceiving, that several seditious and heretical books, both in verse and prose, are daily published, stamped and printed by divers scandalous, schismatical, and heretical persons, not only exciting our subjects and liegmen to sedition and disobedience to us, our Crown, and dignity, but also to the renewal and propagating of very great and detestable heresies against the faith and sound Catholic doctrine of holy mother the church.[60]

1558

Christopher Goodman's *How Superior Powers Oght to be Obeyd* was the chief source of political disobedience theories. One hundred twenty-five years later it was deemed treasonable and burned at Oxford.[61]

1559

Queen Elizabeth reversed Queen Mary's control of Protestants. In her *Injunctions*, she consolidated her control of the press. She appointed churchmen as licensers, thus assigning control of printing to the Protestant Episcopal Church. As head of the Church, Elizabeth decreed that all new books, pamphlets, plays, ballads, and reprints of works on religion and government had to be approved prior to printing by appropriate officials. Even though licensing was weakly enforced, thirteen printers were fined and imprisoned. The Court of High Commission supplemented the Star Chamber in punishing heresy and sedition.[62]

1566

The Star Chamber issued a decree limiting printers to publish only the most innocuous material. The Privy Council ordered enforcement of licensing provisions and added heavier penalties; each printer had to help finance the enforcement efforts and had to provide sums of money to guarantee they would observe all rules and regulations controlling printing. The company could search for and seize printing matter, including that on ships. Elizabeth issued a Star Chamber decree authorizing it to punish unlicensed printing since so many secret presses were in operation.[63]

1567

The Stationers investigators caught six people dealing in prohibited Catholic works. John Stow was accused of possessing unlicensed books after a search found unlawful papist books in 1569.[64]

1570

The Ecclessiastical Court of High Commission handled libel cases. It used a device called the "oath ex-officio" which meant the accused could be imprisoned for contempt or convicted by his required confession. The Licensing act of Queen Elizabeth required that everything printed had to be submitted to a censor "to stop the Press from publishing anything that might discover the Corruption of the Church or State."[65]

Queen Elizabeth used the Star Chamber Court to jail Puritan printer, William Carter who was hanged for his pro-Catholic publications.[66]

1572

John Field and Thomas Wilcocks were sentenced to a year in jail for sponsoring a Puritan pamphlet pointing out errors in ecclesiastical government. They argued that they wrote it during Parliament time, thus interpreting the right to petition Parliament as an argument for the free press.

The Puritans issued the pamphlet, *An Admonition to Parliament*, which attacked the bishops and vestiges of the Roman church hanging on in the English church. The government had to destroy Puritan presses to regain control of the press.[67]

1573

Although Queen Elizabeth ordered all Puritan books be brought to the Episcopal bishop of London for destruction, no books were turned in by anyone.[68]

John Whitgift published a reply to a second *Puritan Admonition* written by

Thomas Cartwright. The public debate delighted the Puritans, but the government arrested Printer John Strand and his assistants. His presses were destroyed.[69]

1575

Peter Wentworth told the House of Commons that "The liberty of free speech is the only salve to heal all the sores of this common-wealth. There is nothing so necessary for the preservation of the prince and state as free speech."

He said:

> I find written in a little volume these words, in effect: "Sweet is the name of liberty, but the thing itself has a value beyond all inestimable treasure." So much the more of it behoveth us to take care lest we, contenting ourselves with the sweetness of the name, lose and forego the thing, being of the greatest value that can come unto this noble realm. The inestimable treasure is the use of it in this House. I was never of Parliament but that last and the last session, at both times I saw the liberty of free speech so much and so many ways infringed and so many abuses offered to this honorable council as hath much grieved me, even of very conscience and love to my prince and state. Wherefore to avoid the like I do think it expedient to open the commodities that grow prince and whole state by free speech used in this place, at least so much as my simple wit can gather of it, the which is very little in respect of that wise heads can say therein, and so it is of the more force. Without it it is a scorn and mockery to call it a Parliament house, for in truth it is none, but a very school of flattery and dissimulation, and so a fit place to serve the devil and his angels in and not to glorify God and benefit the common-wealth.[70]

The Stationers Company adopted an order for the weekly search of London printing houses where printing was concentrated. Pairs of searchers reported on work in progress, the number of orders on hand, the identity of customers, the number of employees, and the wages paid. These searchers were an effective check on extensive bootleg printing.[71]

1576

John Foxe wrote his book about protestant martyrs, *The Ecclesiastical History*, to record the deaths of protestants for their religious beliefs. William Tyndale was burned for his translation of the Bible into English.[72]

1579

Queen Elizabeth became infuriated by a pamphlet discussing her possible marriage. Author John Stubbes, a protestant loyal to the Queen nonetheless, had his right hand cut off, but Printer Hugh Singleton was spared even though also sentenced to lose his right hand.

John Wolfe, a fishmonger, set up several secret presses to publish non-political and non-religious books. He refused to agree to the queen's rules saying he would print any lawful book. He insisted upon his liberty to publish and make a living therefrom. The Privy Council jailed him but doing so caused such an uproar that he was released, promoted, and granted publishing privileges. He called himself "The Father of the Book-Trade."[73]

Arthur Hall was fined 500 pounds, imprisoned five months, and dismissed from Parliament for publishing a pamphlet criticizing the speaker of the House of Commons.[74]

Henry Nicholas and his Family of Love religious sect of non-conformists was condemned by Queen Elizabeth for his writings.[75]

The Martin Marprelate Tracts appeared in the 1580s. They were printed on a secret press and poked fun at the clergy. Queen Elizabeth condemned them. They continued until 1588.[76]

1583

Forty-four commissioners were appointed to a permanent Court of High Commission by the Archbishop of Canterbury to fight the Puritans. Very few of the commissioners were active; only Archbishop John Whitgift really functioned. He used the oath ex officio to force unwilling witnesses to incriminate themselves and others. Subsequent archbishops continued the practices based upon 24-inquisitorial interrogatories. Whitgift drove 200 ministers from their positions. His Ecclesiastical Commission soon "stank in the nostrils of English clergy." If a person refused to take the oath he was expelled from his church and sent to jail for contempt. Whitgift used the process to stamp out whatever ideas he disliked.

John Coppin and Elias Thacker were executed and books by Robert Browne and Robert Harrison were burned. These men were proponents of Congregationalism.[77]

1584

William Carter was hanged in 1584 after a search of his house found "other naughty papysticall bookes." He had earlier been called a lewd fellow and been imprisoned several times "for printinge of lewd pamplettes." He was "dranwe from Newgate to Tribourne and there hanged, bowelled, and quartered." Carter was hanged for printing Dr. Gergory Martin's *A Treatise of Schism*, which authorities said would incite women of the court to assassinate Queen Elizabeth. He refused to answer questions of the High Commission about the books.[78]

1586

A periodicals codification law in England restricted printing to London, Oxford and Cambridge, limited the number of printers, and required that books be approved by the Archbishop of Canterbury or his deputies. It established a printing monopoly for 97 members of the stationers company.[75]

1586

The Star Chamber Court became the agency for dealing with printers and printing of unlicensed books. An order which required all books be licensed by the archbishop, who was empowered to restrict printing presses to the licensing considered necessary, became the most comprehensive licensing system yet. Enforcement was jointly done by the Stationers' Company and ecclesiastical authorities. Enforcement varied, being somewhat efficient in 1588, but weak by 1599.

The Star Chamber decree continued the Stationers authority to search and seize unlawful printing. These searches could destroy presses and deface equipment.

The Star Chamber decree gave vast powers of search and seizure to the government, backed printing monopoly, and required the licensing of all books. The Archbishop of Canterbury and the Bishop of London were appointed licensers and all printing had to be done in London or by Cambridge or Oxford universities. The Stationers Company seized unlawful books, and could not elect new printers unless the licensers approved. Severe penalties for violating the rules were stipulated.[80]

Archbishop John Whitgift believed that many scurrilous libels were daily published against the government and the church. The archbishop thought it necessary to have a strict watch to stop any copies going to the press before they had been seen by the bishop of the diocese, or some reverend. He also forbade printing or publishing anything that impinged on doctrine or discipline, or that made any unworthy reflections upon the queen or the state. In spite of this decree, books about religious or political issues, were printed secretly in Britain or smuggled in from abroad.

1586

John Greenwood was imprisoned four years for his Puritan views.[81]

Henry Barrow was imprisoned for his Puritan views. When tried he demanded to see his accusers, but the archbishop sent him to jail wherein he died. Both he and Greenwood wrote extensively while imprisoned.[82]

1587

John Penry, a Welsh Puritan, was jailed 12 days for his *A Treatise on the Aequity of an Humble Supplication.* He was hanged on May 29, 1593.[83]

Peter Wentworth argued for freedom of discussion in Parliament saying that "how can truth appear and conquer until falsehood and all subtleties that should shadow it be found out?" He was imprisoned in the Tower but Queen Elizabeth pardoned him. He then tried to have the House take up the issue but he was ignored.

Peter Wentworth preceded Milton by six years with viewpoints and efforts to provide free discussion in Parliament.[84]

1588

A printer reported that the bishops handled printers by:
> Daily spoilinge, vesting, molesting, hunting, pursuynge, imprisoninge, yea barringe and locking them up close prisoners in the most unwholesome and ugle prysones, and their deteynige them, without bringing them to their answeres, untyl the Lord by death put an ende to their myseries. Some they have haled from their honest labours in their trades and caste them loaden handes and feete with boultes and fetters of yron into cold and noysome prysons close prisoners. Some they have cast into the "Little Ease": some they have cast into the "Myll" causing them to be beaten with Cudgels in their prysones; others in the nighte tyme they have been apprehended and drawen out to their house yea seperatinge them most ugodbye from their wiefes, laboures to their utter undoinge, and the affanishement of their poor wiefes and children. All this barbarous havacke they make without regard of age, sexe, estate or Degree as may appeare by the lamentable estate of those which remayne, and by the deathes of others by them murthered in the persons, whose blood cryeth out from under the aulter; some of us have bin kepte prysoners these 19 monethes for hearinge the scripture read unto us in one of our houses uppon a Lordes day mornings in all godly and peaceable maner, neyther have we bin all this tyme once produced to our answere, or had either errour or cryme obieted against us.

John Udall became a martyr when he died after cruel imprisonment for his *Diotrephes*, a Puritan book.[85]

1589

A series of anonymous tracts were distributed in England which attacked the bishops of the Church of England. They were signed by "Martin Marprelate." The Privy Council summoned John Udall to answer for the tracts, which he had not written, although he had written criticism of the church and did know who Martin

Marprelate was. Udall refused to take the *oath ex officio* and was jailed. After a farcical trial he was found guilty but the judges were hesitant to sentence him to death, so they put him in jail for six months, after which he was called up for sentencing again. Sir Walter Raleigh interceded and Udall's sentence was turned over to Whitgift. After two years of imprisonment, Udall was given a pardon by the queen and died soon thereafter from the illnesses he endured while imprisoned. The Puritan printers of the tracts used a secret press which they moved frequently, but they were finally apprehended. The Puritans mounted a press campaign in the Martin Marprelate tracts. The government destroyed the press, but the Puritans obtained another one which they moved frequently to avoid its destruction, that happened. John Hodgkins and his two helpers were imprisoned for more than a year at the Tower prison to be racked because he would not confess satisfactorily.[86]

1592

Abell Jeffries was imprisoned for refusing to cooperate with authorities collecting books he had printed. The books were to be burned. The bishop had said "Whosoever wrote books to the defamation of her majesty, and to raise rebellion, doe offende against the statute and are felons. They that wrote for Reformation, make books to diffame the Queen and raise rebellion. Therefore the writers for petition to Queen Elizabeth asked that these strict rules be changed, since the actions of the bishops were really the disloyal acts.

Thomas Kyd, an English dramatist, said, "Evil news fly farther than good."[87]

1593

Queen Elizabeth told Commons its only freedom of speech was to say *aye* or *nay* when voting.

John Penry, a Welsh Puritans, was executed for his part in the Marprelate religious tracts which attacked the Presbyterian control system of the church. Penry was probably the chief author of the tracts.[88]

Sir Fancis Bacon said that if "libels and licentious discourse against the state became frequent it is a sign of trouble. We make them live longer if we try to stop them—instead we should correct the cause of the complaints."[89]

1599

The Archbishop of Canterbury and the Bishop of London ordered the burning of many works, including Christopher Marlowe's translation of *Ovid's Elegies*. These were probably burned because they had been printed and bound in the volume that contained Sir John Davies' *Epigrammes*, which satirized contemporary authorities.[90]

The licensing act was sabotaged frequently by printers using hardworking schemes.[91]

Edward Aldee had his type smashed for printing a popish book.[92]

Queen Elizabeth removed the deposition scene from William Shakespeare's *King Richard II* because it concerned royal illegitimacy.

William Shakespeare wrote, "Better a little chiding than a great deal of heartbreak."

Chapter 3

IRREVERENCE AND NEWSPAPERS
1500 Through 1699

1500

Pope Alexander VI said, "Rome is a free city; everyone may write and speak as he pleases. Evil is often spoken of me, but I let it pass."[1]

Leonardo Da Vinci said, "Anyone who in discussion relies upon authority uses, not his understanding, but rather his memory."[2]

At least 255 European cities had printers in 1500. Twenty-million copies of books had been printed in Europe by 1500

Best sellers included 291 editions of Cicero, 91 of the *Latin Bible*, 95 of Virgil, and 57 of Horace.[3]

1501

Pope Alexander VI proclaimed that unlicensed printing would not be permitted, so that publicity would not be given to evil. He set up preventive censorship in Germany.[4]

1505

Erhard Oreglin, an Augsburg printer, put out a news sheet broadside, announcing the discovery of Brazil.[5]

1506

Posted official reports of the Dalmatian War by the magistry of Venice was an effort to offset gossip and printers. A charge of a *gazetta* was required of readers;

hence, the word *gazette* appeared in newspapers.[6]

1507

Rumanians set up printing presses in monasteries to produce religious works and histories, but by 1565 the Turkish rulers stopped all printing and enslaved the Rumanians.

1515

Pope Leo X ordered censorship applied to all translations from Hebrew, Greek Arabic, and Chaldaic into Latin and from Latin into vernacular languages, under the bishops or their delegates or by the *inquisitores haereticae provitatis*. The decree said readers were being sold books which promoted errors in faith and daily life. Even though the Church and its bishops issued many censorship edicts between 1480 and 1515, the invention of printing was believed to have been divinely inspired.

1517 to 1535

Martin Luther's religious activities and writings launched a religious publishing avalanche. Three separate editions of Luther's *Theses* were published by printers in three different cities in December. The *Theses* were known throughout Germany within two weeks and all of Europe within a month. Louise Halborn reported in 1942 that "scholars complained that the whole book market was devoted to books by Luther and his followers and that nobody wished to print anything for the Pope or any material that would offend Luther."

Martin Luther wrote 92 works and these were re-published 220 times in 1518 and 1519.

Pope Leo X denounced the works of Luther as heretical and ordered them burned. Imperial edicts condemned Lutheran tracts in efforts to stop Protestant heresies. Arthur Dicken said in 1968 that "between 1517 and 1520, Luther's publications sold over 300,000 copies. Through printed books and pamphlets Luther was able to reach the minds of Europe. For the first time in history a large reading public judged revolutionary ideas through mass media which used vernacular languages with the arts of the journalist and the cartoonist." Luther described printing as "God's highest and extremist act of grace, whereby the business of the gospel is driven forward."

Pope Leo X issued the bull *Contra Errores* in an effort to control and censor Martin Luther's publications. Luther showed his disdain for the Pope's order by burning it publicly.[7]

Martin Luther published 4,000 initial copies of his *Address to the Christian Nobility of the German Nation* in 1520, followed by many reprintings.[8]

Charles V of the Holy Roman Empire in his Edict of Worms prohibited the printing, sale, possession, reading, illustrating, or copying of any of Martin Luther's works. Luther asked the Elector of Saxony to censor works by Andreas Bodenstein von Karlstat, who was more anti-Catholic than Luther.

Charles V made church laws about publishing, the law of the state and put the printing under the control of the Holy Roman Empire.

Emperor Charles V in the Edict of Worms included as censorable items as both printed and illustrated and included artists, printers, and authors as subject to punishment. The wood blocks used for printing were confiscated in Nuremberg.[9]

Nuremberg and other Protestant towns balanced local support of Lutheran views and public support of the Emperor, a Catholic. At one point the City Council banned all portraits of Luther.[10]

1520 to 1536

Erasmus was considered an author of the second class by the Catholic Inquisition which meant that his *Praise of Folly* could only be read if parts considered objectionable were removed. He was a humanist favoring reforms of the Catholic Church. The book was published in 35 editions, most of which were printed by various printers since Erasmus had no copyright protection in those years.[11]

Erasmus, a Dutch scholar and author, said, in 1536, "Be careful that you write accurately rather than much."[12]

Between 1520 and 1540, the Sorbonne had condemned only eleven printed books, and twelve manuscripts, despite religious contentions and fears of heresy.

King Francis directed Parliament to set up a system of control for publishing. Parliament used the faculty of the Sorbonne as the agency to approve publications in 1521.

The Sorbonne refused to censor books the king wanted censored, and censored books he didn't want censored.

The Sorbonne faculty of theology condemned four works by Erasmus, including his *Colloquies* in 1525.

King Francis reasserted his authority over censorship. The Sorbonne's authority wavered and was almost ended by the French Reformation of the 1530's.

1523

Catholic censors crossed out the Jewish words for *strange* and *gentile* and even longer passages which they found objectionable in a Jewish law code.[13]

1524

Charles V of Belgium issued a list of censored books, relying on church advice as to what books should be prohibited.

1525 to 1527

Nuremberg censored Erhard Schon's *Eyn Wunderlich Weyssagung von dem Babsturm* for its attack on the Roman Catholic Pope. Officials confiscated 600 copies, required the printer thereafter to obtain approval of works to be printed, and told Schon to retire to his shoe shop. Other works censored in Nuremberg included Lucas Cranach's *The Papal Coat of Arms* and *Passionale and Anti-Christ*.

Hans Guldenrund was punished in 1527, in Nuremberg for printing a book against the papacy.

1527

An Anabaptist preacher was burned to death in Nuremberg in 1527. Anabaptists found their writings to be censored by Protestants and Catholics who opposed the beliefs of this reformation sect. Johannes Dabneh in his *Articuli Anabaptistarum* described their beliefs.[14]

1530

The Edict of the Diet of Augsburg required that printed materials name the printer and the place of publication. But this and other edicts proved quite ineffective. Basel printer Kopfl was jailed because he attributed a censored pamphlet to another printer, but officials traced his type faces.[15]

1539

Fernando Columbus, son of Christopher, built up a library of 15,000 books in Seville, Spain, using some of the Explorer's legacy for the purchases. In contrast, Plutarch could only have a library of two volumes in 1374.[16]

Giovanni Paoli, an Italian, set up a press in Mexico City under license from the Spanish Government and the Catholic Church. He printed a news sheet about a Guatemalan earthquake in 1541, and produced a religious book in 1543.[17]

542

Johann Sleidan, German historian, said, "As if to offer proof that God had chosen us to accomplish a special mission, there was invented in our land a marvelous new and subtle art, the art of printing. This opened German eyes even as it is now bringing enlightenment to other countries. Each man became eager for knowledge, not without feeling a sense of amazement at his former blindness.

Parlement described what types of books and manuscripts were unacceptable, and it reaffirmed its power to ban publishing after John Calvin's *Institution Chretienne* was published. The catalog of censored books in France contained 394 works.

1543

Copernicus in his *On the Revolutions of the Heavenly Bodies* pointed out that the earth revolved around the Sun. Since this view contradicted the Catholic notion that the earth was the center of the universe, the book was condemned and made the *Index of Prohibited Books* in 1616.[18]

1545 to 1547

Even though the French king authorized Francois Rabelais to print. his works, the Sorbonne condemned them. The King extended the license for them until 1560. Parlement meanwhile accepted the Sorbonne's list of condemned books, thus making them illegal in France. Thereafter, edicts were poorly enforced. Only obscure printers or boy helpers were arrested or burned at the stake.

Francois Rabelais was listed as a first-class author by the Inquisition. This meant his books, including *Gargantua*, were completely banned in 1547.[19]

1550

Spain issued at least 78 press control decrees between 1550 and 1800.

1553

In Italy copies of the Talmud and additional Hebrew books were burned as anti-Christian. A papel decree in 1554 forbade possession of books written in Hebrew.[20]

Sebastian Castellion, a Protestant teacher at Basel, published his *Treatise of Heretics* which led to furious religious debate.

1559

The *Index Librorum Prohibitorum* was issued under papel authority. This impeded the circulation of forbidden books if a vigilant bishop insisted, but it failed to prevent the books which it condemned from penetrating areas obedient to Rome.

During the counter-reformation designed to oppose Martin Luther, the Inquisition persecuted heretics vigorously, including suppression of heretical books and tracts.[21]

1564

The Roman Catholic Church *Index Librorum Prohibitorum* authorized by the Council of Trent listed books which contained religious doctrinal error, or anti-clerical, lascivious, pornographic, political, magic, demonology, and occult arts materials. These books could not be read by Catholics.[22]

1566

The French Ordinance of Moulins said no one could print, or cause to have printed, any book or treatise without the permission of the king.

1570

Charles V of the Holy Roman Empire issued the Edict of Speyer to forbid printing in out-of-the-way localities.[23]

1571

Pope Pius V forbade the writing of avvisi (news gossip sheets) because he and other church officials had become incensed with the gossip and scandals reported in many of them. It was even illegal to possess a copy of one.

1579

French Hugenots published *Vindicae Contra Tyrannos* in Scotland to justify revolts against bad princes on the basis of Calvinistic beliefs. The Puritans republished it as justification for their revolt in England and execution of Charles I in 1619.[24]

1580

Montaigne, the French essayist, said, "The truth these days is not that which is, but what every man persuades another man to believe."[25]

Niccolo Machiavelli, author of *The Prince*, qualified the right of every man to think all things, speak all things, write all things by pointing out that popular governments suffer because the people are free to speak ill of them. He said princes were wise to allow the citizen to have opinions which please the prince.

Machiavelli's *The Prince* was produced in London rather than Italy and had to be distributed clandestinally. For many years, authors had their books and pamphlets printed in countries other than their own to escape suppressions. Soon scurrilous books about the ribald sex life of the nobility began appearing throughout Europe as a form of protest of tyranny.[26]

1585

Pope Sextus issued a *bando* strengthening Pope Pius' earlier rule which was ineffective in controlling *avvisi*. Here is how the *bando* was enforced in one instance: Hannibal Capello was accused of slander and arrested for an *avviso* he produced in Pesano. He was brought to Rome and taken to the Bridge of St. Angelo. First, one of his hands was cut off, then his tongue was cut out, then he was hanged because he had been judged "a false *menati* and had for many years been a detractor of the honor of persons of every kind, and because he kept and exhibited obscene figures in various postures and libidinous acts, in despair of God and the saints, and because he wrote *avvisi* to heretic princes." His body and its parts were tossed into the Tiber River. In sixteenth and early seventeenth centuries all *menati* were regarded as criminals.

1595

Montaigne, a French essayist, said, "Every abridgment of a good book is a stupid abridgement."[27]

1598

Hugo Grotius, a Dutch lawyer and statesman, was sentenced to life imprisonment for his part in pleading for religious toleration in Holland just after his nation had won its independence from Spain. While in prison he wrote his *Introduction to Dutch Jurisprudence*. His wife managed his escape by hiding him in a large box that supposedly contained his research reference books. They escaped in a frantic dash to France where he entered diplomatic services, He later wrote his *Law of War and Peace*, which was considered the basis for international law.[28]

1600

Giordino Bruno was burned to death by the Inquisition in an open field near St. Peter's Square because he lectured for a new religion different from Reformation Protestantism and Counter-Reformation Catholicism. His book urging the worship of a natural god was also burned.[29]

L'Ecole des Filles, a pornographic book, was internationally known and read throughout the sixteenth and seventeenth centuries.

1603

Miguel de Cervantes, a Spanish writer, said, "There is not the least thing that can be said or done, but people will talk and find fault."[30]

Cervantes, Spanish author of *Don Quixote*, wrote, "The priest bade the barber hand him the books one by one, so that he could see what they were about; for he might find some of them that did not deserve punishment by fire."

"Truth may be stretched, but cannot be broken, and always gets above falsehood, as oil does water."[31]

1609

Johann Kepler wrote *The New Authority* to demonstrate the orbits of planets around the sun as Copernicus had contended. The book was listed in the *Index of Prohibited Books.*[32]

1616

A Catholic Church decree stated Nicholas Copernicus was contrary to scripture and his views were not to be believed or defended. Paolo Antonio Foscarini, head of the Carmelite order, was silenced by the Catholic Church for arguing, in his Carmelite *Letters,* that Copernicus' views agreed with scripture. Nicholas Copernicus' *Epitome* was placed on the Catholic index of prohibited books in 1617.

Tommaso Campanella was jailed in Naples for his writings, but managed to escape and go to France. His *Apologia Pro Galileo* was smuggled to Germany and was published by the Rosicrucians.

1621

A *bando generale* of the Italian government relaxed the rule against *avvisi* by allowing written government permission to produce an *avviso*. If a *menanti* did not have permission he could be punished by scourging, a heavy fine, and five years in prison. The punishment for libel was death. The relaxation, slight as it was, led to the rise of the professional *menati* in Italian society, and thus to the profession of journalism.

1625

Hugo Grotius explained natural law in Protestant terms as serving the maintenance of a social order which had to be consonant with human intelligence and free will of God, "to which beyond all cavil our reason tells us we must render obedience." Grotius reflected deist thought by pointing out that the power of God does not extend over certain things.[33]

1625

Printing began in Ecuador. All printing and publishing were carefully supervised by the government in all Spanish areas.[34]

1631

Theophraste Renaudot became editor of the *Gazette de France* sponsored by Cardinal Richelieu, who granted him the sole privilege to publish news in France. He declared:

In one thing only will I yield to nobody—I mean in my endeavor to get at the truth. At the same time I do not always guarantee it, being convinced that among 500 dispatches written in haste from all countries, it is impossible to escape passing something from one correspondent to another that will require correction from Father Time."[35]

1632 to 1636

Galileo Galilei had to defend his support of Copernicus to the Roman Catholic Inquisitions. It appeared in his *Dialogo,* which also was placed in the Index of prohibited books. Galileo submitted his book *Discourses* to the Vatican censor who required him to add a preface indicating the ideas of the book did not advocate the theories proposed earlier by Copernicus. The Church fired the censor and convicted Galileo of heresy but allowed him to recant his views which he did quite willingly. *Discourses* was on the Vatican's list of prohibited books for at least two centuries, but was widely distributed in countries beyond the control of the Catholic Church.[36]

Galileo was imprisoned in 1633 it Italy for his writings. René Descartes stopped work on his cosmological treatise when he heard about Galileo's imprisonment. Since Galileo's *Discourse* could not obtain an Italian imprimatur in 1636, it was smuggled to Germany when it was published by the Elseviers in Leiden.

1642

The Gazeta was Portugal's first news sheet after Portugal gained its independence from Spain. But it was suppressed for being untruthful and in bad taste. In 1660, the Boaganzas suppressed Portugal's second news sheet and forced Antonio Macedo, editor into exile.

1644

Pope Urban VIII founded the first school of propagandists to spread the Catholic faith among the Teutonic people. Pope Gregory XV founded in 1622 the *Sacre*

Congregatio de Propaganda Fide to supervise missions. Teutonic Germans during World War I, however, embroiled the world in the curse of propaganda which spread like a pestilence throughout the world.[37]

1650

When Swedish theologians asked the government to condemn local scientists for saying the Baltic Sea shape was changing, the government said that God had made both the Baltic and Genesis. Any contradiction between the two works indicated errors in copies of the Bible, since they had the original Baltic Sea to see.

1647

Baltasar Gracian, Spanish priest, said, "Evil reports carry farther than any applause."[38]

Gracian said, "What the multitude says is so, or soon will be so."[39]

1660

The French government jailed many booksellers who soon relocated in other countries and continued publishing there instead of France.

1667

Jean Baptiste Maliene, French dramatist, asked, "Do you think you could keep people from talking?"[40]

1672

Louis XIV invaded Holland partly because he was disturbed by materials published in Dutch gazettes which he considered libelous.[41]

1676

Paolo Sarpi said, "There is no need of books, the world hath too many already, especially since printing was invented; and it is better to forbid a thousand books without cause, than permit one which deserves prohibition."

1685

Pierre Bayle reported that French censors sometimes held up publication of books for as long as five years.[42]

1692

Two men were executed in France for publishing an engraving showing the king and four women who had been his mistresses.

Chapter 4

SCHISMATISM IN ENGLAND
1600 Through 1643

1600

George Abbot, vice chancellor of the University of Oxford, had many pictures burned because they supposedly were too supportive of Roman Catholicism.[1]

Sir Walter Raleigh said, "Books are written to be read by those who can understand them; their possible effect on those who cannot is a matter of medical rather than literary interest."[2]

Sir John Hayward was tried for treason in 1600 because Queen Elizabeth objected to his *Life of Henry IV*. The Bishop of London had the book burned. Hayward was jailed but Sir Francis Bacon interceded to save his life.[3]

John Wolfe couldn't get a London printing license but he printed and sold whatever he wanted until his presses were seized and he was imprisoned.[4]

Several written materials were burned because of offences against morality. These included: John Marsten's *Pigmalion, Metamorphosis of Pigmalion's Image, and Scourge of Villainy;* Edward Gulpin's *Skialatheia;* Thomas Middleton's *Micro-Cyncion;* John Davies' *Epigrams;* Robert Tafte's translation of *The Booke Against Woemen;* and an anonymous book *The xv Joyes of Marriage.* Two books by Samuel Rowlands were burned — *A Merry Metinge* and *The Letting of Humous Blood in the Headvaine.*[5]

Only two printers—John Twyn and William Anderton—were executed in the seventeenth century for treasonable publications. Twyn was hanged, drawn, and quartered and Anderton was hanged.[6]

1601

Queen Elizabeth announced that the Common Law Courts would handle printing patent questions. She revived the powers of ecclesiastical officers and added the authority to fine, imprison, and excommunicate persons deemed guilty of heretical writings or seditious opinions.[7]

1602

William Shakespeare wrote, "Words pay no debts."[8]

1603

Church law said no plays could be presented in English churches or church graveyards.

1604

Seven-hundred-fifty English preachers asked James I to do away with the *oath ex officio* when he became king, but he was only angered by the request.

1605

Provisions in the English *De Libellis Famosis* law included:
A libeler could be punished at indictment of common law or *ore tenus* on his confession in the Star Chamber. Libel against a common person also was a criminal offense. Invention of libel of any kind was a criminal offense. The dead could be libeled. Publication was libelous since the material was written or printed. Truth was immaterial and persons could be tried in Common Law Courts or in the Star Chamber. A law said actors could not use profanity in plays.[9]

In the *De Libellis Famosis* law, Attorney General Edward Coke and the Star Chamber said that libels made against a private person, and libels made against magistrates or public persons are different in effect because the latter is a greater offense because it concerns not only a breach of the peace, but also the scandal of government.
For what greater scandal of government can there be than to have corrupt or wicked magistrates to be appointed and constituted by the king to govern his subjects under him? And greater imputation to the state cannot be than to suffer such corrupt men to sit in the sacred seat of justice. It is not material whether the libel be true or whether the party against whom it is made be of good or ill fame, for in a settled state of government the party grieved ought to

complain for every injury done him in any ordinary course of law, and not by any means to revenge himself either by the odious course of libeling or otherwise.[10]

Francis Bacon, British essayist and philosopher, said "Liberty of speech inviteth and provoketh liberty to be used again, and so bringeth much to a man's knowledge."[11]

1610

James I promised to appoint commissioners to investigate "what shall be put to the presses, either concerning our Authorities Royall, or concerning our government or the lawes of our kingdome." The law-making power of Parliament was thought limited by the existence of fundamental natural law.

Conrad Vorst's *Tractatus theologuius de Deo* was burned by James I.[12]

1611

Ecclesiastical courts had complete control of all printed materials. King James I ruled, "And also we give full authority to inquire and search for all heretical, schsimatical, and seditious books, libels, and writings, and all other books, pamphlets, and portraitures offensive to the state or set forth without sufficient and lawful authority, and to seize and dispose of the presses and books thus found."

1612

Francis Bacon, British philosopher said, "Some books are to be tasted, others to be swallowed, and some few to be chewed and digested."[13]

Bartholomew Legate and Edward Wightman were among the last persons to die in England for their religious beliefs. They were burned to death in Smithfield for heretical religious views and writings.[14]

1613

Leonard Busher believed few errors and few books would be written and printed, "seeing all false ministers, and most people, have little or nothing else, besides the fathers, to build their religion and doctrine upon."

Busher, an obscure Baptist layman in England wrote, "Even as the chaff before the wind cannot stand, so error before truth cannot abide." He told King James I that "It ought to be lawful for every person or persons, yea, Jews and Papists, to write, dispute, confer and reason, print or publish, any matter touching religion, either for or against whomsoever provided they allege no fathers for proof on any point of religion, but only the holy scriptures."[15]

George Wither was jailed for four months by the Privy Council for his *Abuses Stript and Whipt*, even though the licenser had approved it for publication.[16]

1615

William Martin was forced to remove passages objected to by the king in *Historie and Lives of the Kings of England*.[17]

1616

James I denied freedom of discussion in England when he told the Star Chamber it was presumption and high contempt to dispute what the king could do.

1617

King James I burned Richard Mocket's *Doctrina*. Mocket was so shaken that he died within a year.[18]

1621

Thomas Archer was imprisoned because he published an unlicensed newsbook even though there was no licensing requirements.[19]

Nicholas Bourne and Nathaniel Butter became the only approved newsbook publishers until 1632. They were fined for publishing a decree by the French king. They were fined and had to pay damages to Nathaniel Newberry who had the patent on it.[20]

News sheets and newsbooks were published in England, but James I tried to suppress both Dutch and English corantos. The first coranto approved by the clerk of the council appeared in England. It bore the inscription "Published by Authority."[21]

The Court stripped W. Aldee of his right to be a "liverie man" until he submitted to the English court for having printed books without licenses.[22]

Sir Francis Cottingham, became licenser and censor of newsbooks.[23]

James Floyd, an ardent Catholic and an old man, was abused by Commons for his views, He was arrested and members of the House concocted all sorts of lies about him. So they pilloried him three times, made him ride backward on a horse, labeled with his offense, and fined 1,000 pounds. The king ruled Commons had no authority to do this to Floyd, but The House of Lords stepped in, raised the fine to 5,000 pounds, ordered him whipped from London Bridge to Westminster Hall, and imprisoned for life. The Prince of Wales interceded to eliminate the whipping.[24]

1622

John Chamberlin said, as the reign of James I was ending, that the times are dangerous and the world grows tender and jealous of free speech.[25]

The House of Commons submitted a formal protest against King James I for his denial of its right to discuss issues and "to abridge us of the ancient liberty of Parliament for freedom of speech, jurisdiction, and just censure of the House." The king replied that they only operated from the grace for the crown. He forbade speech which could not be lavish or made by common people about the state.[26]

Oxford authorities burned a book by David Pareus because he advocated that rulers should be called to account for their actions.[27]

1623

William Phillips was jailed for translating a small French pamphlet for printer Nathaniel Newberry.[28]

William Stansby had his presses destroyed for printing a tract for bookseller Nathaniel Butter.[29]

Butter was fined in 1624 for printing corantos contrary to order and fined again in 1625 for unfitting speeches.[30]

1625

George Wither, a poet, attacked the patent and monopoly system of the Stationers and even managed to have his case heard in the Court of Chancery.

Wither won a printing patent for hymns and church songs, but only after years of efforts and two imprisonments for political allusions in his satirical poetry. He fought with the Stationers in 1625 because they wouldn't sell his songs. He claimed the booksellers had enslaved printers, binders, claspmakers, and authors.[31]

Francis Bacon said the invention of printing changed the appearance and the state of the whole world. "We should note the force, effect, and consequences of inventions which are nowhere more conspicuous than in those three which were unknown to the ancients, namely, printing, gun powder, and the compass."

Edward Coke produced *The First Part Institutes of the Lawes of England; or, a Commentarie upon Littleton*. Coke was a brutal judge, as evidenced by his prosecution of Sir Walter Raleigh, but he was independent and defended the common law against pressures from the crown. James I finally dismissed him and stripped him of all his titles; Coke soon became leader of the Constitutional Party and led the fight to gain freedom for parliamentary discussion. He was instrumental in drawing up the Petition of Right in the reign of Charles I. His *Institutes* became the source book for the defense of national liberties and constitutional rule of England.

1625

Works by Alexander Leighton and Richard Montagu were suppressed.[32]

Roger Manwaring, the king's chaplain, was sentenced by Parliament to imprisonment, suspended from the ministry, had his books burned, and had to pay 1,000 pounds for preaching sermons justifying the king's right to levy taxes without Parliament's consent. Although Charles I upheld the sentence, he immediately re-instated Manwaring to the ministry.[33]

The House of Commons recommended punishment for Chaplain Richard Montagu for his book *An Appeal to Cesare* because it offended the Archbishop of Canterbury and encouraged papacy.[34]

The Petition of Right forced on Charles I by Parliament helped establish the sovereignty of Parliament and its rule. The Petition of Right joined the Magna Carta as part of the English constitutional system.

1627

Thomas James, Bodley's librarian, published *Index generalis librorum prohibitorium a Pontificibus* because he believed it was a recommendation for a library to buy all books condemned by the Pope.[35]

1628

John Cowell wrote a dictionary of legal terms, Parliament was offended by some of the definitions. The king confiscated and destroyed the books.[36]

Roger Manwaring had to renounce two sermons which were burned because some royalists considered them an attack on English Laws. Peter Smart also had a sermon burned because it criticized Romanish practices in worship services.[37]

Archbishop William Laud controlled printing tyrannically for King Charles I.[38]

1629

King Charles I imprisoned several members of Parliament in the Tower for opposing him. They were fined and held until they gave bond not to oppose the crown further. John Elliot refused to give surety and died in jail.

Printers Michael Sparke, Nathaniel Butter, William Jones, and Augustine Matthews were accused of printing four works without license. Sparke, who had been imprisoned, challenged the Star Chamber's legality as "directly intrenching on hereditary liberty and being contrary to the Magna Carta, the Petition of Right, and other statutes." He proposed the firm foundation for freedom of the press which John Milton reiterated ten years later. He was arrested many times, and continued his free press contention; no person of his time waged such a sustained and persistent warfare against regulation of the press.[39]

1630

Nicholas Bourne, James Bowler, and Michael Sparke were arrested for selling controversial pamphlets.[40]

Physician Alexander Leighton, for his pamphlet entitled *An Appeal to the Parliament*, or *Zion's Plea Against the Prelaige* criticizing the English clergy as anti-Christian and satanical, was tried by the Star Chamber and found guilty without being given a chance to appear or speak in his own defense. He was degraded from the ministry, pilloried, whipped, one ear cut off, his nose slit, his face branded, and imprisoned. He escaped for awhile, but the sentence was carried out when he was captured. Its severity infuriated the people. The Long Parliament released him.[41]

1631

The Archbishop of Canterbury was angered by mistakes made in the 1631 edition of the Bible. Two read "Thou shalt commit adultery" and "The Lord hath shewed us his glory and great arse." The archbishop said,"I knew the tyme when great care was had about printing, the Bibles especially, good compositors and the best correctors were gotten being grave and learned men, the paper and the letter rare, and faire every way of the beste, but now the paper is nought, the composers boyes, and the correctors unlearned."[42]

Matthew Barker, printer of the king, were fined for mistakes in the Bible to help the Reformed Church of England, and to tighten controls on the press.[43]

1632

William Prynne was fined 5,000 pounds, had his university degrees taken away, and his ears cut off by the Star Chamber and Bishop William Laud for a book which had been passed by the licenser and produced by a registered printer, because Laud and the other judges believed the book contained veiled threats to the crown. Michael Sparke, printer of the book, was fined 500 pounds and had to stand in the pillory. The High Commission had earlier sentenced three men for having false ideas which they blamed on William Prynne, a Puritan. The licenser was fined 50 pounds. Prynne managed to keep up pamphleteering through he was imprisoned for life. One of his ears was cut off at Westminister and the other at Cheapside. The book, *Historio Mastrix*, had criticized a stage play in a manner considered to cast aspersions to the king and queen. [44]

The Spanish ambassador complained to English King Charles I about news books which had offended the Austrian Court. So Charles forbade publication of news from abroad in England. [45]

The Star Chamber prohibited the printing, publishing or selling of gazettes and news pamphlets. [46]

1632

Nicholas Bourne and Nathaniel Butter were suppressed by Charles I who didn't want people to know about reverses on the continent. Charles I ended corantos in England. [47]

John Hern's press in Shoreditch was discovered and destroyed, as was one owned by William Harris in the Minorie, on orders of the Court of Assistants of the Stationers Company because they had been installed without permission. [48]

1634

John Milton, English poet and politician, said, "Thou canst not touch the freedom of my mind." [49]

1637

Charles I began a systematic prosecution of Puritans. [50]

The printing decrees of the Star Chamber expanded the 1586 printing codification in an effort to control Puritan pamphleteers. The Star Chamber ended in 1641, but Parliament then took over the control of printing. [51]

John Bastwick, Henry Burton, and William Prynne were sentenced by the Star Chamber to pay fines of 5,000 pounds and be degraded from their profession, be pilloried, lose their ears, and be imprisoned for life for their writings. The people turned the public execution of the sentence into a demonstration of sympathy for the three men. Prynne was fined another 5,000 pounds, sentenced to perpetual imprisonment and had his ears shaved off again. In symbolic support people strewed flowers in his path and roared in agony as each ear was shaved. William Laud condemned Puritan writers and praised the king and the Star Chamber in a speech during the trial of the three men. The king ordered the speech printed and distributed, but most people bitterly denounced it. [52]

Henry Burton, an English Puritan minister, was sentenced to jail by Bishop Laud and the Star Chamber for libelous books against the church hierchy. Parliament released him in 1640.[53]

John Lilburne was arrested on a London street by the Star Chamber which accused him of importing forbidden Puritan books and pamphlets. He was not guilty of the charge, and refused to take the *oath ex officio*. Lilburne, 20, was accused of importing thousands of illegal books into England from Holland. The Star Chamber sentenced him to pay 500 pounds, be whipped through the streets, stand in the pillory, and stay in prison until he would take the *oath ex officio*. But Lilburne shouted to the crowd watching him. He was then imprisoned for 30 months without funds or friends.[54]

When William Laud became Archbishop of Canterbury he had the Star Chamber issue a decree for complete control of printing so he could prevent and punish unauthorized materials. Laud's efforts failed, so in 1637 the Star Chamber issued its most repressive decree to control printing. All books and pamphlets, including title, epistle, proem, preamble, introduction, table, and dedication, had to be licensed. Printers had to deposit 300 pounds as surety not to print anything unlicensed, and only 20 printers were authorized in London. The Star Chamber decreed it unlawful to make, buy, or keep type or presses or to practice printing, publishing, or book selling without a license from the Company of Stationers. This decree was unpopular and led to the abolishment of the Star Chamber in 1641. The Star Chamber regulations were largely efforts to control Puritan pamphlets. A law was passed limiting what printed materials could be imported into England, and nothing deemed injurious to the church, religion, or the government was allowed to enter the country. These rules generally failed.[55]

Despite increasing press controls with the law of seditious libel and the Star Chamber decree of 1673, Puritans, printers, and politicians evaded them during Charles I's reign.[56]

1638

John Bastwick contended that the English court had decided the case against Henry Burton, William Prynne, and himself before the trial and that its clerk couldn't pronounce Latin words.[57]

Even though John Lilburne was too tall for the neckhole in the pillory, he was forced to stand in the device. He was gagged and his mouth bloodied as he shouted defiance. When he was then imprisoned in England, he had no food for the first ten days. John Wharton was tried with Lilburne for publishing seditious books.

While in prison John Lilburne produced a report of the trial that put him there. Lilburne became the principal crusader for freedom of the press throughout the Puritan

Revolution. He had been convicted of sedition.[58]

1639

The King warned infamous libels and calumnies against his royal authority, and warned of traitorous intentions of the Scots. But the Scots became more active in distributing materials in defiance of the king and the Star Chamber.

1640

Parliament created its system of press controls using provisions that had been followed by the monarchs.

The Long Parliament took over the regulation and control of printing.

Inefficiency and lack of reader interest saw them end efforts in 1640.[59]

Ben Johnson, an English playwright said, "Stand for truth and tis enough."[60]

The Scots descended on London to demand concessions and money from King Charles I. Since he didn't have the money, he summoned Parliament. It set the press free and ended ecclesiastical tyranny. The High Commission Court could no longer seize books or decide on matter about printing.[61]

The Long Parliament of the Puritans released William Prynne, Henry Burton and John Bastwick from prison sentences. The three Puritan pamphleteers were cheered by thousands of Londoners who tossed flowers in their paths when they returned from exile.[62]

1641

John Brookes was sent to Fleet prison for printing *A Scandalous Ballad* about the Queen Mother. The hangman burned the ballads.[63]

Samuel Hartlib said, "The art of printing will so spread knowledge that the common people, knowing their own right and liberties will not be governed by way of oppression."[64]

Richard Herne threatened to kill Nicholas Borne when Borne attempted to find out who wrote a scandalous pamphlet. Borne was master of the Stationers Company.

Richard Herne was jailed but managed to continue publishing pamphlets thereafter. Five mercury women (hawkers of pamphlets) reported they sold the pamphlets for Herne.[65]

John Pocklington published two popish pamphlets which displeased the church. It defrocked him and had the hangmen burn the book. William Bray, who had inadvertently licensed the books, had to preach a recantation sermon.[66]

Michael Sparke was involved in almost all of the seditious printing of his time and went to jail eleven times. He fought Robert Barker, the king's printer and holder of the lucrative Bible patent, as well as the authority of the church and the crown.[67]

John Thomas began publishing parliamentary reports called *Diurnal Occurences*. Samuel Pecke issued a newsbook entitled *Heads of Several Proceedings in both Houses of Parliament* on November 29. Its title was soon changed to *Diurnal Occurences* and later to the *Perfect Diurnal*. In July, Parliament forbade members giving out notes of proceedings.[68]

The first book burning under the Long Parliament was a speech by George Digby who had sought to have the Earl of Stafford convicted of treason.[69]

The Stationers Company continued to search out unlicensed printing; for example, they tried to search John Ashton's home for secret presses, but he and his associates fought off the Stationers with swords, guns, and pistols for two hours until they could burn all the contraband printing in the house.

Committee of the House of Commons on Printing were assigned the duties of prosecuting Archbishop Laud for treason, examining all abuses in printing. The committee heard a number of complaints about pamphlets and published sermons, especially those of the royalists and high churchmen. The committee chairman was imprisoned, dismissed, and tossed out of Parliament for printing a collection of speeches about religion. His book was burned. After proceeding against several printers, the committee developed an ordinance passed by the House to control printing. The House printed and distributed reports of its votes to repudiate printers' reports.

The Long Parliament abolished the Star Chamber and Court of High Commission, which markedly reduced the number of libel prosecutions, but it continued orders for a licensing system for the next two years.

Parliament issued an order which threatened severe punishment for persons who falsely purported their printing to be done by its order or that of the king.

The House of Commons ordered printers to stop printing anything without the name and consent of the author. This was a step toward copyrighting.[70]

1642

Sir Thomas Browne, an English author said, "No man can justly censure or condemn another, because indeed no man truly knows another."[71]

A Speedy Post from Heaven to the King of England violated a regulation forbidding printed material reflection on his majesty. It was burned.[72]

John Bond was imprisoned for writing a false letter about an effort of the Queen to sell her jewels. He had to stand in the pillory for an hour with a paper on his head saying he was a contriver of false and scandalous libels for two days. The letter was burned and a half dozen printers were implicated in the episode.[73]

Edward Dering lost his job as chairman of the committee in printing because he offended Presbyterians in the House of Commons. His book was burned and he was imprisoned in the Tower.[74]

Dering in his *Collection of Speeches* criticized severely Archbishop Laud. The House of Commons ordered the book burned and Dering imprisoned for a short period.[75]

Dering and George Strode were impeached as principal instigators of the Kent petition challenging church practice and having political complications. The petition was ordered burned. The petition had complained that Protestant religious books were suppressed and popish propaganda and practice favored.[76]

Mrs. Gregory Dexter had printed a pamphlet critical of King James. She was sent to the King's Bench prison.[77]

The House of Commons condemned a Scot tract criticizing King James in this order:

> Ordered, that the pamphlet entitled "King James his Judgement of a King, and of a Tyrant," be referred to the Committee of Printing and the Publisher, and that it be burned.[78]

Parliament issued a declaration to suppress seditious and scandalous pamphlets aimed at its members. It outlawed all diurnals which ceased publication for awhile, but reappeared in a few months. The House of Commons issued an order for licensing printing, The House of Lords joined the House of Commons to erase all of the Star Chamber proceedings. They even awarded Lilburne 3,000 pounds which was stolen by bureaucrats. Lilburne continued to defy the government, including Parliament and Oliver Cromwell.[79]

Newsbooks appeared everywhere and contained Parliamentary proceedings. Parliament ordered that every publication had to include the name of the author, because of false information being published about the civil war.[80]

John Lilburne's last prison sentence ended when he was 41. He was so popular that he set patterns in conducting trials fairly for all English courts to follow.

John Milton, a British poet, said, "The best apology against false accusers is silence and sufferance, and honest deeds set against dishonest words."[81]

William Newton was accused of writing a letter reflecting on the honor of the Prince of Orange. The letter was a forgery, but it was burned.[82]

Samuel Pecke was jailed twice for his reports about Parliament's actions.[83]

Henry Walker, once an ironmonger, became England's funny-man printer. He published nearly 200 things which he thought could be sold and which would "rend or shake the peace of either church or state." He evaded one trial for publishing offensive items by promising to go back to his iron works. Soon, however, he tossed handfuls of smart aleck tracts at the king's coach. A rabble from the streets rescued him from the police so he could spend several additional months publishing without license or paying any publishing taxes. He spent this time disguised as a priest and even conducted mass for St. Mary Magdalene Church. The king scolded about his libelous pamphlets and he was jailed in the London Tower. He admitted being guilty of libeling the king but begged for mercy; the king allowed the conviction be only a misdemeanor eligible for a light sentence.[84]

1643

Also jailed were Bernard and Thomas Fawcett who confessed to printing scandalous pamphlets.[85]

Sir John Berkenhead published his *Mercurius Auclicus* to present the king's side in the gathering civil war.[86]

The Scottish church, disturbed by newspapers, decided "to attempt some supervision over what might reach the ears of the people either through the news sheets or by the more careless methods of the 'jade rumour.'" Parliament was asked to employ parish ministers to spread news:

> Because thruch want of sure and tymous intelligence a greate pairt of the people are arther left to uncertane rumoures or flichted by the negligence of common bearers, or abuseit with malignant informationes that thei nather know thair awin danger nor the danger of religion in the countrey. A solide ordour would be set down whereby intelligence may goe furth from Edinburgh to Everie Shyre and so to everie particular pastor that the people may be informed both of thair danger and dewtie.

Women who sold Royalist pamphlets were dragged to Bridgewell prison where they were whipped.[87]

The Committee on Printing devised a bill for Parliament and upon passage licensers were appointed.[88]

Lucius Cary died of gunshot wounds when he crowded through an opening in which English enemies were firing. He had been sent to Newgate prison for having 1300 copies of a letter belittling troops of Parliament. The letter copies were burned.[89]

Joseph Hunscot became a searcher or beagle for the Stationers Company to find unlicensed printing.[90]

Philip Hunton wrote his *A Treatise on Monarchy* which led the end of the divine right notion. But ten years later the book was burned."[91]

John Locke believed that every person had the natural rights of life, liberty, and property.

In June, the Ordinance for the Regulations of Printing was passed by the Long Parliament, This ordinance assured that the Stationers Company would continue. Religious books were to be licensed by Presbyterian ministers, minor publications by the clerks of the Stationers, Parliament proceedings by each house, and books by the Stationer's Register. Parliament and the Stationers could search and seize unlicensed publications and presses with nut, spindle, and materials. Royalists and non-royalists printers alike badgered Parliament which found it could not control the press in 1643. The committee zealously cited printers for violating rules; nonetheless, the ordinance proved ineffective.[92]

Parliament empowered Henry Walley, clerk to the Company of Stationers, to be sole licenser of publication. Thus, although the Star Chamber was abolished, control of the press remained in the hands of the government. The Stationers looked for irregular printers to protect its property rights, and to help the government suppress seditious publications. The newsbooks licensed included "Printed according to order."

Parliament ordered licensing of all printing, and ordered reports of its meeting not be published.[93]

Henry Parker's Political Catechism led to the strengthening of the House of Commons and the end of the king's powers.[94]

Samuel Pecke spent several months in Fleet prison for printing unapproved reports even though he normally was a careful servant of Parliament.[95]

Printers jailed In Fleet prison included William Bray, Henry Walker, John Wells, Francis Leach, Francis Coles, Richard West, Thomas Alsopp, Bernard Faucett, Richard Herme, and Samuel Pecke.[96]

Henry Robinson, an English merchant said, "No man can have a natural monopoly of the truth. [Religious opinion should be] fought out upon eaven ground, on equall termes, neither side must expect to have greater liberty of speech, writing, or printing than the other." Reason, and argument were the only allowable weapons for "Papists, Jewes, Turkes, Pagans, Hereticks, Infidels, Misbelievers, and all others." He recommended freedom of speech and press as a logical extension of the *Laissez-faire* economic doctrine. [97]

Chapter 5

FREEDOM OF EXPRESSION BECKONS IN ENGLAND
1644 Through 1699

Areogapitica was a criticism of the existing law of libel as proclaimed by English court decisions. "To say that the press is free when punishment of publication is certain is to place on trial virtue, honor, and good conduct." John Milton, an English poet and political writer, wrote *Areogapitica*, which has been considered ever since an eloquent and effective plea for freedom of the press. Actually, Milton had considerable difficulty because of his writing favoring divorce. He had married a 16-year-old girl who could not stand him and had run away for two years. *Areogapitica* grew out of his fuss over divorce laws.

He was an active proponent of Puritanism and became secretary of foreign tongues during the Commonwealth. He also supervised the licenser of the press. In some reports he appears as a censor; in others, he is said not to have interferred with content. He was arrested but not punished after the restoration in 1660, although he could have been put to death.[1]

Milton said:
> When complaints are freely heard, deeply considered, and speedily reformed, then is the utmost bound of civil liberty attained that wise men look for. [2]

In *Areogapitica* Milton wrote:
> Give me the liberty to know, to utter and to argue freely, according to conscience, above all liberties. And although all the winds of doctrine were let loose to play upon the earth, so Truth be in the field we do injuriously by licensing and prohibiting, to misdoubt her strength. Let her and falsehood grapple. Who ever knew Truth put to the worse in a free and open encounter? Her confuting is the surest and best suppressing. For who knows not that Truth is strong next to the Almighty? She needs no policies, nor stratagems, nor licensings to make

her victorious; those are the shifts and defences that error uses against her power; give her but the room and do not bind her when she sleeps[3]

Milton said, "Who kills a man kills a reasonable creature, God's image; but he who destroys a good book kills reason itself."[4]

1644

William Laud was executed for his misconduct as Archbishop of Canterbury. William Prynne, who had been severely persecuted and imprisoned and pilloried led the legal fight to condemn Laud, an arrogant, power hungry prelate. Also imprisoned by Laud were John Bostwick and Henry Burton.[5]

William Laud's chaplain had to make a public recantation from the pulpit for Laud's errors of judgment concerning printing. [6]

John Lilburne produced his *A copie of a letter to Mr. William Prynne, Esq.* In which he demanded freedom of the press as a privilege of a free-born English subject. Prynne had him arrested and imprisoned in the Tower until 1648. Lilburne continued with other pamphlets and said the Magna Carta was the supreme charter of popular liberty, including liberty of conscience, freedom of the press, and economic justice. [7]

Marchamont Nedham, publisher of *The Mercurius Britanicus* newsbook, was jailed for two weeks for publishing attacks on the House of Lords, the queen, the king, and Sir John Berkenhead (the king's propagandist) who Nedham ridiculed in a false obituary. In 1647 he became disgusted with the Cromwellites and defected to the Royalists. When the king was executed, Nedham was captured and imprisoned, but subsequently was authorized to publish news for the Commonwealth. When the Commonwealth collapsed, he fled to Holland, but managed to obtain a pardon a year later. He published pamphlets after returning to England from Holland, but lived in fear the rest of his life because both Royalists and Puritans hated him. [8]

Richard Overton was a Leveller pamphleteer who supported the natural rights of man concept, popular government, and freedom of the press. He wrote about them while imprisoned at Newgate for supporting and refusing to answer questions about John Lilburne. He urged Parliament to "let the imprisoned presses at Liberty, so that all men's understanding may be more conveniently formed" in a pamphlet which the government declared scandalous. Overton believed the law of God should be translated into the principles of democracy. In a pamphlet he called the licensing system an absurdity. [9]

Richard Royston, a printer, was jailed for vending books from Oxford, a city where Royalist publications were issued.[10]

William Walwyn argued that only criminal deeds should be punished, not expression. He wrote a series of Leveller tracts on freedom of the mind, liberty of conscience, and freedom of discourse. [1]

The House of Commons had a committee for demolishing superstitious images, pictures, and monuments. [12]

Thomas Audley licensed an issue of *Mercurius Britanicus* in 1645 which contained an article critical of Parliament, which jailed Audley but not the author Marchamont Nedham. Nedham sneaked an issue past Audley and was jailed. [13]

Paul Bent gave a manuscript belittling the Trinity to a minister friend for his reaction. The minister turned it in to the authorities. The House of Commons ordered Bent to be hanged for the manuscript but this sentence was changed to three years in prison.

Lawrence Clarkson was banned from England by the House of Commons for his Anabaptist book *The Single Eye, All Light, No Darkness, or Light and Darkness One*. [14]

Lilliam Larner was jailed by Hunscot, an English searcher for seditious publications for the Stationers Company. [15]

Petitions were signed by 98,064 persons asking the English government to free John Lilburne. [16]

Abigail Rogers, a mercury woman, refused to name the supplier of pamphlets she was selling. She was jailed but beat the rap because she was pregnant. [17]

During the negotiations to end the war between the Scottish Commissioners and Parliament, Robert Bostick, Thomas Blacklock, John Field, Francis Leach and George Chapmen were jailed and fined for printing reports of the negotiations. [18]

Searchers had the tables turned on them by printers and mercury women who sold publications on the streets. The Browns brought suit against Hunscot. Robert Eeles had the master searcher jailed for the treatment his wife received while selling books. [19]

The Scottish Dove was one of several publications judged an affront to both Parliament and the king of France. It was burned. Also burned was a pamphlet, *The Question of the King's Person*. [20]

The Committee on Sequestrations suppressed pamphlets printed at the headquarters of the King in Oxford. [21]

William Walwyn said the licensing system was impractical and freedom of the press should be established to secure religious toleration. Henry Robinson in 1647 wanted freedom of the press to cover other areas. [22]

John Dillingham was jailed by Parliament for an article critical of the Earl of Essex in *Parliament Scout.* [23]

Two books by David Buchman were ordered burned because they revealed negotiations between Scotland and England. [24]

Richard Overton was imprisoned in Newgate because be refused to answer questions about his printed attacks on the House of Lords. [25]

England's first book discussing libel and slander was John March's *Actions for Slaunder.* [26]

English army agencies began a political push that frightened Parliament, which in turn led to several suppressions of newsbooks and a new but ineffective licensing law. [27]

Several satirical tracts were issued to carry on the struggles between Parliament and the king. A Commons Committee was authorized to find the printers, burn the satires, and destroy printing plants. [28]

The ordinance of 1647 was designed to stamp out Royalist publications, especially two newsbooks, *Pragmaticus* and *Eleciticus.*

The Ordinances of 1642 through 1647 failed to strengthen press controls. [29]

1648

John Fry was dismissed from Parliament for publishing *The Clergy and Their Colors* and *A Pair of Bellows* which attacked *The Doctrine of the True Religion.* The books were burned. [30]

Milton's works were suppressed before the Commonwealth was established. [31]

Sir William Petty, an English physician, proposed that all books be condemned into one set of volumes and that all which was "nice, contentious, and merely fantastical be suppressed and brought into contempt with all men." [32]

William Walwyn was convicted and jailed for circulating Leveller pamphlets. [33]

Paul Best was persecuted for his Socinian views. John Biddle and John Fry were other Socinians who battled with the theology of the Trinitarians. [34]

1649

The army took over the control of printing and deputies of the marshall were authorized to search and seize all unlicensed printing presses with or without the consent of the Stationers Company. The oath of only one witness was sufficient for conviction. Half the fine imposed was awarded the arresting officer and the other half went to the poor of the parish. [35]

The Leveller party petitioned Parliament to revoke all ordinances against free printing, saying:

> by giving freedom to the press and in case any abuse of their authority by scandalous pamphlets, they will never want advocates to vindicate their innocency. And therefore all things duly weighed, to refer all books and pamphlets to the judgment, discretions, or affection of Licensers, or to put the least restraint upon the press, seems altogether inconsistent with the good of the Commonwealth, and expressly opposite and dangerous to the liberties of the people. And if you and your army shall be pleased to look back a little upon affairs you will find you have bin very much strengthened all along by unlicensed printing. That you will precisely hold yourself to the supreme end — the freedom of the people — as in other things so as in that necessary and essential part of speaking, writing, printing, and publishing their minds freely without setting of masters, tutors, and controulers over them and for that end to revoke all orders and ordinances to the contrary.
>
> As for any prejudice to Government thereby, if government be just in its constitution, and equal in its distributions, it will be good, if not absolutely necessary for them, to hear all the voices and judgments, which they can never do, and to be carefully awarded, as any other exorbitancy or prejudice in Government.
>
> And generally, as to the whole course of printing, as justly in our apprehensions may licensers be put over all publick or private teaching and discoveries in divine, moral, natural, civil, or political things, as over the press, the liberty whereof appears so essential unto freedom, as that without it, it's impossible to preserve any nation from being liable to the worst of bondage. For what may not be done to that people who may not speak or write, but at the pleasure of licensers?[36]

John Lilburne was a scappy pamphleteer who was first condemned to the pillory for distributing the works of William Prynne. Later he attacked Prynne and the Presbyterians and asserted freedom of conscience and speech and "That the press might be as open to us as you." These efforts established the Leveller movement. Thereafter he was jailed, tried, and acquitted, exiled, and again jailed, tried, and acquitted when he slipped back into England. He was acquitted of charges of having "published treasonable, venimous books." The crowd and the jury were sympathetic with "Freeborn John" even though the judges were not.

John Lilburne proposed *An Agreement of the Free People of England*. This plan was heavily used by William of Orange after the Glorious Revolution of 1688.[37]

The Printing Act of 1649 presented the most detailed list of regulations of the press for the century. Printing was limited to London, Oxford, York, and Finsbury. No house could be rented to a printer nor could any printing equipment be made without notice to the Stationers Company. Scandalous and seditious material was prohibited. All books and pamphlets had to be licensed. All newsbooks were suppressed. The Stationers Company enforced these and other provisions with searches, seizures, fines, and imprisonment. The licensers ignored the views of Parliament and licensed Royalist publications, Leveller publications, the *Koran*, and even *The Man in the Moon* attack on Cromwell. Licenser Mabbott resigned in disgust because his name was counterfeited on publications; he believed licensing was being used illegally and unjustly, because it created a monopoly, and because he believed any person should be allowed to print whatever book he desired.[38]

The Printing Act of 1649 authorized the army to control printing lightly.[39]

Members of Parliament supposedly could initiate any subject for discussion; however, it took until the 1700s included the right to criticize both the crown and the government. Queen Elizabeth simply evaded any efforts of Parliament to provide greater freedoms. [40]

General Fairfax gave the militia warrants to suppress both royalist and Presbyterian printers. The Treason Act made criticism of the government a capital offense. But royalist publications prospered until Parliament Joan set up sting operations to catch the royalists. [41]

Puritans reprinted the Hugenot pamphlet *Vindiciae Contra Tyrannos* to lead to the revolt that included the execution of King Charles I of Great Britain and set up the Puritan Commonwealth. [42]

1650

Lawrence Clarkson spent a month in jail and was banished from England for publishing an impious book called *The Single Eye and Mr. Rainborow's Carriages*.[43]

John Fry was dismissed from Parliament for writing a book which attacked a fellow member and for a second book which was considered a scandalous attack upon the clergy. The Committee for Plundered Ministers brought the action against Fry. He was convicted of heresy for denying the Trinity.[44]

The Ranters was a group of Englishmen in the 1650s demanding freedom of the press. [45]

The Searchers, or Beagles, looked for unlicensed printing. They included "Parliament Joan, a fifty-year-old fat woman; Smith, a tall, thin chapt knave and printer; Holt, who had a trim pair of scratched chaps; Matthews, a cheat; Jack Rudd, a figger-flinger; and John Harris, an actor and printer." Joan Cromwell, the middle-aged woman, was so efficient that Oliver Cromwell and Parliament were able to destroy much Royalist printing. [46]

A Single Eye, a pamphlet written by Abilzer Coppee or Jacob Bauthumley was burned at Westminster and at the Exchange in London. It was a Ranters book which violated the 1650 Blasphemy Act. Other writings by the Ranters faction were also burned. [47]

1651

Thomas Hobbes in his *Leviathan* contended that there should be a contract between a monarch and a subject. He discounted the ideas of the divine right of kings and religion's role in society. His book was suppressed in 1669 when the English monarchy was restored. [48]

Hobbes, an English philosopher, said, "They that approve a private opinion, call it opinion, but they that mislike it, heresy, and yet heresy signifies no more than private opinion." [49]

John Lilburne was fined 7,000 pounds and banished for having been present when a petition had been written about a colliery swindle. The petition author, Joseph Primat, also was fined 7,000 pounds and jailed in Fleet Prison. [50]

Milton served as one of Oliver Cromwell's licensers or censors and the works he handled were corantos or newsbooks which were partisan sheets of current news. [51]

William Bell in a pamphlet said that:
> the most Christian potencies (or Republicks) and Illustrious potentates have thought fit to comprehend the liberty of printing (even as of coyning) within the sphere of their several powers; well perceiving that the eye of understanding might be subject to be deceived by erronous principles in Print, as may the bodily eye by counterfeit coyne; In regard whereof they propagated wholesome orders and decrees for the regulating of printing and printers; which rightly considered, cannot be defaced nor blemished by the notion of Tyranny."

Thomas Hobbes, in his *Leviathan*, proposed a political philosophy justifying absolute authority. [52]

Parliament established a new control of printing act which embodied all the regulations of the 1649 Act and resembled earlier Star Chamber decrees. The Council of State was the main agency controlling the press.[53]

Robert Norwood gave a paper outlining his religious beliefs to his pastor, who arranged for him to be tried for blasphemy. He was excommunicated and sentenced to prison for six months. [54]

Not only were authors, printers, and publishers of unlawful books prosecuted, but so were the buyers and readers, until the Printing Act of 1649 expired in 1651.[55]

1652

Samuel Chidley, a Leveller, said publications which provided falsehoods should not be permitted. [56]

Presbyterian printers and stationers protested popish and sectarian books with a publication, *A Beacon Set on Fire*. The printers were called the "Beacon Firers" and wanted a strong licensing system. The Levellers retorted with a publication called *Beacons Quenched* and became the "Beacon Quenchers." [57]

Lodowick Muggleston, a religious fanatic, was given six months in jail for blasphemy for his book *Transcendent Spiritual Treatise* because it denied the trinity.[58]

1653

A printer blamed the government for not suppressing John Lilburne's charges against Oliver Cromwell in a pamphlet entitled *Sedition Scourg'd, or A View of the Rascally and Venemous Paper, Entituled A Charge for High Treason Exhibited Against Oliver Cromwell, Esq., for several Treasons by Him Committed*. John Lilburne returned to England and was immediately arrested and placed in the tower. He had supposedly accepted 10,000 pounds from the Duke of Buckingham to destroy the Commonwealth, murder Oliver Cromwell, and restore the monarchy, all within six months. This was to be done by importing publications. The printing licensing system failed again because of Lilburne's defiance and leadership. The Council of State indicted him with a 164-page document. Lilburne fought all tyranny including that of the bishops, the Presbyterians, and Cromwell. He thought of himself as championing the rights of common people and as being both a folk hero and a martyr. The Council of State called him the greatest libeler of all; but many others said he was the greatest champion of press freedom. [59]

1655

Oliver Cromwell disregarded criticism aimed toward him and was somewhat tolerant of press attention. He took over as Lord Protector and instituted his own control system of the press; his Council of State became the chief regulation agency. Cromwell suppressed all news books, street hawkers, and mercury women.

Oliver Cromwell issued Commonwealth orders on the control of the press which were almost as stringent as those of Queen Elizabeth a century earlier.[60]

John Goodwin's defense of freedom of the press, *Fresh Discovery of the High Presbyterian Spirit*, indicated that suppression was absurd. His pamphlet was one of the landmarks in the progress of press freedom from governmental control. Goodwin, in reply to the Beacon Firers, said, "The setting of watchmen with authority at the door of the press to keep errors and heresies out of the world is as weak a project and design, as it would be to set a company of armed men about a house to keep darkness out of the night season. [61]

The three commissioners authorized by the 1655 Cromwell's orders suppressed all news books. [62]

1656

Giles Calvert was convicted for publishing a merry (humorous) book and several Quaker publications. The press control managers tried to suppress the Quaker pamphlets but failed. Cromwell ordered the release of seven Quakers from Hosham Jail where they had been imprisoned for Quaker books.

Oliver Cromwell favored full and free discussion of religious matters except for Catholics. Royalists could not attack the Commonwealth, but the Royalist press persisted. The Cromwell Council of State censored news and was the principal publisher in England. [63]

When a plot to kill Oliver Cromwell failed, Colonels Sexby and Titus smuggled in a pamphlet entitled *Killing No Murder* to carry on the plot against Cromwell. John Stargess was jailed for having copies of the pamphlet and died in the Tower of London. He confessed to the plot and responsibility for the pamphlet.[64]

James Nayler rode to London on a mule followed by women chanting, "Holy, Holy, Holy!" He was convicted of blasphemy, but Cromwell stopped the punishment the court had imposed. While Quakers were imprisoned, the jailers allowed them to give speeches. Nayler, however, was cruelly punished by the House of Commons for books the House called blasphemous and had burned.[65]

1657

Cromwell was basically tolerant of the press even though his advisers and the Council of the State were not.

Eighty "Fifth Monarchy" members rose in arms against Cromwell because they thought he was ready to make a deal with the crown. William Medley wrote a pamphlet *The Standard Set Up* to promote their cause. They failed and the 80 were jailed in the Tower of London. [66]

Milton wrote in *A Treatise of Civil Power in Ecclesiastical Causes* that the right of a free and open debate should be reserved to all Protestants including Anabaptists, Socinians, Anglicans, and Puritans, but papists— the only heretics—were to be barred from participation.

1659

John Biddle, father of Unitarianism, was prosecuted by the Presbyterian Beacon Firers for his books. He was jailed several times for publishing blasphemous doctrines. He and two printers were imprisoned for publishing *A Twofold Catechism* which Parliament had declared blasphemous. His books were burned and he was banished to Sicily. [67]

John Croope, a member of the Liberty of Conscience Party, spoke vigorously for dissenters to have the freedom to publish their opinions without prosecution during the time of the Protectorate. [68]

1660

John Goodwin's book about religious matters was condemned and burned publicly at both the Old Bailey and at Oxford. [69]

James Guthrie, a Scots Protester, had his book *Causes of the Lord's Wrath Against Scotland* burned because Charles II considered it treasonable with its Presbyterian content. [70]

After the restoration of Charles II occurred, a "patent" system authorizing publication of the news developed. Ultimate control was divided between the crown and Parliament. The press edicts of 1637 were reaffirmed. Appearing in 1660 was a work entitled *The London Printers Lamentation or The Press Opprest and Over Prest.* [71]

The Privy Council suppressed all newsbooks except Henry Muddiman's *Parliamentary Intelligence* and *Mercurius Publicus.* [72]

Charles II gave Henry Muddiman a monopoly to print news. The House of Lords ruled against publication of its proceedings. [73]

William Prynne became embroiled in controversy with the long parliament which he so antagonized that he was declared guilty of high treason primarily because of his writing and efforts to stamp out opposing views. He finally made abject apologies to Commons, and was forgiven. [74]

For four consecutive weeks from February 21 to March 16, 1660, excepting on Sundays and on one Tuesday, Oliver Williams published *A Perfect Diurnal of the Dayly Proceedings in Parliament*. It was newsbook size and was the first daily news publication in England. [75]

John Garfield was imprisoned for writing *The Wandering Whore. Answer to Plain English* was condemned as a traitorous and fanatic pamphlet by the Council of State, and was suppressed.

1661

William Drake in a pamphlet challenged the legality of Parliament. He was impeached and turned over to the attorney general to be prosecuted in the Court of King's Bench. [76]

1662

Beginning in 1662 and continuing until 1679 the licensing of the press was authorized by Roger L'Estrange.[77]

The Act for preventing the frequent abuses in printing seditious, treasonable, and unlicensed books and pamphlets and for regulating of printing presses lasted until 1694.[78]

A licensing act specified a printer's code and established a surveyor of the press who could suppress unauthorized publications. It limited the number of printing presses in its efforts to control schismatical, blasphemous, seditious, and treasonable material. The act for preventing the abuses of printing unlicensed books lasted until 1694. Enforcement included the use of general warrants and surety bonds from printers.[79]

Parliament provided a law to prohibit the writing of seditious, treasonable, and unlicensed books which were pro-royalty.[80]

Roger L'Estrange wrote *Truth and Loyalty Vindicated from the Reproaches and Clamours of Mr. Edward Bagshaw Together with a Further Discovery of the Libeller Himself and His Seditious Confederates*.

Roger L'Estrange became Surveyor of the Imprimery and Printing Presses and was empowered the sole licensing authority of ballads, charts, printed portraitures, printed pictures, books, and papers. He was granted the right to write, print, and publish all narratives, advertisements, mercuries, intelligenciers, diurnals, books, plays, maps, charts, briefs for collections, playbills, quack-salvers' bills, custom and excise bills, post-office bills, creditors' bills, and tickets. He had the power to search for and seize unlicensed, treasonable, schismatical, and scandalous books and papers.

This licensing Art of 1662 remained in force until 1695.[81]

Roger L'Estrange wrote *Considerations and Proposals in order to the Regulation of the Press Together with diverse instances of treasonous and seditious pamphlets, proving the necessity thereof.* L'Estrange, who was a Tory pamphleteer and licenser of the press, was appointed Surveyor of Imprimery. He inspected printing establishments and strictly enforced the 1662 Licensing Act. He had the monopoly of publishing a newspaper, *The Intelligencer*, which lasted until 1666.

L'Estrange said:

> Supposing the press in order, the people in their right wits, and news or no news to be the question, a Publick Mercury should never have my vote; because I think it makes the Multitude too Familiar with the Actions and Counsels of their Superiors; too Pragmatical and Censorious, and gives them not only an Itch, but a kind of Colourable Right and License to be meddling with the Government. A paper of quality may be both safe and Expedient; truly if I should say, Necessary, perhaps the case would bear it, for certainly there is not anything, which at this Instant more Imports his Majesty's service and the Publick Than to Redeem the Vulgar from Their Former Mistakes and Delusions, and to preserve them from the like for the time to come. The prudent Menager of Gazett may contribute in a very high Degree to the Genius, and humor of the common people, whose affections are much more capable of being turned, and wrought upon, by convenient Hints and Touches in the shape and Ayre of a Pamphlet, than by the Strongest Reasons, and best Notions imaginable under any other, and more sober form whatsoever." [82]

The Printing Act of Charles II became known as the Licensing Act. It required that all writing be submitted to an official licenser prior to publication. It was intended to establish a system of control far more comprehensive than a simple censorship. It subjected the whole printing trade to a series of restrictions so severe as to make expansion impossible. Printing was confined to London, Oxford, and Cambridge and no one could set up a printing press anywhere else in England. Master printers were limited to twenty and the number of presses and apprentices allowed was rigidly controlled. [83]

1663

Simon Dover, Thomas Brewster and Nathan Brooks were sentenced to prison and the pillory and fined on the basis of testimony given by L'Estrange. The judge said they would have been executed for treason for publishing seditious pamphlets but for the king's compassion. [84]

Roger L'Estrange was given a monopoly to publish news. [85]

George Wither, a Puritan writer, was frequently imprisoned. The last time he was sent to the Tower of London for a poem, *Vox Vulgi*. After a year his wife was sent to get him to recant his views. He finally was released by giving bond for good behavior.[86]

Richard Allein, a Puritan minister, printed his *Vindiciae Pietatis* which was illegal unlicensed printing according to a 1663 law. Despite this the book survived and was reprinted in 1664 and 1676.[87]

1664

Benjamin Keach, an Armenian Baptist, was fined, imprisoned, and pilloried in London and his book about infant baptism and criticism of the Church of England was burned. [88]

William Twyn was hanged, drawn and quartered at Tyburn because he would not reveal the name of the author of a book titled *A Treatise of the Execution of Justice*. The book endorsed the right of revolution and was held to be a threat to the king's life. The trial was reported in *An Exact Narrative of the Tryal and Condemnation of John Twyn for Printing and Dispersing of a Treasonable Book*. Chief witness against Twyn was Roger L'Estrange. [89]

All 1500 copies of a book by Benjamin Keach (a Calvinistic Baptist) were destroyed. At one point Keach escaped death when an officer kept mounted troops from riding their horses over him. When he was tried the judge abused him and jurors convicted him to the pillory as a base and dangerous fellow. [90]

1665

Henry Muddiman was summoned to Oxford where the court had gone to escape the London plague. He produced *The Oxford Gazette*. When the plague ended, the newspaper was transferred to London and became *The London Gazette*, official government newspaper. Under the licensing law, secretaries of state had a monopoly of news until 1688. [91]

1666

The House of Commons passed a law to punish theism. Actually, the law really was designed to punish Thomas Hobbes for his *Leviathan*. The king's council ordered suppression of *An Apology of the English Catholics*. In 1680 Hobbes defended his books vigorously. [92]

William Carr, a member of the House of Lords, for writing about the record of Charles Gerard's concealment of the death of several soldiers under his command, was fined 1,000 pounds, to stand in the pillory twice, and to wear a head paper saying he had published libelous and scandalous papers and thereafter suppressed and imprisoned. [93]

John Wickham and Sam Mearne, Stationers Company officials, stole a press belonging to Elizabeth Calvert, but were accused of giving it back to her and of selling unlicensed books for her. Other messengers of the company also were corrupt and frequently took bribes. The company was no longer considered effective by the crown. [94]

1669

Roger L'Estrange was ordered to arrest those responsible for *The Whore's Petition.* [95]

1670

The Surveyor of the Press became an effective press control official and the shared responsibility of control by the crown and Parliament. Ultimately the Stationers Company lost its partnership with the King. [96]

1671

Milton, in *Samsom Agonistes*, wrote, "But what more oft in nations grown corrupt, and by their will brought to servitude, than to love bondage more than liberty — bondage with less than strenuous liberty — and to despise, or envy, or suspect, whom God hath of his special favour raised as their deliverer."

1672

Rector Charles Hatham, a devotee of astrology, directed in his will that his books should be burned because they were monuments of lying vanity and remnants of heathen idolotry. [97]

1675

Coffee houses were suppressed by royal proclamation. Cromwell earlier had considered such a move. The coffee houses were places where political and religious debates were rampant. [98]

Henry Oldenburg resigned in disgust as licenser. Roger L'Estrange did most of the licensing, but the process became so difficult that other licensers would not serve. [99]

1676

English judges were pronouncing publications as being blasphemous under the law laid down by Sir Matthew Hale, who said:

> That such wicked and blasphemous words were not only an offense to God and religion but a crime against the laws of the state, and government, and therefore punishable in the court; for to say 'Religion is a cheat' is to dissolve all the obligations whereby the civil societies are preserved and Christianity is parcel of the laws of England, and therefore, to reproach the Christian religion is to speak in subversion of the law.

The legality of Parliament was questioned in three pamphlets, supposedly written by Lord Halles. Parliament ordered them burned. [100]

Lodowick Muggleston, a religious zealot claiming heavenly visitations, wrote books seeking to revise church dogma and the Bible. The King's Bench in the Old Bailey condemned much of his writing and burned them. He was sentenced to six months for blasphemy for his book *Neck of the Quakers Broken.* [101]

1678

Titus Oates reported a Catholic plot to murder the king. His testimony led to the execution of Edward Coleman, a Catholic writer. The judge who questioned Oates was murdered; newsletters supporting the Popish plot report appeared. The affair was actually concocted by opponents of James II, a Catholic, from becoming king. The newsletters inflamed the nation so much that Charles II dismissed Parliament in 1679. This dismissal ended licensing of the press. [102]

1679

Charles Blount wrote *A Just Vindication of Learning* or *An Humble Address to the High Court of Parliament in Behalf of the Liberty of the Press.* [103]

Benjamin Harris was arrested for articles about the Popish Plot in his *Appeal from the Country to the City* in which the king was openly criticized. Harris was jailed because he had no money to pay the fine, but the Printing Act had expired so he escaped punishment. He then published *Triumphs of Justice over Unjust Judges* which he dedicated to Justice Scroggs who had sentenced him. [104]

Chief Justice William Scroggs invented the theory that the king had the common law right of licensing and declared it a criminal act to publish without royal consent. A bench of twelve English judges declared it a cardinal offense to publish anything derogatory about the government without a license. Chief Justice Scroggs told the king it was criminal to publish any news without first having obtained a license whether the news was true or false, in praise or in censure. Scroggs said the court had "to take care to prevent and publish the mischiefs of the Press; otherwise the country would be at the mercy of the libels of the Papists, the factions, and the mercenaries." [105]

The beginnings of a party press was fueled by religious and political controversy.[106]

1680

Lord Chief Justice Scroggs used a royal proclamation made by Charles II which said the King could prohibit the printing and publishing of all newsbooks and pamphlets of news to prosecute Henry Care. [107]

An English royal proclamation provided that printed news should be agreeable to truth, that the minds of his majesty's subjects should not be disturbed or amazed by lies or vain reports. [108]

The House of Commons ordered its votes to be published. Charles II suppressed newsbooks to placate the Spanish Court. He decreed that the printing of all news was a royal prerogative. [109]

Henry Care was judged guilty of libel for publishing without a permit when he criticized the Pope in his *Weekly Paquet of Advice from Rome*. He escaped punishment because Parliament was prorogued. [110]

Elizabeth Cellier was found guilty of scandalous libel for publishing her *Malice Defeated*, a book celebrating her acquittal of plotting to kidnap the king.[111]

Bookseller Francis Smith was accused of libel for his *An Act of Common Council for Retrenching the Expenses of the Lord Mayor and Sherriffs of the City of London.*

Francis "Old Frank" Smith was a favorite target of Roger L'Estrange, who tricked Smith's arrest and trial by "mean" Judge Scroggs for *Tom Ticklefoot*, a satire on the trial of Sir George Wakeman. [112]

Jane Curtis also was tried for publishing and selling a libel called *A Satyr upon Injustice, or Scroggs on Scroggs*. When he attempted to suppress the Whig press, Chief Justice Williiam Scroggs was "a wild bull who roared that whoever invented the heretical art of printing should be frying in hell." [113]

1681

Stephen Colledge, a fanatical anti-papist, was executed, drawn, and quartered for threatening the king and riding armed to Oxford where Parliament was meeting. His "scandalous" pamphlets led to his arrest. [114]

William Denton criticized the Catholic Church imprimatur requirement as "stifling books in the womb and injuring truth as a trick to keep the laity ignorant."[115]

Edward Fitz-Harris was executed for high treason for publishing a pamphlet critical of the king, *The True Englishman Speaking Plain English in a Letter to a Friend from a Friend*. [116]

Edmund Hickeingill, rector of All Saints Church in Colchester, was tried for blasphemy for his book *The Naked Truth*, which criticized the jurisdiction and ritual of the Church of England. Later he said, "No books vend so nimbly as those that are sold (by Stealth, as it were) and want Imprimaturs." [117]

Joseph Hindmarsh was convicted of blasphemy for printing *The Presbyterian Paternoster*. [118]

Roger L'Estrange became unemployed when the printing License Act expired and a chief licenser was no longer authorized.

1682

Nathaniel Thompson, publisher; William Pain, writer; and John Farewell, writer, were sentenced to the pillory for letters they published which defended Catholics against murder charges in an episode of the Popish Plot. In addition to having garbage hurled at them, they each had to pay a 100 pound fine. [119]

The Privy Council ordered *The Sanquhar Declaration*, a Scots Presbyterian pamphlet which infuriated the Episcopalians, burned along with several other Scots books. [120]

1683

Oxford University issued a decree authorizing the burning of books written by Milton, Goodwin, Baxter, Knox, and Hobbes following the Rye House Plot to kill Charles II. [121]

Thomas De Laune, a Baptist layman, wrote *A Plea for the Non-Conformists*. He was arrested, convicted, fined, and the pamphlets burned. He couldn't pay the fine so he, his wife, and two children went to prison where they all died because of its foul conditions. [122]

Algernon Sidney was beheaded for high treason for writing an unpublished manuscript which stated the king was subject to the laws of God. It was found in his study at his home. [123]

Protestant newsbooks disappeared because of revival press control rules. By 1688 rules required suppression of seditious and unlicensed books and false news. [124]

James Buchanan dedicated his 1579 book *De Juri Regni Apud Scotos* to James

VI of Scotland. The Oxford decree of 1683 condemned it. [125]

John Brown of Wamphrey, Scotland, wrote two books which infuriated the Oxford convention because of their Presbyterian content. One was ordered burned in 1678. But two more including *The History of the Indulgence* were burned in 1683.[126]

Books written by Samuel Rutherford, a Scots Presbyterian, and others were burned because they attacked royalists views and religious sects. [127]

Books condemned by the Oxford Convention included those by Thomas Hobbes supporting the doctrine that possession and strength give a right to govern.[128]

The Oxford Convention condemned to burning Thomas Cartwright's *A Second Admonition to the Parliament*. He was driven out to Cambridge by Queen Mary and spent an exile on the continent. Queen Elizabeth took away his Cambridge professorship in 1571. His book was condemned a hundred years after it first appeared. [129]

The Oxford Decree of the Convocation condemned the book *Naphtali* which cited Biblical references from Phineas contrasting with English rulers. James Mitchell, a minister, botched his attempt to kill the Archbishop over the controversy. Mitchell was executed in 1678. [130]

Mene Tekel, a book refuting the succession of the king's heirs to the throne, was condemned by the Oxford Convocation. [131]

Daniel Whitley, the Reconciler, had his book, *The Protestant Reconciler*, burned. Later he recanted his views and was sarcastically called "Whigby" by protestant activists. [132]

The Judgement and Decree of the University of Oxford ordered the burning of 27 books called pernicious containing damnable doctrines destructive to the sacred persons of princes, their state and government, and of humane society.[133]

The Oxford Convention reached back to a 1574 book by Walter Travers, a sixteenth century Puritan to condemn it to burning. [134]

1684

There were sixteen trials for seditious libel in an eight month period. Chief Justice William Scroggs and John Holt continued prosecutions despite the expiration of the Printing Act in 1694. Luttell's *Diary* recorded 16 trials for seditious libel in 1684. [135]

Langley Curtis was sentenced to stand in the pillory, pay a 500 pound fine, and sent to Marshalses prison, and have his silly *The Night of Bloomsbury* burned. [136]

1685

English courts had forever abandoned procedures which could force a person to incriminate himself. "Freeborn John" Lilburne did most to establish this principle which is central to American jurisprudence. His ordeals and achievements began with freedom of the press issues.

1686

Samuel Johnson, a clergyman, was convicted of publishing anti-Catholic pamphlets. He was whipped with 317 lashes by the common hangman from Newgate to Tyburn. The Ecclesiastical Commission revoked his clerical status so as not to embarrass the church by whipping a clergyman. In 1689, Parliament declared the sentence, the proceedings, and the commission all illegal and the punishment cruel. Johnson was thereupon given a pension by the king.

Samuel "Julian" Johnson was an avid anti-Catholic who believed the Duke of York was like Emporer Julian whom he considered a pagan. His book *Julian* caused him to be hailed to the Court of King's Bench. His clerical status was ended so he could be fined 500 marks, imprisoned until paid, stand in the pillory several days, and whipped by the hangman from Newgate to Tyburn. In 1689, the Committee of the Commons decided the sentence was cruel and illegal and that Johnson be appointed to an appropriate ecclesiastical position. [137]

1687

The 1662 Royal Society of England had published many scientific works under the leadership of Robert Boyle. Dutch printers had also published scientific books which sold well. Isaac Newton wrote his *Principia* in 1687 to refute Cartesian science. [138]

1688

The trial of the Seven Bishops with its not guilty verdict became a prediction of what would happen to libel law as the jury was empowered to determine the libel itself. [139]

Elizabeth Cellier, a mid-wife, was found not guilty of high treason accusations that she was involved in the Titus Oates plot even though some relevant papers were found in a meal-tub of her home. She soon wrote an account of the trial titled *Malice Defeated*. For this she was found guilty of scandalous libel and was fined 100 pounds, to sit in the pillory for several days, and be jailed until the fine was paid, and see her books burned when in the pillory. [140]

1688

The archbishops of Canterbury, St. Asaph's, Ely, Chicester, Bath and Wells, Peterborough, and Bristol were acquitted of publishing a seditious libel. This verdict pushed England's Glorious Revolution forward. The Glorious Revolution in 1688 brought a change in the monarchial institution, which in turn brought more freedom to journalists. [141]

Richard Baxter's book on *The Holy Commonwealth* was burned at Oxford. Earlier he had spent two years in prison for failure to pay a 500 pound fine assessed in 1665 for his criticism of orthodox Christianity in his *A Paraphrase of the New Testament*. [142]

1689

The English Bill of Rights secured to members of Parliament their freedom of speech after a century-long struggle begun by the Wentworths under Elizabeth and highlighted by the martyrdom of Sir John Eliot. After 1689, the problem was not that Parliament's freedom of speech was not infringed, but that Parliament would not permit freedom of speech to nonmembers.

The Bill of Rights joined the Magna Carta and the Petition of Right to form the basis of the unwritten English constitution. After the Glorious Revolution, the crown relinquished its authority governing the press. Although the Bill of Rights in 1689 provided for freedom of speech in Parliament, no mention of freedom of the press was made. [143]

The House of Commons ordered the printer of *Mr. Duncombe's Case* be burned by the hangman. Richard Janeway was arrested for printing a committee action of the House of Commons. [144]

John Locke argued that "no opinions contrary to human society or to those moral rules which are necessary by the preservation of civil society, are to be tolerated by the magistrate." But he proposed punishing people who "will not own and teach the duty of tolerating all men in matters of mere religion." The proper form of punishment was not prior government censorship. [145]

John Selden said:
> A lie will make the circuit of the globe while truth is putting on its boots to follow. Though some make slight of Libels, yet you may see by them how the wind sits; as take a straw and throw it into the Air, you shall see by that which way the Wind is, which you shall not do by casting up a Stone. More solid things do not show the Complexion of the times so well as Ballads and Libels.[146]

The House of Commons published its votes but forbade any republication of a report in newspapers. John Dyer defied such proscription for years and had to go in hiding to avoid arrest. [147]

Hubert Lanquet's 1579 book *Vindiciae contra tyrannaus* was condemned in the 1683 Oxford decree but reappeared in 1639 as England's attitudes toward the king's rule had changed. [148]

1690

The Convocation of the University of Oxford condemned Arthur Burg's *The Naked Gospel* to be burned for heresy and blasphemy. [149]

John Locke, an English philosopher, said, "New opinions are always suspected, and usually opposed, without any other reason but because they are not already common." [150]

Locke said, "He that judges without informing himself to the utmost that he is capable, cannot acquit himself of judging amiss." [151]

The English ecclesiastical comprise indicated the government would tolerate only minimal dissent and enforce maximum uniformity.

1692 to 1694

Charles Blount used much of Milton's *Areogapitica* as the basis for his pamphlet urging a free press. John Locke in turn used Blount's work in his demand in Parliament to end the licensing of the press.

Charles Blount's opportunistic moves created such opposition to the press licenser that the Licensing Act was only renewed for two years. Edward Bohun was lightly fined for offending the House of Commons.

John Locke relied on Blount's pamphlet for his document asking the House of Commons to end licensing. Blount probably had more to do with ending licensing than did Locke and Milton combined. Through trickery, he even got licenser Edmund Bohun fired.

Charles Blount, a diest and republican who had his tracts burned by the hangmen, summarized the Seventeenth Century English thought on the scope of permissible writing. His writings such as *Reasons Humbly Offered for the Liberty of Unlicensed Printing* in 1693 aided in ending preventative censorship in 1694. [152]

Anthony Wood's works were suppressed, as were Charles Blount's *A Just Vindication of Learning, Anima Mundi,* and *Life of Appadorius Tyareus.*

Charles Blount's 59-page book and Gilbert Buret's *Pastoral Letter* were ordered burned by Commons. [153]

The Society for the Reformation of Manners was founded to monitor and control the press. [154]

William and Mary extended the 1685 Press Control Law and continued the policies of the Stuart kings and queens in press matters. [155]

1693

William Anderton was hanged for refusing to name the authors of two books considered treasonable. The investigator had to fight off the printer's wife and mother-in-law when he found Anderton's secret press and the books titled *Remarks upon the present confederacy and late revolution in England* and *A French conquest neither desirable nor practicable.* [156]

John Locke told the House of Commons that there were at least 18 reasons to end government censorship. The House of Lords wanted to renew the Printing Act, but the House of Commons would not agree. Locke objected to government prior censorship because it injured the printing trade, was administratively cumbersome, and was unnecessary because the common law gave adequate protection against licentiousness.[157]

In his *Essay Concerning Human Understanding,* John Locke said:
> Since men are forced to operate in a twilight zone of knowledge, when truth and certainty are scanty, it would be wisest to maintain peace and the common offices of humanity and friendship in the diversity of opinions. We should do well to commiserate our mutual ignorance, and to endeavor to remove it in all the gentle and fair ways of information, and not instantly treat others ill as obstinate and perverse because they will not renounce their own and receive our opinions, or at least those we would force upon them, when it is more probable that we are no less obstinate in not embracing some of theirs. For where is the man that has uncontestable evidence of the truth of all that he holds, or of the falsehood of all he condemns, or can say, that he has examined to the bottom all his own or other men's opinions?

John Locke believed the natural state of man provided absolute independence, freedom, and equality because all men were ruled only by natural law. Men could judge and punish those who took these away from him. This concept justified revolution from the improper applications of punishment by the crown. The purpose of government is the good of mankind. This concept became the creed of the American revolutionists in 1776. [158]

Parliament refused to re-enact the Printing Act. The English common law as declared by the courts prevailed in press and libel law after the Licensing Act expired. In William and Mary's reign the House of Commons did more for liberty than the Magna Carta and the English Bill of Rights; from that time onward, no English government had claimed or practiced the right to license the press. Although the English Regulation of Printing Act expired, this did not mean the press had become free, because it was still subject to the restraints of common law.[159]

1694

The rise of a two-party political system destroyed the press licensing system, and Parliament would not provide laws for Queen Anne to stop critical pamphlets and newspapers.[160]

1695

Edmund Bohun published a pamphlet by Charles Blount which was based on high church views. The House of Commons had the book, *King William and Queen Mary Conquerors*, burned and Bohun fined. [161]

The printing act of 1662 was renewed every two years until 1679, but even then no one had the right to print political news. In 1685 the act was renewed until 1692, but Parliament would not renew it in 1695. The press had been licensed for 157 years in England. Newspapers multiplied and became political party advocates. Strong opposition to these newspapers developed among governing classes. From 1695 until the end of Queen Anne's reign, publishers of domestic news were comparatively free.[162]

1696

John Toland in his *Christianity Not Mysterious* contended that the doctrines of the trinity and transubstantiation were only nonsense. His book was condemned for blasphemy in London in 1699 but widely circulated for many years. [163]

William III and other Stuart kings issued proclamations controlling printers, books, and pamphlets. [164]

1697

The Act of 1697 said any deviation from orthodox Christianity to Unitarianism or other heresies made such persons ineligible for office.

The House of Lords reprimanded John Churchill for publishing a report of proceedings and issued an order that reserved such rights to the House only. This order was effective until the end of the 1700s. [165]

A London jury condemned John Toland's *Christianity not Mysterious: or a Treatise Shewing That There Is Nothing in the Gospel Contrary to reason Nor Above It*, as being blasphemous because it said the mysteries were only nonsense.[166]

The House of Lords issued an order forbidding reports of actions taken therein. This order prevailed throughout the next century. [167]

Coffeehouse conversation by members of Parliament was a chief source of information about actions taken as coffeehouses personnel eavesdropped. [168]

1698

Jeremy Collier's *A Short View of the Immorality of the English Stage, together with the Sense of Antiquity upon this Argument* helped establish a permanent system of stage censorship. [169]

Francis Gregory, rector of Hambleden, said in his *A Modest Plea for the Due Regulation of the Press* that a toleration of all opinions and practices in matters of religion was never thought to be lawful, and consequently such an unlimited liberty of the press, to bring in, and spread errors and heresies, ought not be allowed. This contention was a reply to Matthew Tindal's anonymously published *A Letter to a Member of Parliament Shewing That a Restraint of the Press Is Inconsistent with the Protestant Religion, and dangerous to the Liberties of the nation*. Tindal reproduced Milton's *Areogapitica* and parts of Charles Blount's adaptation of it in the 32-page document which created considerable Parliamentary opposition to licensing the press.[170]

1699

Daniel Defoe published a *Letter to a Member of Parliament Shewing the Necessity of regulating the Press*, "chiefly from the necessity of Publick establishments in religion, from the rights and Immunities of a national church and the trust reposed in the Christian magistrate to protect and defend them." [171]

Chapter 6

LIBEL IN ENGLAND
1700 Through 1759

1700

John Erskine argued in 1700 that people seeking to enlighten others, and not intending to mislead, should be able to address the universal reason of a whole nation on what is believed to be true.[1]

English publishers provided, by popular demand, sermons, science, books, penny novels, hymnals, almanacs, masterpieces, pornography, political tracts, attacks on the king and the aristocracy, or the clergy.[2]

Daniel Defoe was a turn coat political propagandist, Jonathan Swift, Joseph Addison, Robert Steele, Henry Fielding, and Tobias Smollet were the political propagandists.[3]

Jonathan Swift was courted by the Whigs but ended up as a moderate Tory in his newspaper writing.[4]

John Toland's work *Christianity Not Mysterious*, was condemned and burned.[5]

Matthew Tindal, England's leading deist, was interested in an unlicensed liberty of the press in religious controversy, and believed freedom of the press was a natural right.[6]

1702

Charles Delafaye edited *The London Gazette* as a political paper. He offended such persons as Admiral Graydon, Prince George, and Lord Marlborough (John Churchill). By 1717, circulation dropped to 2,000 copies since the content became rather drab.[7]

The Common Law criminal libel definition meant the press was free of advance censorship, but was subject to subsequent punishment. Judge Holt established the court view that the judge would determine if something was libelous, and the jury would only determine the fact of publication.

Chief Justice John Holt defined seditious libel thus:

> This is a very strange doctrine to say that it is not a libel reflecting on the government, endeavoring to possess the people that the government is maladministered by corrupt persons. To say that corrupt officers are appointed to administer affairs is certainly a reflection on the government. If people should not be called to account for possessing the people with an ill opinion of the government, no government can subsist. For it is very necessary for all governments that the people should have a good opinion of it. And nothing can be worse to any government than endeavor to procure animosities as to the management of it; this has always been looked upon as a crime, and no government can be safe without it.

Even so convictions for seditious libel were difficult to obtain. [8]

The English bishops refused to censor John Toland's *Vindicious Liberius* which the House of Commons considered a pernicious and theistical book. [9]

1703

Abel Boyer published *The Political State of Great Britain*, a monthly publication he continued until 1729. His reports of Parliament were delayed until after adjournments so he did not violate publishing prohibitions. [10]

Many newspapers, including *The Observer* of John Tutchin and the *Courant* of Samuel Buckley, were cited by the House of Commons for uncomplimentary references to it. [11]

James Watson served a short jail term for his book *Scotland's Grievance Respecting Darien*. [12]

Among works condemned and burned by the House of Commons was Daniel Defoe's *The Shortest Way with Dissenters*. [13]

Defoe was convicted of libel for *The Shortest Way with Dissenters*, fined 200 pounds, had to stand in the pillory three times, and imprisoned in Old Bailey. [14]

Daniel Defoe devoted his talents to political propaganda. From the Whigs he obtained government appointments for such service; later he catered to the Torys. His works were suppressed but he was pardoned in 1703 for helping the Torys. He shifted again to the Whigs after the queen's death. [15]

The House of Lords jailed William Fuller as a cheat and imposter for publishing spurious letters supposedly from the late King William. [16]

1704

Two books by William Coward, a metaphysician, were considered heretical because of numerous passages discussing religion. Commons had the books burned.[17]

Daniel Defoe started his *Review* which lasted nine years wherein his editorials were the prototype of contemporary newspaper editorials. Defoe said licensing lent itself to arbitrary actions and bribery. He suggested a law with specific indication of non-publishable items instead of relying on the whims of a magistrate. Defoe's *An Essay on the Regulation of the Press* said taxing printing news would only encourage newswriters to vent their own opinions and the sum collected would be too small to mention.

Defoe said in his *Review*, "Government will not be jested with, nor reflected upon, nor is it fit that they should always lye at the mercy of every pen." [18]

John Haw, Benjamin Brogg, and John Tutchin all absconded rather than face punishment by the House of Commons for a second article about conformity they published in their *Observator*. [19]

Dr. James Drake's book, *Anglo-Scotia*, was suppressed. His books and tracts were frequently burned for seditious libel. [20]

The House of Commons prohibited publication of its proceedings. The House had permitted publication of its votes from 1680 to 1703, with brief suspension in 1689 and 1703. The House of Lords ordered one of its officials to publish its votes.[21]

Daniel Defoe was fined and sentenced to 18 months in prison. During his life he was jailed frequently for attacking the Tories and the High Church. Defoe's prosecution was caused by the antagonism of his judges at the Old Bailey. These judges were men whom he had satirized in print in scathing terms for public and private vices. Defoe had written *The Shortest Way With Dissenters* as a funny spoof but church leaders were infuriated. [22]

Daniel Defoe wrote *A Hymn to the Pillory* extolling freedom of the press and proclaimed it an honor to stand in the pillory as did Prynne, Burton, and Bostwick. While he was in the pillory for his *Shortest Way with Dissenters*, his pamphlet was being sold on the streets. Londoners treated him like a hero as he sat in the pillory by drinking toasts to him and bringing him flowers. On the last day of his sentence, the pillory itself was decorated with plants. [23]

John Tutchin, charged in *The Observer*, that French gold was bribing national leaders. A jury convicted him of composing and publishing the material but not having written it; however, he was dismissed on a technicality. His works were suppressed, and he died as a debtor in 1707 in the Queen's Bench Prison. [24]

1705

Parliament burned books written by William Atwood, who wrote political books that antagonized almost everyone. [25]

Roger L'Estrange died at the age of 84 after having been associated with printing and newspapering most of his life. He had owned several newspapers and had championed liberty of the press, but as soon as he became licenser he brutally controlled the press as he had proclaimed in the first issue of his *Intelligencer* which he established as one of his first acts. He had spent six years in prison for his earlier papers, and had been under sentence of death at Newgate prison for four. His plan to destroy liberty of the press included death, mutilation, imprisonment, banishment, corporal pains, disgrace, the pillory, stocks, whipping, carting, standing under the gallows with a rope about the neck at a public execution, wearing some badge of infamy, condemnation to work in the mines, or others. In 1688 he was jailed at Newgate prison for publishing treasonable papers, three years after he had been knighted by James II. [26]

Efforts to enact press licensing laws in Parliament failed in 1696, 1697, 1698, 1699, 1702, and 1704.

Matthew Tindal produced a pamphlet entitled *Reasons Against Restraining the Press* in which he indicated neither religious nor civil reasons were sufficient to license or restrain the press. [27]

James Drake in his *Mercurius Politicus* said:
> He must confess, that to have the most weighty and important affairs, and the conduct of the Great Council of the Nation convass'd in this publick manner, is an invasion of the prerogatives of the Crown, and the authority of Parliament, which may in time prove fatal to 'em both. Some subjects, which in strictness ought not to be prostituted in this manner, to the censure and examination of the indiscreet, incompetent rabble. [28]

The Privy Council forced the publisher of the Edinborough *Evening Courant* to promise to print "nothing concerning the government till first the same be revised by the clerks of Her Majesty's Privy Council." [29]

1707

Irishman John Asgill was expelled from the Irish Parliament in 1703 and from the English Parliament in 1707 for publishing a heretical book arguing that a person may be translated into eternal life without passing through death. He was nicknamed

"Translated." In *An Essay for the Press*, he ignored the law of seditious and blasphemous libel under which he had been censured and his books burned. He believed freedom of the press was the natural right of mankind. [30]

The House of Lords arrested several persons in a London coffee house for distributing newsletters about its proceedings. [31]

In his *Rehearsal*, Charles Leslie said:
> But the law will not allow men to asperse and villify those in post and quality, though their accusations were true. For private men are not judges of their superiors. This would confound all government. And the honour and dignity of our governors is to be preserved without which they could not govern, nor would they be obeyed as they ought to be if they were rendered contemptible to their subjects. [32]

An Act of Parliament provided that it was high treason to assert that the Pretender had any right to the throne of the kingdom, or maliciously, advisedly, and directly, by writing or printing, to maintain and affirm, that our Sovereign the Queen that now is, is not the lawful and rightful Queen of these realms. [33]

1708

The publisher of *The Fifteen Plagues of a Maidenhead*, was freed from a civil court because obscenity had to be tried in an ecclesiastical court. The disappearance of the Privy Council was a great step toward emancipation of the press.

1709

The first English Copyright Act was passed in 1709. [34]

John Humfrey, an advocate of comprehension, and a non-conformist, had his books burned. [35]

Lady Mary Wortley Montagu, a British essayist, said, "Miserable is the fate of writers: if they are agreeable, they are offensive; and if dull, they starve." [36]

London authorities tried Richard Sare, a London bookseller, and the author of the book, Matthew Tindal, for *Rights of the Christian Church Asserted*. [37]

1710

The English Revenue Act of 1710 imposed a tax on printed matter. It was aimed at almanacks and calendars. [38]

A sermon by Dr. Henry Sacheveral favoring passive resistance and non-resistance caused the House of Commons to suspend him and jail him for three years. This move toppled the Whig government and the Tories took over again. Dr. Sacheveral was then given a life-time pastorate. [39]

John Toland's *Christianity Not Mysterious* was banned. [40]

Sir Robert Walpole said:

> The great licentiousness of the press, in censuring and reflecting upon all parts of the government, has of late been given too just a cause of offence; but when any pamphlet and common libels are matters of complaint; when none but mercenary scibblers, and the hackney pens of a discontented party, are employed to vent their malice, it is fit to leave them to the common course of the law, and to the ordinary proceedings of the court.

1711

Charles Ripley Gillett lists 275 or more books, etc. burned publicly in England between 1641 and 1711. [41]

Queen Anne set up a stamp act to restrain and crush small newspapers. Queen Anne told the House of Commons that "Her majesty finds it necessary to observe, how great license is taken in publishing false and scandalous libels, such as are a reproach to any Government. This evil seems to be grown too strong for the laws now in force. It is therefore recommended to you to find a remedy equal to the mischief." The House of Commons responded to the queen in this statement by Gilbert Dolben: "We are very sensible how much the liberty of the press is abused, by turning it into such a licentiousness as is a just reproach to the nation; since not only false and scandalous libels are printed and published against your Majesty's government, but the most horrid blasphemies against God and religion." The House of Commons attempted to pass a bill to control the press but the House of Lords would not join it. [42]

James Boyce, an Irish Presbyterian, disturbed the Irish House of Lords with his sermon on scripture and vexed bishops so much that it was burned. [43]

Joseph Addison, English journalist and writer, wondered why his countrymen were more interested in news than humor. [44]

Addison, a moderate, believed with the Whigs that "there never was a good Government that stood in fear of freedom of speech which is the natural liberty of mankind; nor was ever any administrations afraid of satire but such as deserved it." Addison opposed requiring the identification of authors of even scurrilous works since such law would destroy all learning and "root up the corn and the tares together." [45]

Sir William Blackstone in his *Commentaries* said:

Every freeman has an undoubted right to lay what sentiments he pleases before the public: to forbid this is to destroy the freedom of the press: but if he publishes what is improper, mischievous or illegal, he must take the consequences of his own temerity. To subject the press to the restrictive power of a licenser is to subject all freedom of sentiment to the prejudice of one man. But to punish (as the law does at present) any dangerous or offensive writing is necessary for the preservation of peace and good order, of government and religion, the only solid foundations of civil liberty. Thus the will of individuals is left free; the abuse only of that free will is the object of legal punishment. [46]

Samuel Buckley, publisher of a daily newspaper, was arrested for an article he had copied from a Dutch paper which offended Commons. [47]

George Ridpath and William Hurt were jailed in Newgate for printing and publishing the *Flying-Post*. Ridpath was convicted of three libels published in the paper; in the next year he paid a fine of 600 pounds. [48]

Henry St. John, who was Viscount Bolingbroke, suppressed the press when in power but became a libertarian and free press advocate to launch political criticism when he established *The Craftsman*. [49]

Daniel Defoe, English author and journalist, said, "Doubtless liberty of speech, which is a British privilege, extends no further than to speak truth; otherwise pretend to reckon the liberty of lying to be a privilege of an Englishman. [50]

1712

Under Queen Anne the first stamp act was enacted. Printers found so many loop holes in the stamp act that it was largely ignored. Attempts to create a press registration act failed in Commons.

Sir Richard Steele, in commenting on the stamp act, said: "This is the day on which many eminent authors will publish their last words." This first stamp act led to taxes on paper, advertising, and publications primarily as control devices. [51]

Daniel Defoe did not believe that the 1712 stamp duty on printing would improve news journals and said that taxing any trade so it could not subsist under the payment was not a means to raise money, but to destroy the trade. As a source of revenue the stamp duty would be futile and there is no doubt that the intentions were to suppress the newspaper. The stamp tax was a substitute for the defunct Regulation of Printing Act and was instituted by Queen Anne at the request of ecclesiastic authorities to control the press. The tax covered newspapers and pamphlets, advertising, and paper, and set up regulation and enforcement provisions. Real purpose of this stamp tax was suppression of the Whig press. [52]

Jonathan Swift wrote:

> Do you know that Grub Street is dead and gone last week? No more
> ghosts or murders now for love or money. I plied it pretty close the last
> fortnight and published at least seven penny papers of my own, besides
> some of other people's; but now every single half sheet pays a half
> penny to the queen. The *Observator* is fallen; the *Medlays* we jumbled
> together with the *Flying Post*, the *Examiner* is deadly sick; the
> *Spectator* keeps up and doubles its price; I know not how long it will
> hold. Have you seen the red stamp the papers are marked with?
> Methinks the stamping it is worth a half penny. [53]

Lord Mansfield said, "To be free, is to live under a government by law. The
liberty of the press consists in printing without any previous license, subject to the
consequences of the law." [54]

1713

Daniel Defoe was accused of treason, but managed only to be convicted of a
common law information, and won a pardon so he could write in favor of the French
Commerce Bill in his publication, the *Mercator*. [55]

William Hurt, the printer, was jailed two years, pilloried, and fined 50 pounds for
printing the *British Ambassador's Speech to the French King*. [56]

1715

Daniel Defoe believed in laws against seditious libel and tried to destroy the
principal Whig paper (*The Flying Post*) by trying to get the attorney-general to bring
sedition charges against it.

Daniel Defoe, mercenary political journalist, peddled his talents and opinions to
the highest bidder. He was fined, pilloried, and jailed in 1703 for a tract on religious
dissent, jailed again in 1713 for his published remarks, and convicted in 1715 once
more. [57]

The Post-Master General was told to stop distribution of the *Weekly Journal*
because it contained the "Scotch Manifesto." [58]

1716

For publishing *The Shift Shifted*, George and Mary Flint and Isaac and Mary
Dalton were convicted as Jacobite sympathizers. Flint managed to escape to France.[59]

1717

Joseph Addison, English essayist and publisher, said, "Our news should indeed be published in a very quick time, because it is a commodity that will not be kept cold." [60]

John Toland in his proposal for regulating newspapers said:

> Thus, my Lord, without incroaching in the least on the liberty of the press (which ought to be sacred) or confining to any one party the privilege of supplying the public with news, I fancy the method here laid down [requiring stamped paper] will answer the end proposal, and especially deliver the common people from the distracting plague of those Journals, which are the scandal of King George's reign, in which they all had their rise to disturb, and to the best of their power, to destroy it. [61]

1718

Thomas Emlyn, Unitarian minister, was sentenced to a year in jail, fined heavily, and put on life probation by a court in Dublin, for publishing *An Humble Inquiry into the Scripture Account of Jesus Christ*. He wasn't even allowed to speak in his own defense at the trial. [62]

John Matthews, an 18-year-old printer, was hanged for high treason for publishing a pamphlet, *Vox Populi, Vox Dei*, which said the Pretender to the English throne had a legitimate claim. Two apprentices had tattled on him. When one apprentice died, a huge crowd of printers and editors came to the funeral to insult his body. [63]

Richard Steele made most of his money as a political writer and a partisan journalist. The Whigs gave government positions as a reward after Queen Anne's death. [64]

1719

James Craggs wrote the English ambassador in Paris that the liberty of the press in England "arises even to a licentiousness, and that we have no redress against the impertinent reasonings of any writer, the law having only provided against false matters of fact."

John Trenchard and Thomas Gordon, disenchanted Whig journalists, became investigative reporters examining the South Sea Eattle scandal. They were fined in 1722. [65]

1720

Cato, pen name for John Trenchard and Thomas Gibson, produced 158 essays between 1720 and 1778 first published in the *London Times* to espouse a libertarian theory of a free press. They said, "The exposing therefore of publick Wickedness, as it is a Duty which every Man owes to Truth and his Country, can never be a libel in the Nature of Things." [66]

Cato believed that government officials should be subject to popular criticism and should welcome having their activities openly examined. Their essay "Of Freedom of Speech: That the same is inseparable from Publick Liberty" was especially popular. It said:

> Without Freedom of Thought, there can be no such Thing as Wisdom; and no such Thing as publick Liberty, without Freedom of Speech: Which is the Right of every man, as far as by it he does not controul the Right of another; and this is the only Check which it ought to suffer, the only Bounds which it ought to know.
>
> This sacred Privilege is so essential to free Government, that the Security of Property; and the Freedom of Speech, always go together; and in those wretched Countries where a Man cannot call his Tongue his own, he can scarce call any Thing else his own. Whoever would overthrow the Liberty of the Nation, must begin by subduing the Freedom of Speech; a Thing terrible to publick Traytors.
>
> That Men ought to speak well of their Governors, is true, while their Governors deserve to be well spoken of; but to do publick Mischief, without hearing of it, is only Prerogative and Felicity of Tyranny: A free People will be shewing that they are so, by their Freedom of Speech.
>
> The Administration of Government is nothing else, but the Attendance of the Trustees of the People upon the Interest and Affairs of the People. And as it is the Part and Business of the People, for whose Sake alone all publick Matters are, or ought to be, transacted; so it is the Interest, and ought to be the Ambition, of all honest Magistrates, to have their Deeds openly examined, and publickly scanned; Only the wicked Governors of Men dread what is said of them.
>
> It is only they who fear a free press. Libels are the inevitable result of a free press and Evil Arising out of a much greater good, bringing advantages to society that far outweigh potential harm.
>
> Misrepresentation of publick Measures is easily overthrown, by representing publick Measures truly: when they are honest, they ought to be publickly known, that they may be publickly commended; but if they be knavish or pernicious, they ought to be publickly detested. Freedom of Speech is the great Bulwark of Liberty; they prosper and die together: And it is the Terror of Traytors and Oppressors, and a Barrier against them. It produces excellent Writers, and encourages Men of fine Genius.
>
> All Ministers, therefore, who were Oppressors, or intended to be Oppressors, have been loud in their Complaints against Freedom of Speech, and the License of the Press; and always restrained, or

endeavored to restrain, both. In consequence of this, they have brow-beaten Writers, punished them violently, and against Law, and burnt their Works. By all which they shewed how much Truth alarmed them, and how much they were at Enmity with Truth. [67]

Lord George Grenville said, "The seditious writers of the present day, who deluge the country with their wicked and blasphemous productions, do not make it a question of whom the government is to be administered by whether government should exist at all."

Joseph Hall, an Anti-Trinitarian, wrote a book, *A Sober Reply to Mr. Higgs Merry Argument*. His views so disturbed the House of Lords that it had a 99-member committee search out whence it came. The publisher, Mrs. E. Smith, was let off but three men were tried. The book was ordered burned. [68]

Jonathan Swift, in commenting on Steele's *The Crisis*, said, "I am told by those who are expert in the trade that the author and bookseller of this twelvepenny treatise will be greater gainers than any one edition of any folio that hath been published these twenty years." [69]

The British government suppressed the *True Briton* and the *Freeholder's Journal*. Publishers of the *Evening Post* and of the *Weekly Journal* were fined for libel by Commons. [70]

1722

The *British Journal* said:
When words used in their true and proper sense, and understood in their literal and natural meaning, import nothing that is criminal, than to strain their genuine significance to make them intend sedition is such a stretch of discretionary power, as must subvert all the principles of free government, and overturn every species of liberty. [71]

Cato (Trenchard and Gordon) ridiculed government officials who call:
every opposition and every attempt to preserve the People's Rights, by the odious names of Sedition and Faction; libels rarely foment causeless discontent against the government; the benefits from what the law denominated libels, by keeping great men in awe and checking their behavior, outweigh their mischiefs. Without freedom of speech and press, there could be neither Liberty, Property, true Religion, Arts, Sciences, Learning, or liberty of expression. There may be a risk in allowing freedom of expression. Let men talk freely about philosophy, religion, or government, and they may reason wrongly, irreligiously, or seditiously; but to restrain their opinions would simply result in Injustice, Tyranny, and the most stupid Ignorance. They will know

nothing of the nature of Government beyond a Servile Submission to Power.

1723

Parliament ordered "no publication of its minutes or other items, and that the press not intermeddle with debates or proceedings of either house, or any committee."[72]

1726

Anthony Collins, an English deist, believed:
> as it is every man's natural right and duty to think, and judge for himself in a matter of opinion; so he should be allowed freely to profess and publish his opinions and to endeavor, when he judges proper, to convince others of their truth; provided these opinions do not tend to the disturbance of society. Suppressing opinions that differ from one's own only sheds doubt on the opinions of the suppressor. [73]

The Craftsman in its No. 4 issue of Friday, December 16, said Lord Bolingbroke had this press attitude:
> I must do the persons then in power the justice to own that they generally suffered writings against them to be published with impunity, and contented themselves with applying agrument to argument, and answering one piece of wit and satire with another. The only instances of any severity which we meet with, are burning the Bishop of St. Asaph's immortal *Preface*, and expelling Sir Richard Steele from the House of Commons; but we meet with no grievous imprisonments, no expensive prosecutions or bothersome fines, in the history of that Administration.

Henry St. John, Viscount of Bolingbroke, a Jacobite politician, writer and philosopher, contributed to the 18th Century thought used by American revolutionaries. Bolingbroke, in his weekly or every two-week issues of *The Craftsman*, taunted Robert Walpole's administration with ridicule and denunciation.[74]

The House of Commons attempted to arrest David Jones as author of *A New Description of England and Wales with Adjacent Islands* which it believed libelous. But Jones had died, so the publishers and printers were reprimanded and fined. [75]

1727

An English court ruled that Edmund Curll's *Venus in the Cloister* or *The Nun in Her Smock* was an obscene book that could be punished as a common law crime and said:

Destroying morality is destroying the peace of the government, for
government is no more than publick order which is morality. My Lord
Chief Justice Hale used to say, 'Christianity is part of the law, and why
not morality too?' I do not insist that every immoral act is indictable,
such as telling a lie, or the like; but if it is destructive of morality in
general, if it does, or may, affect all the King's subjects, it is then an
offence of a publick nature.

The King's attorney-general ruled that a thing is offensive against common law if it
goes against the constitution or the government, reflects upon religion, or destroys
morality. Curll was condemned to the pillory. This conviction established the English
civil law misdemeanor of obscene libel. [76]

Parliament considered it a crime for the press even to mention names of its
members. The *London Journal* complained that:

Though the publication of a speech in Parliament looks like a piece of
affectation at anytime, yet it has a much worse aspect at present; coming
as it does so long after the occasion on which it was made, and after all
the measures taking place it was calculated to oppose, it can have no
other view than to render the necessary expense of the government, and
the loyalty of the House of Commons, odious to the people.

1728

Twenty-two persons were arrested in London for letters they had written in
support of Nathaniel Mist and published in *Mist's Weekly Journal* on August 24.
Mist's Weekly Journal, No. 175, earned the pillory and six month's jail for three
printers and one month's jail for three apprentices for printing reflections on the
government. Richard Francklin was fined, imprisoned for a year, and bonded for seven
years good behavior. He had been fined and jailed several times. [77]

Robert Raikes, publisher of the *Gloucester Journal*, and informant Edward Cave
were fined and imprisoned for publishing Parliament proceedings. The next year his
printers published a similar item, and Parliament fined a postal clerk and the
distributor for the item. [78]

1729

Joseph Carter and Richard Nutt, apprentices, were jailed for a month and had to
wear paper hats depicting their offences; publisher Nathaniel Mist already was in jail.

John Clarke and Robert Knell were jailed and pilloried for publishing *A Letter* by
Amos Dudge criticizing King George II. [79]

John Wyckliffe in Middlesex, England, said he was shocked that:

there should be any men so deaf to Religion and Common Sense, so regardless of the natural rights of mankind as to attempt to break in upon that Liberty which every man ought freely to enjoy, of thinking of himself, and of publishing such thoughts to the World, in all instances where such Publication is not prejudicial to society. I do not write in behalf of infidelity; but I contend for a Liberty for other men to unite in behalf of it, if they think fit. [80]

Thomas Woolston said that the liberty of publication provided the opposition of others which sharpens wit and brightens truth. He was sent to jail for a year for his *A Moderator Between an Infidel and an Apostate* and his *A Defense of the Thundering Legion*. Since he had no money to pay his fines, he remained in the English jail until his death in 1733.

When trying Thomas Woolston as a scandalous deist, Chief Justice Raymond said:

Christianity in general is parcel of the Common law of England, and therefore to be protected by it. Now, whatever strikes at the very root of Christianity tends manifestly to a dissolution of the civil government; so that to say an attempt to subvert the established religion is not punishable by those laws upon which it is established is an absurdity.[81]

1730

Edmund Curll was tried for libel for his *Ker of Kersland Memoirs*. [82]

A compilation of libel cases indicated that English monarchs were involved in at least these: Queen Anne, 8 times; King Charles I, 22 times; King Charles II, 15 times; King Edward III, 2 times; Queen Elizabeth, 4 times; King Edward IV, 4 times; King George I, 3 times; King Henry VI, 2 times; King Henry VII, 3 times; King James I, 10 times; King James II, 6 times, and King William, 2 times.

Nathaniel Mist, publisher of *Mist's Weekly Journal*, changed the name to *Fog's Weekly Journal* when the authorities were after him. He escaped to Boulogne and continued his publication for several years. *Mist's Journal* had a circulation of more than 10,000 in London. He had been arrested several times from 1717 on for objectionable articles. [83]

Robert Nixon was imprisoned for publishing acts passed by Parliament. [84]

1731

An indictment for seditious libel was made against Richard Francklin, publisher of *The Craftsman*, wherein he published "A letter from the Hague" critical of the government's foreign policy. A Bolingbroke partisan wrote a tract condemning the government's practice of stretching phrases to find an innuendo to base sedition charges upon. Francklin was jailed a year for criticizing the treaty in *The Craftsman*.

The Lord Chief Justice would allow the jury to decide only if Francklin were the publisher and if the article referred to the king and his ministers. He was fined 100 pounds and had to post 2,000 pounds for good behavior. He was frequently prosecuted and imprisoned by the courts and Parliament for libel. [35]

1732

Thomas Fuller, an English physician, said, "Speak what you will, an ill man will take it. Nowadays truth is the greatest news." [86]

The phrase "freedom of the press" became popular and appeared in English courts in 1732 and in Commons in 1738. Reports of the John Peter Zenger trial in New York and republishing Milton's *Areogipatica* led to this movement. [87]

1733

James Branston in *The Man of Taste* said, "Can Statutes keep the British Press in awe, When that sells best, that's most against the law?" [88]

1735

Efforts to convict someone of seditious libel became too difficult for the government to pursue. [89]

Using the 1730 English Juries Act, the government finally convicted, fined, and imprisoned Richard Francklin for the *Craftsman* for seditious libel with a packed jury. *The Political State of Great Britain* journal said the cheering for Francklin in the streets around the court demonstrated the fondness of the people of England for the liberty of the press. [90]

The Doctrine of Innuendo's Discussed, or *The Liberty of the Press Maintained*, "being some thoughts upon the present Treatment of the Printer and Publishers of the Craftsman" was published. William Arnold published *The Case of Opposition Stated between the Craftsman and the People.* [91]

1736

Samuel Buckley, proprietor of the *Daily Courant* of London, received large rewards for his support of the government. Actual payments to newspapers were recorded under Robert Walpole's administration in the findings of the Secret Committee of 1742. [92]

The *London Magazine* ssaid:
>Every subject not only has the right, but is duty bound, to enquire into the publick measures pursued; because by such enquiry he may discover

that some of the publick measures tend towards overturning the liberties of his country; and by making such a discovery in time, and acting strenuously according to his station, against them, he may disappoint their affect. This enquiry ought always to be made with freedom and even with jealously.[93]

The Privy Council set up rules "to prevent the dispersing of prophane or scandalous Papers, none shall presume to expose to sell any papers or pamphlets (except as are published by authority) until they be seen or approved of by the magistrates or any whom they shall appoint for that purpose, on pain of imprisonment." Actually, the Privy Council was generally ignored and its "thunderings were as the sound of a shot in an empty barrel."

1737

Henry Fielding exposed the great corruption of Parliament. Walpole retaliated by gagging the English stage. [94]

Henry Haines, printer of *The Craftsman* was jailed for an article comparing King George II with Shakespeare's King John. He was sent to jail for a year, but faced perpetual imprisonment because his employer wouldn't pay a fine for him. The editor of *The Craftsman* said, "The great benefit of the Liberty of the press consists in the freedom of discussing matters of religion and government, all disputable points, with a proper regard for decency and good manners, though even they ought to give place in case of extremity, to the publick good."

The Duke of Newcastle provided warrants to arrest and try persons associated with *The Craftsman* and other publications.

Henry Haines was indicted for comparing the King to characters in Shakespeare's play *King John* and articles relating to Spanish depradations. Sarah Stevens and Nicholas Amhurst were charged also.

He was fined for printing Cardinal Mazarine's Epitaph in his *Old Common Sense* as were Samuel Slaw and Dormer for their pamphlet *The Trial of Robert Nixon.* [95]

Robert Nixon was found guilty of ridiculing five acts of Parliament and was sentenced to tour the law courts with a label on his head indicating his offense, fined 200 marks, imprisoned five years, required to post bonds totaling 750 pounds, and put on good behavior until death. [96]

1738

The House of Commons ruled:
> that it is an high indignity to, and a notorious breach of the Priviledge of, this House, for any News-Writer, in Letters or Other Papers, or for any printer or publisher to presume to insert in the said Letters or papers, or to give therein any account of the debates, or other proceedings of this

House or any committee thereof, as well during the recess, as the setting of Parliament; and that this House will proceed with the utmost severity against such offenders. [97]

Sir William Wyndham said:

I do not know but that the people may have a right to know somewhat more of the proceedings of this House than what appears on your votes; and if I were sure that the sentiments of members were not misrepresented, I should be against our coming to any resolution that could deprive them of a knowledge that is so necessary for their being able to judge the merits of their representatives in doors. [98]

1739

A book of Henry Brooke's play about a fictional Swedish king became a bestseller in England because the authorities had censored its stage performance under the 1737 Licensing Act. [99]

Samuel Johnson wrote a satirical pamphlet attacking the Robert Walpole government and the Lord Chamberlain thus:

Let the poets remember, when they appear before the licenser, or his deputy, that they stand at the tribunal from which there is no appeal permitted, and where nothing will so well become them as reverence and submission. A more sure and silent way to control the spread of ideas without a direct attempt on freedom of the press would be to make it a felony to teach children to read without a license from the Lord Chamberlain. [100]

James Lacy, an actor, became the propagandist in opposition to the Stage Licensing Act of 1737. His propaganda led to the war with Spain and a rising opposition in Parliament which secured freedom of the press in 18th-century England.

1740

British authors Henry Fielding and Tobias Smollett received compensation from political leaders for support in their journalistic writings. [101]

John Hervey probably wrote the statement appearing in London which said, "Freedom of the press was not intended to protect scandal, defamation, falsehood. And to poison minds of mankind with idle thoughts; nor was it intended to teach disrespect and disobedience of the law. The freedom of the press was given to instruct, not to destroy."

David Hume said a free press would allow the employment of all learning, wit, and genius to foil tyrants. [102]

John Menes' *Daily Post* was burned by the hangman. Publishers of other publications were imprisoned until they paid fines. Burning of publications continued until the 1780s. [103]

1741

"Treachery Baseness and Cruelty Displayed to the Full in the hardships and Sufferings of Mr. Henry Haines, Late Printer of the *Country Journal* or *Craftsman*, Who is now, and for above two years has been, in close imprisonment in the King's Bench, for a fine of Two Hundred Pounds at the Suit of the Crown, for publishing the *Craftsman* of July 2, 1737," was published. [104]

1742

Lord Chancellor Hardwicke began the practice of fining and punishing newspaper editors for publishing remarks critical of judges. [105]

The Horace Walpole administration heavily subsidized favorable newspapers.[106]

1746

Edward Cave was fined and reprimanded for reporting Parliament proceedings concerning the treason trial of Lavat. His *Gentlemen's Magazine* had managed to report Parliament directly at first, then figuratively from 1731 on as its competitor, *The London Magazine*, did beginning in 1732. The figurative reporting was developed in 1738 when Parliament also forbade reports during times when it was not in session.[107]

The printer of the *National Journal* was instructed to publish news in this order:
Articles from France, Spain, Portugal, Italy, Switzerland, Vienna, Hungary, Germany, Poland, Muscovy, Sweden, Denmark, Holland, Flanders, Turkey, Asia, and Africa.
Domestik news from the *London Gazette* was to be presented in the same order as the *Gazette* and before foreign news.
News from the *London News* was to follow thus: foreign articles, articles of consequence to the Publick, shipping news, casualties, news from any port or place in England, or from Scotland, or from Ireland, or from the Plantations, Gibralter or Portmahon. [108]

1747

Henry Fielding said:
> In a free country the people have a right to complain of any grievance which affects them, and this is the privilege of an Englishman; but

surely, to canvass those high and nice points, which move the finest wheels of state, matters merely belonging to the royal prerogative in print, is in the highest degree indecent, and a gross abuse of the liberty of the press. [109]

1748

Horace Walpole said:

The press is dangerous in a despotic government, but in a free country may be very useful, as long as it is under no correction, for it is of great consequence that the people should be informed of every thing that concerns them; and without printing, such knowledge could not circulate either so easily or so fast. And to argue against any branch of liberty from the ill use that may be made of it, is to argue against liberty itself, since all is capable of being abused. [110]

1750

Lord Chesterfield, British statesman, said, "Words are the doers of thoughts, which should no more be presented in rags, tatters and dent than your person should." [111]

Samuel Johnson, an English writer, said, "The torch of Truth shows much that we cannot, and all that we would not, see." [112]

1752

William Owen, bookseller, accused the House of Commons of acting unjustly for imprisoning Alexander Murray for publishing conducted during an election. He was judged not guilty by a jury against the judge's will. A great cheer was shouted in the court and in the streets around it. [113]

Edmund Burks, British orator and writer, said, "A man is allowed sufficient freedom of thought, provided he knows how to choose his subject properly." [114]

1757

William Pitt, British statesman, said, "The press is like the air, a chartered libertine." [115]

1759

Thomas Hayter, Bishop of London, believed freedom of speech was "a hierarchy off nonreligious values, a right belonging to and essential to liberty. Printing being only a more extensive and improved kind of speech, freedom of the press was to be cherished because it derived from the Natural Right and faculty of Speech." Hayter believed even noxious opinions with which he disagreed should not be punished. He believed the benefits of free expression outweighed its mischiefs and should not be sacrificed merely to ward off imaginary dangers to peace and security. [116]

The Stamp tax was made more efficient to help raise revenue for the Seven Years War, but London printers still found ways to evade it. William Pitt had the stamp act enacted for George II. [117]

Samuel Johnson said, "A newspaper writer is a man without virtue, who writes lies at home for his own profit. For mere compositions is required neither genius or knowledge, neither industry nor sprightliness; but contempt of shame and indifference to truth are absolutely necessary." [118]

John Shebbeare, an English physician, was sentenced by Lord Mansfield to three years in jail for his *Sixth Letter to the People of England* because satires of dead kings were punishable. Shebbeare had served a sentence for his novel *The Marriage Act*, a criticism of Parliament. [119]

Chapter 7

REPRESSION AND TYRANTS
1700 Through 1799

1700

In Austria, the *Allgemeine Zeitung* of Augsburg had to change its name and move frequently because it offended the government. [1]

In Prussia, Frederick II paid 100 ducats to have a Cologne gazette printer beaten up in 1700. [2]

Emperor K'ang Hsi of China followed up on a suggestion of Jesuit priests and had 250,000 examples of copper type to be used by the government printing office. [3]

1703

Peter the Great established the first Russian newspaper and even read proof for it. Catherine the Great halted all freedom of expression and would not allow materials to enter her domain. [4]

1715

A book *A Long History of a Short Session of a Certain Parliament in a Certain Kingdom* was burned in Ireland. [5]

1720

In Austria the *Allgemeine Zeitung* had to move frequently to escape government suppression. [6]

1724

Bernard Mandeville's *The Fable of the Bees* was denounced as heretical and a public nuisance, and it was hanged in France. [7]

1748

Baron Charles-Louis Montesquieu believed no criminal prosecution could take place unless the thoughts a person had were accompanied by a criminal act. His major work *The Spirit of the Laws* added much to political theory.

De Montesquieu, French philosopher, said, "The enjoyment of liberty, and even its support and preservation consists in every man's being allowed to speak his thoughts, and lay open his sentiment." [8]

1750

The Jesuits and their University of Vienna controlled censorship in Austria until state officials governed secular publications. Maria Theresa wanted the Jesuits to control both. A government censorship commission imposed rules and surety bonds on publications in mid-century. The police banned 2,500 publications in one two-year period.

The *Nouvelles ecclesiastiques* listed undesirable publications for condemnation.[9]

Madame Doubilet's *novelles a la main* were based on gossip about false news, assumptions, and calumnies for forty years despite pressure from the king to knock it off. She produced the most amusing journalism of her epoch. [10]

Paul I, Czar of Russia, closed all printing houses and forbade the importation of foreign literature. [11]

1751

Montesquieu's *L'Esprit des lois* was added to the *Index of Prohibited Books*. He said, "The tribunal (for the index) is unsupportable in all governments. In monarchies it only makes informers and traitors; in republics, it only forms dishonest men; in a despotic state, it is as destructive as the government itself."

1753

Pope Benedict IV was liberal, favored free expression, and asked for censorship reforms on the basis of his *Constitution Sollicita ac provida*.

Samuel Johnson, an English lexicographer and essayist, said that a newswriter is a man without virtue, who lies at home for his own profit. [12]

1755

The Abbe de Prades had his degrees taken away, his diocese taken, and was severely chastised by a furious mandement. He fled to Prussia and became chaplain to Frederick the Great. He had said religion is a development of natur... boast too much about their miracles, and Christ's miracles were equivoc... shook his religious superiors severely.

1756

More than 800 authors, printers, booksellers, and print dealers were jailed in the Bastille between 1600 and 1756.

1759

Oliver Goldsmith, an Irish writer, said, "Books teach us very little of the world. The true use of speech is not so much to express our wants as to conceal them." [13]

1760

Claude Adrien Helvetius, a French philosopher, said, "When a government prohibits writing on matters of administrations, it makes a vow of blindness." [14]

1761

Jean-Jacques Rosseau in his novels *Emile* and *Julie, ou la Novelle Heloise* displayed equality of the French classes. Both were censored not only in France but throughout Europe. [15]

1762

The Paris Parlement condemned Jean-Jacques Rosseau's *Emile* and tried to arrest him. When he was found in Geneva he was expelled.

Rosseau, a French philosopher, said, "Man is born free, and everywhere he is in chains."

Jean-Jacques Rosseau's novels, *Julie* and *Emile*, were both censored, but *Julie* was a best seller which was published in fifty editions by 1789. *Emile* was published seventy times, and was burned by the Parlement de Paris. [16]

In his *The Social Contract* Rousseau said the only rightful rulers were ones chosen by the people. The monarch's right to rule was given by the people and not by God. "Might never makes right; we have a duty to obey only legitimate powers. The only good state is a democratic one."

1763

Francois de Malherbe was the French official in charge of censorship. He was lenient and used his power primarily to limit the number of copies circulated. He was fired in 1763, even though he had limited the circulation of books. [17]

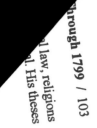

1764

...eported to the Pope that banned books in his city ...not venture to assert that none are ever sold. That ...where various booksellers have ample privileges ...iversity city like this and granted either by His ...ed Supreme Congregation of the Holy Office. In ...keep and sell prohibited books of any sort on the ...view and not selling them except to those who ...ossess them." In 1753, the Inquisitor was afraid ...*œconomy of Human Life* because it had been popular in heathen countries. The cardinals approved the book. Voltaire's (Francois Arouet) *Dictionaire Philosophique* was burned in Berne by the public executioner.

Voltaire, French philosopher, said, "We have a natural right to make use of our pens as of our tongues, at our peril, risk and hazard." [18]

Voltaire, the French philosopher pointed out that in the case of the news, we should always wait for the sacrament of confirmation. [19]

1766

William Bolts, a merchant from Holland, was expelled from Calcutta when he announced plans to start a newspaper. [20]

1770

In Denmark, Johann Struenesse, a German physician who became the principal minister of the Danish king, granted freedom of the press. Even after he fell from grace and was executed, freedom of the press continued. Struenesse was executed in 1772 for having a love affair with Queen Caroline; Danish newspapers revealed the scandal when censorship was ended. [21]

D'Holbach's *Systeme de la Nature* was burned by the French Parlement.

1771 - 1785

A series of pornographic books appeared as the century was ending about the immorality of the nobility. These included:
> *Le Gazetier Cuirasse* by Charles Thevenot de Morande, *Memoires authentiques de la Comtesse du Barry* and *Chronique scandaleuse* by Guilama Imbert.

1772

Voltaire said his oft-quoted statement "I wholly disapprove of what you say and will defend to the death your right to say it." [22]

1775

Pierre-Augustine Beaumarchais, a French dramatist, said, "Vilify! Vilify! Some of it will always stick." [23]

Novels depicting the exploits and depravity of the nobility and aristocrats as a political attack were widely circulated and read in France despite efforts to suppress them. Censored books were aggressively promoted and eagerly sought by an avid reading public.

1779

Richard Brimsley Sheridan, an Irish dramatist, said, "The newspapers! Sir, they are the most villainous, licentious, abominable, infernal — not that I ever read them! No, I make it a rule never to look in a newspaper." [24]

Dutch gazettes produced by expelled Hugenots were filled with bitter attacks on France. French postal officials were easily bribed to circulate them. At least nine of these clandestine journals circulated regularly in France. [25]

1780

Warren Hastings prosecuted Publisher James A. Hickey for criticism in the *Bengal Gazette* which was banned from the mails. [26]

Abbe Raynal's *Histoire philosophique des etablissements et du commerce dans les deux Indes* was such a severe criticism of Europe's exploitation of the West Indies that it was seized and condemned. It was burned by the French Parlement in 1782. [27]

James A. Hickey, founder of the *Bengal Gazette*, was sued for libel, imprisoned, and stripped of his citizenship papers by the government. [28]

1787

The Dutch press was placed under severe censorship in 1787 after the patriotic revolution.

1788

Censorship more or less collapsed in France. Earlier King Louis XIV employed censorship against criticism and even controversy. [29]

1789

When the Estates General of France met to liberalize Louis XIV's government, one of its first demands was to establish freedom of speech and freedom of the press, the prime requisites of a free people. The French translation of the Virginia Declaration of Rights made in 1789 later became the basis of the French Declaration of the Rights of Man and Citizens. The Rights of Man said, "No one shall be disturbed on account of his opinions providing they do not derange public order. The free communications of ideas is one of the precious rights of man and every citizen can freely speak, write, and print, subject to responsibility for the abuse of that freedom as determined by law." [30]

1790

Rigas Fereos and the Poulious brothers produced a weekly Greek language newspaper in Vienna which was smuggled into Turkish-ruled Greece. [31]

Alexander Radischev of Russia said press freedom would keep rulers from departing from the way of truth, lest their policies, wickedness and fraud be exposed.

Johann Wolgang von Goethe, the German poet, said, "Daring ideas are like chessmen moved forward; they may be beaten, but they may start a winning game."[32]

1791

Beaumarchias, French satirist, wrote in his *Figaro*:
They tell me that if in my writings I mention neither the government, nor public worship, nor politics, not morals, nor people in office, nor influential corporations, nor the opera, nor the other theatres, nor anyone who has aught to do with anything, I may print everything freely, subject to the approval of two or three censors. [33]

Louis XVI was forced to accept the new French constitution but its free press provisions had been destroyed by the revolutionaries, who controlled and censored the press very tightly.
The French constitution guaranteed freedom to every man to speak, write, print, and publish his thoughts without having to submit his writings to any censure or inspection before publication. But this provision was not observed by the government.[34]

1792

Catherine the Great of Russia forbade all French printing and even obliterated French names. Tsar Paul I outlawed importing all literature and music. The Russian government burned 20,000 books because it was frightened by the French-Jacobin threat.

The Paris Commune defined ambiguously *sedition* and *libel*, so the press freedom promised in Article XI of the Declaration of the Rights of Man disappeared. The 1793 French Constitution indicated freedom of the press did not exist. By 1797, all French newspapers were controlled by the police.

1793

The French National Convention decreed the death penalty for writing for the dissolution of the assembly or for the restoration of the monarchy. Two journalists were executed, 45 publishers and editors were exiled, 42 journals were suspended, and eleven printing plants destroyed. By 1800, only thirteen newspapers were permitted in Paris. [35]

Jean-Paul Marat published slander and investure during the French Revolution. He was assassinated; a successor in this violent style, Herbert, was guillotined. [36]

1795

An African saying: Scandal is not like bread; there is never any shortage. [37]

A Burmese proverb: Too much talk will include errors. [38]

William Duane was escorted to the first available ship as he was deported for publishing the *India World*. (He became editor of the *Aurora* in Philadelphia.) [39]

1799

Napoleon cut the number of Paris newspapers from 72 to 13. He forbade printing anything contrary to good morals or against his government's principles. He warned that if he loosened the reins on the press, he could not stay in power three months. [40]

Hebert made his *Pere Duchensce* so slanderous that he was guillotined. [41]

Isaac d'Isreli wrote:
> The censors of books in France were a kind of literary inquisitors, which have long been unknown in England. The original institution of these censors was merely disguised as a guard of those publications which might be injurious to society. Their laws were simple, and their approbation at first was drawn up in this concise manner. They declared they found nothing in the work contrary to religion, government, or morals. They had not even a right to judge of its intrinsic merit. It was not long before this system was corrupted. To gratify a faction, these censors assumed the liberty of loading their approbations with high

eulogisms and impertinent criticisms. [42]

A Spanish proverb: It is better to appear in hell than in the newspaper. [43]

Chapter 8

PARLIAMENT AND THE KING'S MINISTERS
1760 Through 1799

1760

Lord William Mansfield said that the jury was concerned only with the fact of publication, and not with other aspects of libel.[1]

Chancellor Hardwicke, the king's minister, prosecuted John Wilkes for sedition in 1760 for his No. 45 issue of his newspaper. A writer said, "Let us not endeavor to enlarge the press's power of doing good. But since it is confessedly capable of producing much mischief, let it be restricted by that power of law, which make the boundaries of the prerogatives, and in all other instances, the Rights of the People."[2]

1761

John Kidgell published a stolen copy of a parody written by Wilkes intended as a private obscene joke titled *An Essay on Woman*. Kidgell published it with changes and became a witness against Wilkes.[3]

1762

John Wilkes argued for press freedom in his *North Briton*. In issue 45 he attacked King George III. He and several other persons were arrested. This act created widespread demonstrations in London and elsewhere. Wilkes won 1,000 pounds for wrongful arrest.[4]

Peter Annet was sentenced to a month in jail, two sessions in the pillory, and an additional year at hard labor, and to post bond for good behavior for his publication *The Free Inquirer* which was accused of blasphemy.[5]

1763

Wilkes, a member of Parliament, was arrested illegally when he criticized

Parliament in his *North Briton*. The authorities couldn't get a conviction of seditious libel from an English jury, so they charged him with obscene libel for his *Essay on Woman* which was a risque parody of Pope's *Essay on Man*. Wilkes was expelled from Parliament even though the work was not published.

Wilkes in the *North Briton* attacked the favoritism and partiality and odious laws of King George III. Wilkes was jailed, but since he was a member of Parliament he was immune from prosecution until he lost his seat and had to flee the country. He was convicted in absentia of seditious and obscene libel and outlawry. When he returned in 1768 to clear himself he was jailed for 22 months, even though the outlawry charge was dismissed. He was such a popular hero that the public contributed more than 10 times what was needed to pay the 1,000 pound fine. Wilkes and 40 of his associates, including 14 journeymen printers, were arrested on a general warrant in the spring for publishing seditious libels. [6]

1764

John Wilkes, fearful of London mobs, fled to Paris. Earlier Voltaire had been beaten by ruffians hired by persons offended by his writings. [7]

Charles Churchill, an English poet and clergyman, wrote:
    Though by whim, envy, or resentment led,
    They damn those authors whom they never read. [8]

The Father of Candor defended the right of the press to criticize a bad government administration. The English jury, not the judge, should decide the question of libel and truth should be an absolute defense. John Almon, publisher of a pamphlet by Father of Candor was tried in 1770 for issuing it. [9]

William Blackstone supported Edward Coke's view of the absolute power of Parliament, saying all forms of government, "However they began, or by whatsoever they subsist, there is and must be in all of them a supreme, irresistible, absolute, uncontrolled authority, in which the *jura summi imperii*, or the rights of sovereignty reside."

John Williams, a publisher of *North Briton* No. 45, was sentenced to the pillory, fined, and sent to jail for six months. A huge crowd collected money for him and demonstrated against the government. [10]

1765

Justice Wilmot considered John Almon's attack upon Lord William Mansfield to be a sacrilege as well as a libel. His comments were not published because the case against Almon was dropped, but the comments were finally published and influenced libel judgments in the United States until at least 1908. [11]

The House of Commons voted 273 to 111 that John Wilkes' *North Briton* was a false, scandalous, and seditious libel and ordered it burned by the common hangman. England passed a law which made it illegal for government agents to search out and seize writers accused of libel. [12]

1767

The first magazine to feature cartoons was John Almon's *Political Register*.[13]

1768

William Bingley was sent to Newgate prison for two years for contempt without a trial, conviction, or sentence for selling No. 50 and No. 51 of John Wilkes' *North Briton*. He refused to answer questions from interrogators appointed by Lord Mansfield. After years of pressure and a threat of Parliamentary investigation, Mansfield released him. [14]

A London barrister said, "The liberty of the press is one of the most valuable privileges of Englishmen; and, when employed to patriotic purposes, merits the patronage of the courts and judicature. As the interests of every member of society is concerned in the proper administration of public affairs, he has a right to publish his thoughts upon them."

The English Government devised the doctrine under Mansfield that the greater the truth the greater the libel and that the court is the judge of the law and the judge of the libel. The jury was allowed to decide only whether or not the article was published by the defendant.

John Wilkes was found guilty of obscene libel for his *North Briton* and was fined 500 pounds and given a 10 month jail sentence. He couldn't attend an earlier trial because he was in Paris recovering from a duel wound. He became a popular hero for freedom of the press as a result of his trials. Wilkes returned from exile in 1768 and was elected to Parliament, but he was not allowed to serve because he espoused views opposed by the crown. By 1769, the American Colonials believed that "the fate of Wilkes and America must stand or fall together." [15]

John Wilkes was sentenced to 22 months and fined 1,000 pounds for his earlier conviction of libel since he fled to France in 1763. British troops killed eleven people in the huge crowds milling around Wilkes' prison.[16]

Sir John Willes, a British jurist, said, "A writer's fame will not be the less, that he has bread, without being under the necessity of prostituting his pen to flattery or party to get it." [17]

1769

The British government was assessed damages of 100,000 pounds in various cases brought by printers against actions taken by Lord Halifax. The court decisions finally ended the arbitrary powers of the Regulation of Printing Act. [18]

Richard Steele and John Wilkes were expelled from Parliament for subversive political writings. [19]

John Horne Tooke had a libel conviction and a fine of 400 pounds set aside by an appeal. He had escaped an earlier sentence on a legal technicality. [20]

A series of letters written by an anonymous author appeared in Henry Woodfall's *Public Advertiser*. They were signed "Junius." They brought seditious libel charges, prosecutions, and convictions. Woodfall, who published the *Junius Letter*, was convicted only of publishing but not of sedition. Juries in two other cases brought by Lord Mansfield found those publishers not guilty. William Mansfield's rulings in these libel cases provoked a heavy debate for years about the right of the jury to determine the truth in libel cases. Junius said:

> We owe it to our ancestors to preserve entire those rights, which they have delivered to our care: we owe it to our posterity, not to suffer their dearest inheritance to be destroyed. [21]

Sir Joseph Yates, a British jurist, said:

> Ideas are free. But while the author confines them to his study, they are like birds in a cage, which move but he can have a right to let fly: for till he thinks proper to emancipate them, they are under his own dominion. [22]

1770

John Almon was arrested and fined for selling a copy of the *London Museum* which had reprinted *Junius' Letters to the King*. He also published the *Father of Candor* letters, anti-government statements in his *Political Register*, and an account of the Zenger trial. [23]

The *Letters of Junius* said, "Let it be impressed upon your minds, let it be instilled into your children, that the Liberty of the Press is the Palladium of all civil, political and religious Rights of Freedom." The *Letters of Junius* threatened disposal of the king. Lord Mansfield tried five publishers who used the letters, but was only able to maintain one conviction. [24]

John Miller, a publisher of the "Junius" letter written by Wilkes to champion freedom of the press, was acquitted by the jury, as were other publishers of the letter. [25]

1771

"Father of Candor" was a pen name for a person refuting a booklet written by Candor, an unidentified lawyer, which had justified Wilkes' prosecution. The reply booklet went through several editions between 1764 and 1771. The Father of Candor believed truth should be an absolute defense against libel. [26]

Commons yielded to public pressure and demonstrations to end its ban on reporting its procedures. John Wilkes engineered the strategy which saw Parliament attempt to jail John Wheble and R. Thompson for articles. The mayor and other city officials helped their cause which included an arrest and dismissal of Wheble. Parliament attempted to arrest the officials, Wilkes, and others. The arresting messenger was imprisoned by the mayor. Finally a mob released two city magistrates as they were being taken to the Tower for imprisonment. [27]

Philelentherus Anglicanus, who was probably Henry Woodfall, criticized the English courts for the way his and Almon's libel cases were handled. The point he made was that an Englishman cannot be found guilty of a crime except by a jury. [28]

George Rous criticized Justice Mansfield's ruling that juries had no role to decide anything but publication in libel cases. Rous presented historical documentation to prove juries had the right to determine if the matter was libelous under common law jury right and that William Mansfield was wrong. [29]

Tobias Smollett, Scottish novelist, said, "As for liberty of the press, it must be restrained." [30]

Henry Woodfall presented a report entitled *Vox Senatus*. "The Speeches at large Which Were Made in a Great Assembly When J.C. Phipps Made a Motion, 'For Leave to Bring in a Bill to Amend the Act of William the Third, Which Empowers the Attorney General to File Informations Ex Officio,' and When Sergeant Glynn Made a Motion, 'That a Committee Should be Appointed to Enquire into the Proceedings of the Judges in Westminster Hall, Particularly in Cases relating to the Liberty of the Press, and the Constitutional Power and Duty of Juries.' " [31]

1772

Reasons to restrict the press in England included the contentions that freedom of the press had served its purpose and could be discontinued, that the press was not free during England's Glorious Elizabethan Age, that licensing would suppress immoral and treasonable writings, that no anonymous works would be published, and that increasing the newspaper tax would make newspapers pay for villification.

William Murray, a British jurist, said, "As for freedom of the press, I will tell you what it is: the liberty of the press is that man may print what he pleases without a license." [32]

1773

Samuel Johnson, a British writer, said that the world always lets a man tell what he thinks his own way. [33]

Loop holes in the stamp and tax plans were finally plugged. The House of Commons forbade reporting its debates. [34]

1774

John Miller was fined 2,000 pounds for libel for a letter published in the *London Evening Post*. [35]

Printers Sealy and Hodson of the Salisbury, England, *Journal*, were found guilty of libeling Justice of the Peace William Buckler when they published an anonymous apology to him. [36]

Henry Woodfall identified John Horne Tooke as author of an article offending the House of Commons. The author discredited Woodfall's testimony, so the house kept Woodfall in jail for several days and fined him 72 pounds. [37]

1775

Thomas Hayter, bishop of London, said freedom of the press was an outgrowth of the natural and constitutional right of free speech. Personal slander is a subordinate evil and criticism of men in public life should not be a public offense. A free press reveals the designs of evil men as they can be detected and restrained. The advantages of freedom outweigh the disadvantages. [38]

The House of Lords stopped its efforts to keep the press from reporting its sessions. The House of Commons had given up in 1771. [39]

A book, *The Present Crisis with Respect to America* was burned along with a newspaper because it advocated military action against the American colonies. [40]

In England, John Horne Tooke was fined 200 pounds and a year in jail for seditious libel for denouncing the British killings at Lexington and Concord as murder and proposing a public subscription fund to benefit widows and orphans. [41]

1776

English law divided unlawful publications as defamatory libel: (defamation of personal or professional reputations); seditious libel (defamation of public officers, government, institutions, or laws); blasphemous libel (defamation of Christianity); or obscene and immoral libel (defamation of England's standard of public morality). The King's bench was the criminal court having jurisdiction over these criminal prosecutions for libel. Remedy for libel was either a civil action for damages by persons, or criminal prosecution for seditious, blasphemous, or obscene libel. In civil action, the defendant had to prove the truth of his publication; in criminal libel truth or falsity was of no consequence. In libel trials, the judges determined whether material was libelous and the jury was forbidden to discuss such an issue; instead the jury only determined if the defendant had published the matter. English common law separated liberty of the press from licentiousness of the press. The King's Bench judges ruled on the tendency of publications, true or false, to excite and move people to change the existing order. The grounds of the criminal proceedings was the public mischief, which libels were calculated to create in alienating the minds of the people from religion and good morals, and the country. This summary by Sir Walter Russell depicted the law of libel in Great Britain at the beginning of the American Revolution.

Francis Maseres insisted that the dangerous tendency "must be proved real and manifest to the jury's satisfaction." [42]

Sir James Fitzjames Stephen said:

> Two different views may be taken of the relation between rulers and their subjects. If the ruler is regarded as the superior of the subject, as being by the nature of his position presumable wise and good, the rightful ruler and guide of the whole population, it must necessarily follow that it is wrong to censure him openly; that even if he is mistaken his mistakes should be pointed out with the utmost respect, and that whether mistaken or not no censure should be cast upon him likely or designed to diminish his authority. If on the other hand the ruler is regarded as the agent and servant, and the subject as the wise and good master who is obliged to delegate his power to the so-called ruler for the time being exercises in his own person the right which belongs to the whole of which he forms a part. He is finding fault with his servant. If others think differently they can take the other side of the dispute, and the utmost that can happen is his place, or perhaps that the arrangements of the household will be modified. To those who hold this view fully and carry it out to all its consequences, there can be no such offence as sedition. There may indeed be breaches of the peace which may be incitements to such offenses, but no imaginable censure of the government short of a censure which has an immediate tendency to produce such a breach of the peace, ought to be regarded as criminal. [43]

1777

David Hume, an English philosopher, believed England enjoyed complete press freedom. His essay for several printed editions minimized the dangers of abuse of free press and claimed it as a common right of mankind. But in 1770, this idea was omitted and by 1777 the edition condemned an unbounded liberty of the press as one of the evils of government. [44]

During the century newspapers were looked down on by many. In 1739 Monteguire condemned London newspapers as scurrilous; Dr. Samuel Johnson attacked journalists who "sold out to one or other of the parties that divide us without a wish for truth or a thought for decency, without care of any other reputation than that of a stubborn adherence to their Abbetors." The Lincoln Inn Benchers refused membership to anyone who had ever been associated with newspapers. Reverend William Dodd, accused of forgery, was condemned for having sunk so low as to have become a newspaper editor. And Sir Walter Scott said, "nothing but a thorough-going blackguard ought to attempt the daily press unless it's some quiet country diurnal."

John Horne Tooke was jailed for seditious libel for criticizing Britain's conduct of the war which included inhuman butchering of American Patriots by British troops. [45]

1778

"Now the popular Clamour runs so high about our Disgrace in America, Our Debt at home, our Terrors of Bankruptcy, and fear of French War what signifies all this canting, says the Doctor? The world goes on just the same as it did, who eats the less, or who sleeps the less? Or where is all this consternation you talk of but in the Newspapers? Nobody is thinking or feeling about the matter, otherwise 'tis somewhat to talk about."
Thus Dr. Samuel Johnson complained about the bad news aspects of newspapers.

1779

Patrick Duffin was imprisoned two years and Thomas Lloyd was pilloried and jailed three years for posting libelous and seditious notices, which supposedly supported the French Revolution, in the Chapel of Fleet Prison. [46]

Thomas Erskine defended Thomas Carnan and the House of Commons rejected a bill to take away Carnan's almanac monopoly. Thomas Erskine was dismissed as attorney general to the Prince of Wales because he defended Paine in the trial which found Paine guilty in absentia.

1780

The Duke of Wellington complained that news reports threatened military operations in Spain. [47]

Samuel Johnson, English poet and essayist, said, "The mass of every people must be barbarous where there is no printing and consequently knowledge is not generally diffused. Knowledge is diffused among our people by newspapers."

Johnson said, "Every man has a right to utter what he thinks truth, and every other man has a right to knock him down for it." [48]

1784

The Irish House of Commons adopted a formal resolution that the *Volunteer's Journal* was a daring, false, scandalous, and seditious libel on its proceedings, tending to promote discontent among his majesty's subjects, to create groundless jealousies between the kingdom and Great Britain, to alienate the affection of the people from his majesty's government, and to excite an opposition to the laws of the land. The printers and publishers of the *Volunteer's Journal* were arrested, and the printer of *Freeman's Journal* also was arrested. The chancellor submitted a bill to prevent abuses in the press, precipitating the first serious clash between the Irish press and the government.

Lord William Mansfield said:
> The liberty of the press consists in printing without any previous license, subject to the consequences of law. The licentiousness of the press is Pandora's Box, the source of every evil. Miserable is the condition of individuals, dangerous is the condition of the state if there is no certain law, no certain administration of law to protect individuals or to guard the state.

William Davies Shipley, Dean of St. Asaph's, was tried for seditious libel for publishing and distributing *Principles of Government, in a Dialogue between a Gentleman and a Farmer* which had been written by his brother-in-law William Jones asking for reform in parliamentary representation. His attorney Thomas Erskine argued that the 12-man jury was entitled to determine if Shipley actually published the material, whether the words were actually libelous, or whether Shipley had intended to libel anyone. The court rejected this argument, however, on the grounds that "the greater the truth, the greater the libel." Erskine contended that a limited verdict would be unfair, and that court precedents clearly established all of the principles he presented. Erskine denied that the English press was truly free under the common law because people could be convicted on the mere fact of publishing. Erskine became libertarian champion of truth as a defense. The jury so confused the trial with its verdict of "guilty of publishing only" that the case was ultimately dismissed. [49]

1785

Manassah Dawes, a lawyer, was one of the first English writers to advocate the overt acts test in political libel which provided that an expression was not actionable unless it advocated the commission of a crime. [50]

John Walter, publisher of the *London Times* had to direct his paper's operations while serving a 16-month sentence because he had been convicted of libeling the Duke of York. [51]

1786

The *Volunteer's Journal* in Dublin bragged that in nine months it had had two informations ex-officio filed against it, three rulings to show cause, two indictments for misdemeanors and four indictments for high treason.

1787

George IV proclaimed the need to suppress licentious prints, books, and publications disbursing poison to the minds of the young and the unwary, and to punish the publishers and vendors thereof. William Wilberforce and his Proclamation Society suppressed Sunday newspapers and financed the prosecution of Thomas Paine's *Age of Reason.* [52]

Lord George Gordon was sentenced to jail for a pamphlet and a libel of the judges. He escaped to France, but returned to England where he was sent to Newgate prison until his death in 1793 since he could not raise the securities for his release. Thomas Wilkins was given a two-year jail sentence for printing Lord Gordon's *Prisoners Petition.*

1789

John Bennett said, "Delicacy is a very general and comprehensive quality. It extends to everything where a woman is concerned. Conversation, books, pictures, attitude, gesture, pronunciation should all come under its salutary vestments. A girl should hear, she should see, nothing that can call forth a blush, or ever stain the purity of her mind."

Thomas Erskine, English trial lawyer, said:
> The liberty of the press on general subjects comprehends and implies as much strict observance of positive law as is consistent with perfect purity of intention, and equal and useful society; and what the latitude is cannot be promulgated in the abstract, but must be judged of in the particular instance. [53]

Philip Withers wrote a pamphlet revealing that the Prince of Wales had been secretly married to Mrs. Maria Ann Fitzherbert; he called her a "Catholic whore." Mrs. Fitzherbert had the pamphlet suppressed, so Withers produced another pamphlet using his own name and the same accusations. He was arrested for libel but continued writing pamphlets about her while in jail, during the trial, and after the sentence of a year in Newgate prison because he believed his duty to church and state required that he expose Mrs. Fitzherbert. He said the English law was hostile to the discovery of truth and freedom of the press. [54]

1790

Edmund Burke, an eighteenth-century English statesman, coined the Fourth Estate phrase saying: "There are three estates in Parliament but in the reporters' gallery yonder sits a fourth estate more important far than they all. It is not a figure of speech or a witty saying; it is a literal fact, very momentous to us in these times." The phrase also has been attributed to Thomas Macauley in this form: "The Fourth Estate ranks in importance equally with the three estates of the realm, the Lords Spiritual, the Lords Temporal, and the Lords Common."

John Magee paid 2,000 pounds damages in a libel trial after the jury decided the 8,000 pounds asked was excessive. The judge, Baron Earlsfort of Dublin, kept Magee in jail with high bail requirements. [55]

A writer said William Mansfield's:
> intention was simply to maintain power and to act as a soldier for the crown, and in doing this he became lost in a labyrinth of absurdity. The maxim he left is that truth is a libel. In the wide and dark and troubled ocean of what is now demonstrated to be libel, nothing can be said in private, nothing can be written of living or even dead persons but what may be liable. If History be not impeached, if Epithets be not prosecuted, and if Religious Discourses be not arraigned at the bar, it is carelessness that passes them over — for as the law now stands — Every human thing, that is not Panegyric, is indictable. [56]

A right-wing Association for Preservation of Liberty and Property Against Republicans and Levellers was organized to fight reform efforts. [57]

John Bowles believed that the jury in a libel trial should decide only the fact of publication since the judge should determine if the material was libelous. [58]

The Courier de l'Europe was published in London and Boulogne as a clandestine publication to cause English dismay from 1776 to 1792. Francis Maseres in Dublin urged the overt acts test to determine if a work was seditious and occassioned the disturbance which it seemed to be intended to create. [59]

Fox's Libel Act of England of 1792 provided that a jury could give "a general verdict of guilty or not guilty upon the whole matter put in issue upon the indictment and shall not be required to find the defendant guilty merely on the proof of publication." The dissenting view of Justice Willes in the Dean of St. Asaph's case and the views of Thomas Erskine were the basis of the Fox libel act of 1792. The common law rules of seditious libel were rendered useless by the Act which accepted the Zenger truth principle. But there were 200 informations filed in England for seditious libel as a reaction to the French Revolution. Penalties were heavy upon conviction. [60]

> Lord Chief Justice Kenyon, in discussing James Perry's *Morning Chronicle*, said: I think this paper was published with a wicked, malicious intent to villify the government and to make the people discontented with the constitution under which they live. That is the matter charged in this information. That it was done with a view to nullify the constitution, the laws, and the Government of this country, and to infuse into the minds of his majesty's subjects a belief that they are oppressed; and on this ground I consider it as a gross and seditious libel. [61]

William Roberts had to pay a fine of 100 pounds for libeling Thomas Walker of Manchester. Edmund Freeman, editor of the *Herald of Freedom*, was a verdict of not guilty of a libel charge even though the chief justice had charged the jury to apply the William Blackstone concept of libel. [62]

John Stockdale, a London bookseller, was acquitted of libel charges because Judge Kenyon instructed the jury to look at the effect of the whole pamphlet containing charges against Parliament. [63]

H.D. Symonds served a two year jail sentence for having published Thomas Paine's *Rights of Man* while his partner Thomas Rickman fled to France. [64]

Thomas Paine produced his *Rights of Man* in London as a rebuttal to Edmund Burke's condemnation of the French Revolution. Thomas Paine's work was a textbook of radical thought and basic principles. Paine was convicted of seditious libel in England for attacking the British monarchy in *The Second Part of the Rights of Man*. He fled to France. In his defense of Paine, Thomas Erskine contended:

> Other liberties are held under governments, but liberty of opinion keeps governments themselves in due subjection to their duties. This has produced the martyrdom of truth in every age, and the world has been only purged from ignorance with the innocent blood of those who have enlightened it. The proposition I mean to maintain as the basis for the liberties of the press, and without which, it is an empty sound is this: that every man, not intending to mislead, but seeking to enlighten others with what is his own reason and conscience, however erroneously, have dictated to him as the truth, may address himself to a universal reason of a whole nation, either upon the subject of government in action, or upon that of our own particular country."

Paine said that the English government "stepped in only when cheap copies of the *Rights of Man* were published. The officials feared the common man. It is a dangerous attempt in any government to say to a Nation, Thou Shalt Not Read."[65]

1792

An English jury convicted Thomas Paine of seditious libel for his ideas in *The Rights of Man*. Booksellers could be prosecuted for selling the book, but Thomas Erskine's remarkable defense speech of Paine and freedom of the press could be circulated because it was part of a court proceeding. [66]

John Walter, publisher of the *Times* in London, was fined, pilloried, and sent to Newgate for a year for stating the Duke of York and his two brothers were insincere in expressing joy for the king's recovery. While in jail, he was convicted of more libels and given additional fines and jail terms. The king pardoned him in 1791. [67]

The friends to the Liberty of the Press was organized on December 19. Thomas Erskine presided as he did at the second meeting in January. His speeches extolling freedom of the press were enthusiastically applauded. [68]

1793

John Bowles, a barrister and a member of the Association for Preserving Liberty and Property against Republicans and Levellers, said, "Those who serve licentious excess to which the Friends of the Press is still daily carried, will be of the opinion that it stands in no great need of the proffered protection of this new formed phalanx of defenders." He attacked the free press principles of the Friends of the Liberty of the Press, but Thomas Erskine refuted his views with legal arguments. [69]

Archibald Bruce, a theologian, said no English proclamation to suppress freedom of writing was a mistake. [70]

Thomas Erskine's speech on January 19, 1793, became a Declaration on Freedom of the Press and was widely distributed. Erskine believed in the unabridged liberty of utterance for which no one could be punished, so long as the mere verbal portrayal of ideas was the only factor involved. [71]

William Frend was banished from Jesus College of Cambridge for his pamphlet *Peace and Union Recommended to the Associated Bodies of Republicans and anti-Republicans*. The Court of the Vice-Chancellor believed it was seditious. [72]

Robert Hall, a prominent Baptist minister, worked for freedom of the press. He said, "All men should have absolute liberty to discuss every subject which can fall within the compass of the human mind." His *An Apology for the Freedom of the Press* separated words from actions. "The law hath amply provided against overt acts of sedition and disorder, and to suppress mere opinion by any method than reason and argument, is the height of tyranny." he said. [73]

Thomas Hardy and John Horne Tooke were acquitted of treason charges. Ten others had been indicted, but no further actions occurred. Earlier several judges participated in very repressive prosecutions because of reaction to the French Revolution. Hardy and Tooke were defended by Thomas Erskine. [74]

Thomas Muir, a pro-French revolution English writer, was sentenced to fourteen years banishment from England to Botany Bay penal colony in Australia for criticizing Thomas Paine's works. [75]

Thomas Fyshe Palmer, a Unitarian minister, was sentenced to fourteen years exile for publishing a seditious pamphlet for the Dundee society, and for encouraging people to read Thomas Paine. Also sentenced was William Skirving. They were exiled to Botany Bay in Australia where Skirving died. Palmer died on the way home after serving his fourteen years. George Mealmaker, author of the pamphlet, spent five years at Botany Bay. [76]

A jury returned a verdict of guilty of publishing with no malicious intent when John Lambert, printer, and James Perry, editor of the *Morning Chronicle*, were tried for libeling the king. Judge Lord Kenyon refused to accept such a verdict, so the jury declared them not guilty. This was the first trial under the new Fox Libel Act. [77]

Joseph Towers said the hypocrisy of the Association for Preserving Liberty and Property against Republicans and Levellers depriving men of the freedom of the press, and of the freedom of speech was not maintaining liberty or the English Constitution. [78]

1794

Thomas Hardy, secretary of the London Correspondence Society, was acquitted by a jury of high treason for circulating pro-Jacobin propaganda in England, including his Patriot publication. Eight others were arrested; two won acquittals and the charges on the other six were dismissed. Daniel Holt, however, was fined and imprisoned for four years for publishing two pamphlets asking for parliamentary reforms. [79]

The editor and eleven proprietors of the *Northern Star* were arrested for having published the "Dublin United Irishman's Address to the Volunteers." They won acquittal by showing a progovernment newspaper had published the address a day earlier. [80]

James Montgomery was sent to jail for three months for a 1789 poem with favorable references to France, because the judge believed it had become seditious in 1794 when he published it. [81]

1795

Lord Eldon, attorney general, wrote the Act of 1795 which said publication which intimidated the Houses of Parliament or the King's Ministers were treasonable, and that persons could be expelled from England for causing hatred or contempt of the nation or its constitution on a second offense. [82]

Thomas Holcroft was charged with high treason along with Thomas Hardy, John Horne Tooke, and John Thelwell. The House of Commons discontinued its prosecutions rule concerning the press. [83]

Thomas Spence was arrested at least four times for selling objectionable works including Thomas Paine's *Rights of Man*. [84]

John Horne Tooke was acquitted of sedition and charges against Jeremiah Joyce of treasonable practices for his publishing in behalf of the London Correspondence Society, the English Jacobins, and alleged sympathy for the French Revolution were dropped by the government. [85]

John Thelwell, an actor and writer, was once indicted for treason, and was also convicted of seditious libel for radical agitation. [86]

1796

James Adair, a liberal Whig lawyer, and Erskine defended William Stone against charges of publishing treasonable materials. An English jury found John Reeves not guilty of seditious charges placed against him by Parliament. The jury did say his pamphlet critical of both houses of Parliament was improper. [87]

John Smith was tried in London for selling a work entitled *A Summary of the Duties of Citizenship*. [88]

1797

Lord Kenyon told the jury in the prosecution of a publisher of *Age of Reason* that "the Christian religion is part of the law of the land." Justice Ashurst said blasphemy was not only an offense against God but was against all law and government because of its tendency to dissolve all the bonds and obligations of civil society.

The Pitt government attempted to suppress radicalism and seditious pamphleteering with prosecutions of Tooke, Cobbett, the Tory warrior, Eaton, Cartwright, Thelwell, Frend, Spence, and others. [89]

1798

James Callender and his associates (Walter Berry and James Robertson) were indicted in Edinburgh for publishing the *Political Progress of Great Britain*. [90]

Thomas Erskine became the prosecuting attorney who helped convict Thomas

Williams, an impoverished printer, of sedition for publishing Paine's *Age of Reason*. Erskine did so at the request of the Society Opposed to Vice and Immorality. He believed Paine had attacked Christianity with contempt and falseness to promote civil liberties. Williams was sentenced to three years. Erskine was appalled at the refusal of the society to recommend leniency so he refused payment and talked the judge into reducing the sentence to one year. [91]

Peter Finerty, a minor who was printer for the *Dublin Press*, was jailed two years for his paper's criticism of the government. British law banned material which tended to excite hatred and contempt of the person of his majesty and of the constitution and government. In England, there was only one verdict of not guilty returned under the numerous prosecutions under the sedition act. John Walter, publisher of the *London Times*, had to direct his paper's operation from Newgate prison for sixteen months for libeling the Duke of York. [92]

1799

John Cuthell was found guilty of selling a pamphlet written by Rev. Gilbert Wakefield who attacked the Pitt administration. Defense Attorney Thomas Erskine said Cuthell had no criminal intent because Cuthell did not know the pamphlet's contents. [93]

The Dean of the St. Asaph's law case in which Judge Lord William Mansfield denied a motion for a new trial, redefined liberty of the press as "the liberty of the press is that man can print what he pleases without a license." [94]

Lord Kenyon said:
> The liberty of the press is dear to England. The licentiousness of the press is odious to England. The liberty of it can never be so well protected as by beating down this licentiousness. The liberty of the press is neither more nor less than this, that a man may publish anything which twelve of his contemporaries think is not blameable, but that he ought to be punished if he publishes that which is blameable.

Chapter 9

SUPPRESSION, VICE,
STAMP TAXES, BLASPHEMY
1800 Through 1899

1800

Benjamin Flower was sent to jail in 1800 by the House of Lords for an article in his *Cambridge Intelligencer*. English newspaper editors charged a contradiction fee so anyone could attack enemies for the price of an ad. [1]

Parliament withdrew from the field of punishing publications. [2]

Thomas Erskine in his defense of Thomas Paine, said "The liberty of opinion keeps governments themselves in due subjection to their duties." [3]

1801

Thomas Spence was jailed a year for seditious libel when he proposed breaking up English royal estates and distributing the land to the parishes. He had been expelled from the Newcastle Philosophical Society for such ideas in 1775. He also was sentenced to three years for his *Restorer of Society in Its Natural State*.[4]

1802

William Blake, British poet, said, "The man who never alters his opinion is like standing water, and breeds reptiles of the mind." [5]

The Society for the Suppression of Vice and for the Encouragement of Religion and Virtue throughout the United Kingdom was established. It had 800 members by 1803, and had managed 700 convictions of persons in the courts including seven obscene libel convictions. By 1825 its membership had declined to only 240 members.[6]

1803

William Blake, British poet, said, "A truth that's told with bad intent beats all the lies you can invent." [7]

Sir James MacIntosh said:
> Those who slowly built up the fabric of our laws, never attempted anything so absurd as to define by any precise rule the obscure and shifting boundaries which divide libel from history or discussion. It is a subject which, from its nature, admits neither rules nor definitions. [8]

Lord Ellenborough said, "Any publication which tends to degrade, revile, and defame persons in considerable situations of power and dignity in foreign countries may be taken to be treated as a libel, and particularly where it has a tendency to interrupt the amity and peace between two countries." [9]

The Society for the Suppression of Vice was founded in London to combat immoral, obscene, or blasphemous conduct or publication. [10]

The Society for the Suppression of Vice and the Encouragement of religion and Virtue absorbed the Proclamation Society. Its work was preventive the first year before it directly attacked obscenity. [11]

1805

English Whigs frequently toasted, "The liberty of the press — 'tis like the air we breathe — while we have it we cannot die." [12]

1808

Henry Crabb Robinson, first accredited war correspondent for a modern newspaper, aroused heavy criticism from the Duke of Wellington who believed Robinson's letters gave information to the enemy. [13]

1810

John Stockdale, publisher of the *Annual Register* in London, was fined $200 for a statement saying "the Methodists may be fools but their present historian is a knave."[14]

William Cobbett was reprimanded for publishing an account of the proceedings of Parliament, considered a libel of a member. He was tried for libel before Lord Ellenborough. [15]

Thomas Erskine said:

The press must be free; it has always been so and much evil has been corrected by it. If government finds itself annoyed by it, let it examine its own conduct and it will find the cause.

Peter Finerty was sentenced to eighteen months in the court of the King's Bench for libeling Viscount Castlereagh. [16]

John and Leigh Hunt were acquitted of seditious libel in England for criticizing military flogging. [17]

"Philagatharches" said:
By granting the free exercise of the press, the reasoning powers of men will be cultivated and thus the public mind will be fortified against the insidious attacks of sophisticated politicians. By the freedom of the press, the publick are constituted a tribunal, to which we may appeal, as a last resort upon the merits of a case. Blasphemous crimes against God are not proper subjects for a magistrate's concern; corrupt politics is best counteracted by argument in the press only seditious libel is suppressible. Portrayal of vice is not a crime per se, unless it constituted palpably contrived obscenity. The only legitimate restraints to a free press lie in the realm of sedition, personal libel, and inculcation of vice.[18]

In Commons, Richard Sheridan said.
Give me but the liberty of the press and I will give to the minister a venal house of peers. I will give him a corrupt and servile House of Commons, I will give him the full serving of the patronage of office, I will give him the whole host of ministerial influence, I will give him all the power that place can confer upon him, to purchase up submission and overawe resistance; and yet, armed with liberty of the press I will go forward to meet him undismayed; I will attack the mighty fabric of that mightier engine. I will shake down from its height corruption and bury it beneath the ruins of the abuses it was meant to shelter. [19]

1811

Baron Wood said:
It is said we have a right to discuss the acts of our legislature. That would be a large permission indeed. Is there, gentlemen, to be a power in the people to counteract the acts of Parliament? And is the libeler to come and make the people dissatisfied with the government under which he lives? This is not to be permitted to any man; it is unconstitutional and seditious.[20]

1812

Daniel Isaac Eaton was sent to Newgate prison for eighteen months for publishing Thomas Paine's *Age of Reason*. While in jail he wrote a pamphlet exposing prison conditions. This brought a second charge, but he escaped trial because of his old age. In 1793 and 1794 he won acquittals for selling Paine's *Rights of Man* and *Letter Addressed to the Addresser.* [21]

John and Leigh Hunt were jailed two years and fined 1,000 pounds for libeling the Prince regent by calling him an Adonis of Fifty, a libertine, and a man who had just closed a half century without a single claim on the gratitude of his country or the respect of posterity. [22]

Thomas Starkie's libel law book refuted William Blackstone's view of libel by pointing out that the liberty of the press needed more than absence of prior restraint to achieve freedom since subsequent punishment also was a restraint. [23]

1813

The liberty of the press did not become a legal right protected by the English courts until the rulings of Lord Ellenborough in 1808 and 1813 cases, commenced what is called the law of "fair comment on matters of public concern." [24]

John Magee, Jr., editor of the *Dublin Mail*, was jailed two years for charging the Duke of Richmond with corruption. When he published resolutions by Catholics condemning the sentence, another six months were added, and his mailing stamps denied until a brother took over the paper. [25]

1815

Thomas Bowdler said, "Civil liberty is not liberty to think and do what one will; this is license. Rather it is to be able to do what he ought to will." [26]

John and Leigh Hunt, for criticizing the Prince Regent's habits and tastes were tried four times, acquitted three times, but finally fined 1,000 pounds each and jailed in separate prisons for two years. [27]

Mr. Drakard, an English printer of *The Stamford News*, had commented on what he called the most heartrending of all exhibitions on this side of hell, an English military flogging. He was sentenced to eighteen months imprisonment, fined 200 pounds, and bonded for three years thereafter not to publish disapproved materials. In England, military floggings could not be commented on in editorials. William Cobbett was fined 1,000 pounds and jailed for two years for doing so. [28]

Jesse Sharpless and several associates were convicted of exhibiting a "certain wicked, scandalous, infamous and obscene painting representing a man in an obscene, impudent, and indecent posture with a woman, to the manifest corruption and subversion of youth, and other citizens against the peace and dignity of the commonwealth." The judges weren't allowed to see the picture.

1817

Thomas Bowdler, an English doctor, and his family edited or "bowdlerized" literature to eliminate indelicate passages. Their *The Family Shakespeare* was a best seller with its sanitized presentation of the Bard's works to protect young children from reading about bawdy England. [29]

William Cobbett left England for the colonies when habeas corpus provisions were suspended. This flight weakened Lord Sidmouth's efforts to control the press.[30]

William Hazlitt, an English essayist, said, "Political truth is a libel — religious truth blasphemy." [31]

William Hone was arrested for blasphemous libel in his *Reformer's Register* and other printing but he was acquitted three times by juries. [32]

Percy Byssche Shelley's *Queen Mab* was so disliked by authorities that they used it as evidence to deny him the right to rear his children after his divorce. Shelley was expelled from Oxford later for a pamphlet denying the existence of God. [33]

Lord Sidmouth, English secretary of state, proposed that justices of the peace could jail anyone accused of blasphemous or seditious libels without bail. [34]

When the Society for Suppression of Vice and the Encouragement of Religion and Virtue began campaigning against blasphemy, it was heavily criticized. [35]

1818

Thomas Bowdler published his *Family Shakespeare* excised whatever could not be read aloud in the family or read aloud by a gentleman to a company of ladies. [36]

Francis Ludlow Holt, an English lawyer, considered freedom of the press to be one of the "rights of nature; that is, to say, of the free exercise of our faculties."[37]

William Hone was tried three times for blasphemy, once for a parody on the Apostle's creed, the Lord's Prayer, and the Ten Commandments; once for a political parody of the Litany in the *Book of Common Prayer* and once for a parody of the "Athansian Creed." He was acquitted and sold 300,000 copies of his parodies. Richard Carlile had to serve eighteen months in jail for publishing William Hone's parodies. [38]

An English jury refused to allow a judge to declare Mary Tocker guilty of libel; instead, the jury read the alleged libelous statement and declared her not guilty. [39]

An English court ruled that Robert Southey's poem, "Wat Tyler," was actually libelous and thus not entitled to be his controllable property. Richard Carlile began a fight against censorship in England by hawking *The Black Dwarf* by Wooler and by publishing "Wat Tyler," when the poet laureate was trying to suppress his embarrassing work. [40]

Thomas Wooler was judged guilty of libel for his *Black Dwarf* publication, which was popular among laborers. Wooler was spared a jail sentence because of faulty trial proceedings even though he had been found guilty of seditious libel and high treason. [41]

1819

William Benbow, a bookseller, was charged twice for libel. But the government withdrew from prosecution because the actions were based on the private association, which disintegrated in 1822. [42]

Jane Carlile, whose husband was in jail for libel, was indicted for selling *The First Day's Proceedings upon the Mock Trial of Richard Carlile*, upon the request of the Society for the Suppression of Vice. She had to buy back her furniture from the police, who confiscated almost everything in her shop, which she reopened. But she was charged with libel for publishing Sherwin's *Life of Paine*. Her lawyer got her indictment and sentence quashed on a technicality. [43]

Lord Byron, English poet, said, "Words are things, and a small drop of ink, falling like dew, upon a thought, produces that which makes thousands, perhaps millions, think." [44]

Six publishing indictments against Richard Carlile were in the English Courts. They sentenced him to six years in jail. His wife and sister and many of his friends working in the shop also were jailed.

Carlile developed a book vending machine which delivered a book for coins. This made it impossible to arrest an identifiable bookseller and helped Carlile's shop be a financial success despite jail sentences and harassment.

Carlile was found guilty for the first time. He had published Thomas Paine's *Age of Reason*. He also was found guilty of publishing Palmer's *Principles of Nature*, but his trial for libel in *Sherwin's Register* was not pursued by the government. Since he couldn't make the excessive bail he was jailed. He was sentenced to three years, fined 1,500 pounds, and assessed good behavior bonds for life of 1,200. His printing shops were raided and his equipment and publication stocks confiscated. He actually was never tried for anything he wrote. Carlile said:

> My whole and sole object, from first to last, from the time of putting off my leather apron to this day has been a Free Press and Free Discussion.

When I first started as a hawker of pamphlets I knew nothing of political principles. I had never read a page of Paine's writings; but I had a complete conviction that there was something wrong somewhere, and that the right application of the printing press was the remedy. [45]

The Constitutional Association was founded by English Tories to suppress disloyal and seditious publications. The courts generally rejected its efforts to prosecute publications. [46]

In *A Dialogue between a Methodist Preacher and a Reformer*, the reformer said: The *Two Penny Trash*. And pray, is there no *Sixpenny Trash*? Cannot truth and reason and sound argument be sold for twopence? And if books become dangerous when they are cheap, how are we to defend our cheap religious tract Societies? Now if Cobbett, Wooler, Sherwin, and other popular writers of political tracts, promulgate false doctrines, the press is open, refute them. If they publish misstatements, overwhelm them by the production of irrefutable facts. If their laughing be low and vulgar, expose them in a style more chaste and eloquent. Defeat them upon their own ground. But do not run in an affected fright to a police officer and join associations for the purpose of arguing with swords and batoons. Your God-fearing friends, the yeomanry, have indeed sabred the people, but they have not thereby convinced them of error. [47]

Thomas Dolby was arrested and charged for libels in both his *Pasquin* and his *A Political Dictionary*. [48]

Thomas Flindell was jailed eight months for libeling the Queen in the *Western Luminary* by discussing charges against her in a trial instituted by the House of Commons. [49]

W.J. Fox, in a sermon discussing the trial of Carlile for republishing Paine's *Age of Reason* in England, said, "If Deists will listen to you, persuade them; if they will reason, argue with them; if they misrepresent, expose them; but in the name of Christ do not persecute them; do not abet or sanction persecution." [50]

William Hone, satirist and parodist in England, said, "The printing press is the thing, that in spite of new Acts, and attempts to suppress it, by soldiers or tax, will poison the vermin, that plunder the House that Jack Built." When Joseph Russell was hauled into court for a political libel for selling one of William Hone's parodies, the jury became so amused and laughed so hard it refused to find him or it libelous.

Hone created a parody of a speech by the Prince Regent which he called *Man in the Moon, a Speech from the Throne to the Senate of Lunataria*. Another of his parodies was called *The Political House That Jack Built*. Although these parodies were clearly seditious under English laws, the government would not prosecute for fear of popular ridicule. [51]

John Hunt, a radical, was jailed for libel; this was Hunt's fifth conviction for seditious libel. News vendors selling Richard Carlile's publications were jailed a few weeks each, put on good behavior for three years, and fined. [52]

John Poynder said London Sunday newspapers were an evil religious and political impiety. [53]

Bookseller Russell was convicted for selling William Hone's parodies, another person was judged guilty of libel for selling part of the *Black Book* and his *Republican*. [54]

Lord Sidmouth, English home secretary, urged Parliament to provide measures to regulate the press which "at present is a most malignant and formidable enemy of the English constitution, to which it owes its freedom." [55]

1819

Lord Sidmouth said, "But you are doubtless aware that itinerant vendors of seditious and blasphemous libels may be apprehended and held to bail, and by these means the dissemination of this the worst description of poison, has been considerably checked in many parts of the Kingdom.

Sidmouth said, "It was well-known that a conspiracy existed for the subversion of the constitution and the right of property. Among the means adopted for the accomplishment of this end, the press was one of the principal." Lord Sidmouth, Lord Castlereagh, and Lord Eldon, all government leaders, and Parliament managed to pass six acts. Three pertaining to the press were the act for the more effective prevention and punishment of blasphemous and seditious libel, the act to subject certain publications to the duties upon newspapers, and the act to prevent delay in the administration of justice in cases of misdemeanor.

Thomas Wooler was jailed fifteen and George Edmonds nine months for Edmond's *Weekly Register* and Wooler's *Black Dwarf.* [56]

The "Peter-Loo Massacre" account claiming four hundred persons had been killed, or wounded, or injured at Manchester was cause for arresting James Wroe who was jailed for a year and fined, while his wife and other family members were released on bail. These convictions bankrupted Wroe. [57]

1820

Samuel Bailey appealed for freedom of the press in England as a factor in the natural progress of knowledge and the adaption of institutions to changes in opinion. "No power can arrest the silent march of thought made possible by a free press." [58]

In sentencing the publisher of the *Manchester Observer* to jail for a year, Sir

W.D. Best said:
> With the truth or falsehood of libel, the jury had nothing to do. If this narrative were false, there could be no manner of doubt that it was a gross and abominable libel. If it were true, what was the duty of the defendant as an English subject? Not to make a paragraph of the transaction, to get a livelihood by vending his exaggerations, but to have taken steps for securing the offenders and bringing the affair before the proper tribunal. By publications in his newspaper, what did this man do? He rendered the administration of justice impossible because he rendered a fair trial impossible.

An English jury found the Rev. Blacow guilty of criminal libel for publishing that "the queen was a Goddess of Lust who polluted the Holy Sepulchre itself, the Church at Hammersmith, by her presence." [59]

George Canning said the Libel Act was a dike that should hold off the despotism of the press, but the dike was broken, and the government ministers had to bow before the deluge. [60]

News vendors selling Richard Carlile's publications were jailed a few weeks each, put on good behavior for three years, and fined. [61]

Jane Carlile was sentenced to Dorchester Prison for two years to join her jailed husband because of blasphemous libel for selling Sherwin's *Life of Paine.* [62]

Mary Anne Carlile, sister of Richard Carlile, was acquitted of seditious libel for selling her brother's pamphlets. But she was convicted of blasphemous libel and sent to prison for two years. [63]

John Cleland's book *Fanny Hill* was brought into court on an obscenity charge. [64]

The Constitutional Association for Opposing the Progress of Disloyal and Seditious Principles, which was founded in 1920, said:
> The Press, that great and invaluable blessing of civilized life — that mighty engine for diffusing the light of Liberty and the Gospel — has unhappily become, in the hands of evil men, a lever to shake the foundations of social and moral order. Its power, which within the last century has been multiplied as hundredfold, may now be almost said to reign paramount in the guidance of public opinion; and to those friends of their country who reflect deeply on this fact it cannot but be a matter of serious alarm to observe that a very large proportion of our periodical publications is under the direction, either of avowed enemies of the constitution, or of persons whose sole principle of action is their own private and selfish interest.

Members of the association believed that the lower orders and laborers had understanding barely enabling them to distinguish between a cabbage and a potato.[65]

Thomas Davison said that those who said the Bible was part of the law were bigoted old women and the Bible was derogatory of God, destructive to morality, and opened to the best interests of society. For this he was heavily fined and jailed for two years. [66]

Thomas Dolby was convicted in England of libel in his newspaper and of selling *A Political Dictionary*. He avoided being sentenced by promising to give up book selling. [67]

John Hunt was jailed for a year for publishing that House of Commons members were "venal boroughmongers, grasping placemen, greedy adventurers — in short, containing a far greater portion of public criminals than public guardians.[68]

Between 1807 and 1821 there were 101 prosecutions for seditious libel in England.

Gilbert McLeod was jailed four months for commenting on the Kinloch address in his *The Spirit of the Union*. Two conservative journalists had done the same thing in their Edinburgh *Correspondent*. One was fined and the other jailed. McLeod was exiled to Australia with two hundred convicts. [69]

James Mill said, "Even when it (freedom of the press) is converted to abuse, it is not for the advantage of an innocent man to seek to restrain it; he will find his advantage in continuing through life to despise its excesses." [70]

"Phocion" contended that the press did not cause but only reflected the revolutionary spirit, as was its proper function. [71]

John Thelwell was arrested and tried for seditious libel for attacking the Constitutional Association in the *Champion*. He was acquitted. [72]

Arthur Wellesley, Duke of Wellington, said, "Publish and be damned!" [73]

Mrs. Susannah Wright was sentenced to jail in England for selling issues of Richard Carlile's pamphlets which he had written while serving a jail sentence. [74]

1821

Samuel Bailey of Sheffield said:
> Whoever has attentively meditated on the progress of the human race, cannot fail to discern that there is now a spirit of inquiry amongst men which nothing can stop or even materially control. Reproach and obloquy, threats, and persecution, will be vain. They embitter

opposition and engender violence; but they cannot abate the keenness of research. There is a silent march of thought which no power can arrest; and which is not difficult to see will be marked by important events. Mankind were never before in the situation in which they now stand. The Press has been operating on them for several centuries, with an influence scarcely perceptible at its commencement, but daily becoming more palpable and acquiring accelerated force. It is rousing the intellect of nations, and happy will it be for them if there be no rash interference with the natural progress of knowledge. [75]

Sir Francis Burdett of Westminster was found guilty of writing threatening letters because the letters constituted publishing. He was sentenced to three months in a minimum security prison in which he entertained twice weekly. He was cheered by a great throng on the way to jail, but had to pay a 2,000 pound fine.

In the Burdett trial, Justice Best said:

Libel is a question of law, and the judge is the judge of the law of libel as in all other cases, the jury having the power of acting agreeably to his statements of the law or not; the Liberty of the press is this: That you may communicate any information that you think proper to communicate by print; that you may point out to the government their errors, and endeavor to convince them their system of policy is wrong and attended to disadvantage to the country, and that another system of politics would be attended with benefit. It is from such writings that the religion of this country has been purified; it is by such writings that the constitution has been brought to the perfection that it now has. And God forbid I should utter a sentence to show that a man speaking with that respect which he ought to speak with of established institutions may not show that some reform may be necessary or that the military ought not to be used in the manner in which they are. But the question always is as to the manner.

He told the jury that if it found a paper *to appeal to the passions of the lower orders of the people, and not having a tendency to inform those who can correct abuses*, it is a libel. [76]

Lord Byron gave up his career as an English poet to edit Greek revolutionary papers and was killed in the war against Turkey. [77]

Mary Ann Carlile, sister of Richard Carlile, was convicted of libel for selling *Appendix to Paine's Theological Works*. She was fined and jailed for a year. [78]

James Mills prepared such a cogent explanation of liberty of the press for the fifth edition of the *Encyclopedia Britannica* that it was widely reprinted in pamphlet form. He said it was beneficial to allow the press to make people so unhappy with bad government that the ruling officials would find it imprudent to disregard the discontent of the many. [79]

More than 120 prosecutions for seditious and blasphemous libel occurred from 1819 through 1821.

1822

John Barkley, a shop man working for Richard Carlile, was sentenced to six months in jail for operating Carlile's bookshop while Carlile was in jail. William Holmes, who volunteered to work at Richard Carlile's bookshop while Carlile was in prison, was sentenced to two years for selling seditious books. When he got out of jail he opened his own bookstore selling the same books. [80]

For publishing an alleged blasphemous and seditious libel, Humphrey Boyle was imprisoned eighteen months, a Mr. Rhodes, who refused to give his name, was sentenced two years as a Mr. Holmes was. [81]

Richard Carlile revived his *Republican* while still in prison. The Constitutional Association bankrupted itself by spending 30,000 pounds primarily to prosecute Carlile.
He said, "The printing press may be strictly denominated a multiplication table as applicable to the mind of man. The art of printing is a multiplication of the mind."[82]

William Clarke was prosecuted by the Society of the Suppression of Vice for his *Reply to the Anti-matrimonial Hypothesis and Supposed Atheism of Percy Byssche Shelley*. But the judge said the jury was to decide "whether such a book had any other tendency than that of undermining the divine system of Christianity and substituting atheism in its room." The jury could not, and found Clarke guilty. He got four months in jail and five years good behavior.

Charles Lamb, an English essayist, said, "Newspapers always excite curiosity. No one even lays one down without a feeling of disappointment." [83]

Samuel Waddington was found guilty of blasphemy by a jury that accepted Chief Justice Abbot's view that his pamphlet saying Christ was an imposter and a murderer was a blasphemous libel.[84]

An English jury refused to convict John Ambrose Williams of criminal libel for bringing the Church of England and its clergy into disrespect even though the judge urged conviction. Williams was publisher of the *Durham Chronicle*. [85]

Mrs. Susannah Wright was sentenced to Newgate for selling the pamphlet, *Address to the Reformers*. She had to take her six-month-old baby to jail with her. The English authorities added eighteen more months to her sentence because she believed Christianity could not be part of English law. She wasn't allowed to complete her defense in the trial. [86]

1823

Jeremy Bentham declared that the existence of a free government depended in part of the freedom with which:

>Malcontents may communicate their sentiments, concert their plans, and practice every mode of opposition short of actual revolt, before the executive powers can be legally justified in disturbing them. [87]

Richard Carlile had spent nine years in jail for his publications. These Carlile helpers served jail sentences: William Campion, three years; Richard Hassell, two years; Thomas Jeffries, two months; John Clarke, three years; Mr. Haley and Mr. Perry, three years; and Thomas Cochrane, six months. [88]

Abram Combe in Edinburgh said much of the distress of the world is caused by ignorance and that the periodical press has a responsibility to give full and accurate information on all sides of a controversy so that truth may be perceived.

Edmund Kimball said, "The question is not whether this evil is of equal magnitude with that which would ensue from a tyrannical restraint. An arbitrary corrupt, or weak government cannot long resist criticism from the press. A good government will not fear it." [89]

William Turnbridge, one of Carlile's bookshop volunteers, was imprisoned for two years as a result of prosecutions arranged by the Society for the Suppression of Vice in England. [90]

Leicester Stanhope in London said:

>All history demonstrates that nothing tends so much to avert revolutions, as those timely and temperate reforms which result from free discussion.

James Watson spent a year in jail for selling a copy of Palmer's *Principles of Nature* in Carlile's bookshop and selling materials written by Thomas Paine. [91]

1824

James Affleck, a grocer, was indicted for selling Thomas Paine's *Age of Reason*, a Chinese prayer, a book about the character of Jehovah and the prophets, a letter to the chief rabbi, the *Republican*, and Shelley's *Queen Mab*. He was jailed three months.

John Hunt published a poem, "Vision of Judgment," ridiculing the dead king. He was indicted and Chief Justice Abbott said that a publication tending to disturb the minds of living individuals and to bring them into contempt by reflecting upon persons who were dead, was an offense against the law. Hunt was fined and required to post good behavior bonds. [92]

> Hunt said the distinction between liberty and license was a sham. He said:
> The licentiousness of the press is every disclosure by which any abuse,
> from practice of which they (in whose hands the supreme power of the
> state is vested) draw any advantage, is brought to light and exposed to
> shame — whatsoever disclosure it is, or is supposed to be their interest
> to prevent. The liberty of the press is such disclosure, and such only
> from which no inconvenience is apprehended. [93]

When Robert Hall, a popular Baptist preacher, republished his *Apology for Freedom of the Press and for General Liberty*, a vigorous debate from other clerics followed. [94]

1825

Jeremy Bentham said that "licentiousness of the press is charged when suppression is to the advantage of the government. Liberty of the press is the right of any expression that does not inconvenience those in power." [95]

Richard Carlile was finally freed after serving six years in jail for libel. [96]

Charles Caleb Colton, an English clergyman and writer, said, "We owe almost all our knowledge not to those who have agreed, but to those who have differed."[97]

Charles Knowlton's *Fruits of Philosophy*, which was a book on birth control, was ruled obscene. Annie Besant and Charles Bradlaugh were prosecuted in England for selling the Knowlton book. [98]

The Society for the Suppression of Vice financed trials of fourteen blasphemous publications and twenty obscene publications between 1817 and 1825. [99]

1827

Samuel Cook, a Worcester merchant, was found guilty of seditious libel for a handbill in his window accusing the government ministers of contributing to hunger and recommending they be beheaded on Tower Hill. [100]

Lord Tenterden was refuted by the *London Magazine* for saying that "for Christianity is part and parcel of the law of the land." When Robert Tyler was convicted of blasphemy, the magazine said it is "no more part and parcel of the law of the land than it is part and parcel of Lord Tenterden's wig. It is solely a belief in the truth, subject to critical inquiry."

1828

Thomas Babington Macauley, an English historian, said, "The gallery in which the reporters sit has become the fourth estate of the realm." (This catchy phrase is often misapplied to the role of the press in the United States, which in no way functions as the English press does in relations with its government.) [101]

1829

The Duke of Wellington and his political allies lost in a propaganda war when they instituted libel prosecutions which resulted in *Morning Journal* Editor Alexander being fined and jailed for a year.

1830

Richard Carlile published his *Prompter* and was soon indicted for seditious libel. The jury was tortured and intimidated into a guilty verdict so Carlile could be sentenced to eight more months in jail. [102]

William Cobbett was able to escape libel charges for a letter published in *Cobbett's Weekly*. The jury could not reach a verdict and the case ended as a *nolle prosequi*. [103]

William Makepeace Thackeray, an English novelist, said, "Yesterday's preacher becomes the text for today's sermon." [104]

The 1819 English Libels Act was repealed.

Richard Carlile, athiest publisher in England, was jailed for nearly ten years for circulating such writings. [105]

The Society for Promoting Useful Knowledge was founded in England to offer good literature. It didn't survive. [106]

1831

Richard Carlile was sentenced to two years in jail for his unstamped newspaper the *Prompter*. [107]

William Carpenter was fined and jailed for failing to pay the stamp tax for his *Political Letters* which he claimed were separate publications and thus not a periodical. [108]

Henry Hetherington in his *Poor Man's Guardian* said, "No more evasion: We will not trespass: but deny the authority of our 'lords' to enclose the common against us; we will demand our right, nor treat but with contempt." He was fined for it, and also later for his *People's Conservative* for tax stamp evasion. [109]

Newspapers in England cost seven pence. The stamp cost was four pence. This priced newspapers beyond the reach of most people. Many person published newspapers without paying the tax, and many suffered severe penalties for doing so. A newspaper vendor told the court in England that:

> I stands here, your worships, upon right and principle, on behalf of the poor working, uneducated classes of this country. They are called ignorant, but what is the cause of their ignorance? Why the tax which prevents them from getting information. Your worships pretty well knows the reason them in power puts on the tax; it is to keep the poor from knowing their rights; for if poor working people knowed their rights, they would soon annihilate the corrupt institutions that oppress them.

1832

The first magazine that became a truly mass circulation media with 100,000 copies was the *Penny Magazine* of London. Abel Haywood was imprisoned for distributing the *Poor Man's Guardian* in defiance of the English Newspaper Stamp Act. [110]

Thomas Carlyle, a Scottish essayist, said, "Speech is too often not the art of concealing thought, but of quite stifling and suspending thought, so that there is none to conceal." [111]

Josiah Phillips was found guilty of libel for printing and publishing a book, *The Authentic Records of the Court of England for the Last Seventy Years*, in which the Duke of Cumberland was charged with murdering his valet who had surprised him in unnatural practices with another servant. The murder occurred 22 years before the book was published. [112]

1834

William Blackwood said, "(The press) has effected a greater change in human affairs than either gunpowder or the compass."

Henry Peter Brougham pointed out that the British stamp act tax on newspapers was an evil to society, the impolicy of the government in continuing it, and its interference with the spread of useful knowledge. [113]

In opposing stamp duties, Edward Bulwar, told the House of Commons:

> You create two newspaper monopolies — one a monopoly of dear newspapers, and another monopoly of smuggled newspapers; you create

two publics; to the one public of educated men, in the upper and middle ranks, whom no newspaper could, on moral points, very dangerously mislead, you give the safe and rational papers; to the other public, the public of men far more easily influenced — poor, ignorant, distressed — men from whom all the convulsions and disorders of society arise (for the crimes of the poor are the punishment of the rich) — to the other public whom you ought to be most careful to soothe, to guide, and to enlighten, you give the heated invectives of demagogues and fanatics.[114]

Richard Carlile had spent nine years, seven months, and seven days in prison for using unstamped paper; however, much of the reason really hinged on the content of his publications. [115]

Joseph Forster, a crippled news-vendor, was jailed three months in the House of Correction of Cold Bath Fields, England, for selling unstamped newspapers (*The Mass, Police Gazette, Twopenny Dispatch, Pioneer*, etc.). [116]

Henry Hetherington produced his *Poor Man's Guardian* for three years and defied the stamp act. More than five hundred persons were arrested and fined for selling it, but a jury found it to be a legal publication and not punishable with the decision really not based on English law. [117]

There were 74 informations for libel filed by the crown law-officers between 1816 and 1834. There were 133 prosecutions for seditious and blasphemous libels, and libels defaming the king or his ministers or officials. Only 24 of 204 cases of these happened after 1826.

John Wilson said, "We have never felt that liberty of the press was so essential to our existence as the air we breathed or that without it we should have died."

1835

Between 500 and 750 prosecutions resulted from violations of the British stamp tax between 1800 and 1835. Richard Carlile was fined, imprisoned, his business closed, and $10,000 worth of pamphlets and books confiscated. Others were heavily fined and sentenced to long jail terms. [118]

Robert Dave Owen's *Moral Physiology* about birth control circulated freely until strict new anti-obscenity laws in both Britain and the United States made it illegal from 1857 on. [119]

1835

At least 500 publications with a weekly circulation of 200,000 defied the English stamp tax from 1830 to 1836, despite the jailing of 800 newspaper vendors and publishers. One seller said, in 1835, "Were I to give up selling the Unstamped, my customers declare they will get them of some other reason; as they are determined to have an Untaxed Newspaper, even if they subscribed among themselves to purchase the material for printing, for cheap knowledge they would have." England conducted 728 prosecutions for selling unstamped publications between 1830 and 1836 (219 of them were in 1835). Edward Bulwar told his colleagues in the House of Commons that, instead of silencing fanaticism, they had exalted the fanatic into a martyr. There were about 150 unstamped papers being produced regularly. When the 1819 Publications Act ended between 1815 and 1836 many illegal, unstamped newspapers appeared in England fueled by reform movements and radiical publishers. Through a compromise, the newspaper stamp tax was reduced. In 1836, there were 46 prosecutions for stamp tax evasions.

There were 728 prosecutions in England for unstamped papers between 1830 and 1836. Heavy fines and prison sentences were imposed on several printers who soon were considered martyrs. [120]

1837

Albany Fontblanque said:
> In considering the subject of Taxes on Information, it should never be forgotten, that the newspaper is the poor man's book of knowledge. He has no other means of becoming acquainted with the law, the opinions of society, and the facts with which his own interests are connected. In this country it is a maxim, that ignorance of the laws is no excuse for violation of them; and yet there is no attempt at promulgation, not a show or pretense of it! The laws are supposed to be made in secret, the publication of debates being a breach of privilege; and when passed, the King's Printer has the monopoly of selling the Acts of Parliament in the most expensive form, and at a price far above the means of many. The newspaper publishes the debates, and makes those who can afford to buy them acquainted with new laws and the operation of them; but the newspaper is taxed above the means of the poor, who must suffer for their ignorance. Parliament puts beyond their reach the only instrument which can warn them of its laws. It makes a darkness, digs a snare, and punishes those who fall in it. [121]

James Hansard was accused of libel because the fact that the House of Commons had directed him to publish all their papers was no justification for publishing a part containing a libel against anyone. This action grew out of a controversy between Parliament and the courts. [122]

Harriet Martineu, a British writer, said that readers are plentiful but thinkers are rare. [123]

1838

E.G. Bulwer-Lytton, an English novelist, originated the oft-quoted concept that the pen is mightier than the sword. [124]

1840

Matthew Arnold, an English critic, said, "Journalism is literature in a hurry."[125]

Henry Hetherington, an English newspaper editor, was tried for blasphemy for selling pamphlets in which Charles Haslam said the Bible was abominable trash. He pointed out that citing only specific passages would condemn the Bible although he declined to read his list of objectionable Bible words. [26]

1841

Publisher Edward Maxon was found guilty of blasphemy in England for publishing Shelley's works. [127]

Charles Southwell derided the Bible as the Jew Book in his English athiest publication, *The Oracle of Reason*. For this he got a year in jail for blasphemous libel.[128]

1842

George Holyoake, interim editor of the *Oracle of Reason*, was jailed for six months in Gloucester for blasphemy in Cheltenham. The regular editor, Charles Southwell, was already in jail on a blasphemy conviction. Thomas Patterson, third editor of the *Oracle of Reason*, was sent to jail for his account of the blasphemy trial of George Holyoake.[129]

1843

Lord Lyndhurst said, "I have never yet seen, nor have myself been able to hit upon, anything like a definition of libel, and I cannot help thinking that the difficulty is not accidental, but essentially inherent in the nature of the subject-matter." [130]

Thomas B. Macauley believed that a volume of plays by William Wycherley, William Congreve, and John Vanbrugh should not be suppressed though it could not recommend as an appropriate Christmas present for the young ladies. [131]

1844

· Charles Dickens had his character Jefferson Brick describe New York journalism thus:

"Here's this morning's New York Sewer!" cried one. "Here's this morning's New York Stabber! Here's the New York Family Spy! Here's the New York's Private Listener! Here's the New York Peeper! Here's the New York Plunderer! Here's the New York Keyhole Reporter! Here's the New York Rowdy Journal! Here's all the New York papers! Here's full particulars of the patriotic locofoco movement yesterday, in which the Whigs were so chewed up; and the last Alabama Gouging Case; and all the Political, Commercial, and Fashionable News. Here they are! Here's the papers! Here's the papers!" [132]

Matilda Roalfe said, "To resist bad laws is no less a duty than to respect good ones. The law which forbids the publication of heterodoxy shall never be obeyed by me. I will publish irreligious opinions, be the consequences to myself what they may."

Thomas Patterson, when he got out of jail on a blasphemy sentence, went to Edinburgh and proclaimed he would sell blasphemous books. He was arrested on eleven blasphemy charges and spent fifteen months in jail. Thomas Finley, who owned the bookshop soon thereafter, got a 60-day sentence. Then it was Matilda Roalfe's turn to get a 60-day sentence. Next, a Mr. Baker of the United Order of Blasphemers took over the superintendency of the Atheistic Depot. They gave Sunday school classes a discount. [133]

1847

Disraeli, British prime minister, pointed out that a majority is always the best repartee. [134]

Peter Finerty, publisher of the *Dublin Press*, was convicted of libel for publishing a criticism of the trial and execution of William Orr. [135]

1848

Several hundred radical publishers and printers in England were prosecuted for sedition between 1792 and 1848. Many were acquitted, but still several were sentenced to prison terms. [136]

Thackery turned down Elizabeth Browning because "our readers would make an outcry over the account of a man's passion for a woman." [137]

1849

Perhaps a report in *The Morning Post* of March 9 tells of the last burning of a book by English authorities. It was Froude's *The Nemesis of Faith* publicly burned in the College Hall. [138]

The People's Charter Union was founded and eventually became the Association for the Repeal of the Taxes on Knowledge. A ten-member Newspaper Stamp Abolition Committee was formed. Collet Dobson Collet founded the London Association for the Repeal of the Advertising Duty. [139]

Herbert Spencer, English philosopher, said, "Opinion is ultimately determined by the feelings and not by the intellect." [140]

1852

Passage of the English Common Law Procedure Act made it legally impossible for English attorney-generals to hold editors accused of libel without trial for long periods in vile prisons. Another practice had been to hang men, cut them down, disembowel them, and cut them up in four pieces for saying or writing words that were held to have been uttered to encompass the death of the king. This doctrine of constructive treason was used to punish almost any kind of political debate.

James Grant, a British journalist, said that printed material would become the great ruling power not only in England but throughout all of civilization. [141]

The London Times, in replying to an attack made upon it in the House of Lords, said that the power of the press could not in anyway be compared with the power of government or could newspapers be required to adopt codes as governments must. It said:

> We cannot admit that *The Times'* purpose is to share the labours of statesmanship, or that it is bound by the same limitations, the same duties, the same liabilities as that of the Ministers of the crown. The purpose and duties of the two powers are constantly separate, generally independent, sometimes diametrically opposite. The dignity and freedom of the press are trammelled from the moment it accepts an ancillary position. To perform its duties with entire independence and consequently with the utmost public advantage, the press can enter into no close or binding alliances with the statesmen of the day, nor can it surrender its permanent interests to the convenience of the ephemeral power of any government. The first duty of the press is to obtain the earliest and most correct intelligence of the events of the times, and instantly, by disclosing them, to make them the common property of the nation. The statesman collects his information secretly and by secret means, he keeps back even the current intelligence of the day with ludicrous precautions, until diplomacy is beaten in the race with publicity. The Press lives by disclosures; whatever passes into its keeping becomes a part of the knowledge and history of our times; it is daily and forever appealing to the enlightened force of public opinion — anticipating if possible the march of events — standing upon the breach between the present and the future and extending its survey to

the horizon of the world.

The duty of the journalist is the same as that of the historian — to seek out the truth, above all things, and to present to his readers not such things as state craft would wish them to know but the truth as near as he can attain it. The ends which a really patriotic and enlightened journal should have in view are, we conceive, absolutely identical with the ends of an enlightened and patriotic minister, but the means by which the journal and the minister work out these ends and the conditions under which they work are essentially and widely different. The statesman in opposition must speak as one prepared to take office; the statesman in office must speak as one prepared to act. A pledge or a dispatch with them is something more than an argument or an essay — it is a measure. Undertaking not so much the investigation of political problems as the conduct of political affairs, they are necessarily not so much seekers after truth as after expediency. The Press on the other hand has no practical function; it works on the ends it has in view by argument and discussion alone, and being perfectly unconnected with administrative or executive duties may, and must, roam at free will over topics which men of political action dare not touch.

Cardinal Newman was convicted of libeling a defrocked Roman Catholic priest by falsely accusing him of extensive sexual immorality. The priest, G.C. Achilli, had been lecturing on the general immorality of the Catholic clergy. [142]

Henry Reeve, an English writer, said:
To find out the true state of facts, to report them with fidelity, and to call down the judgement of the world on what is false, or base, or tyrannical, appears to me to be the first duties of those who write. [143]

1853

The duty on advertising was repealed by the House of Commons by a vote of 200 to 169. Milner Gibson used a parliamentary trick in the House of Commons to substitute the word "naught" for the tax amount. The change sailed through and the advertising tax died. [144]

1855

The newspaper stamp tax was ended in England. [145]

The Saturday Review said:
No apology is necessary for assuming that this country is ruled by *The Times*. We all know it, or, if we do not know it, we ought to know it. It is high time we began to realize the manificent spectacle afforded by British freedom—thirty millions of *Cives Romani* governed despotically

by a newspaper. Even the direct rivals of *The Times* in the daily press implicitly admit its autocracy. As for the weekly newspapers, they have degenerated into the toadies of the great daily journal, and if there be one form of this toady is more ecstatic than another, it is that exhibited by the jokers of the hebdomadal press. [146]

Father Petcherine, a Catholic priest, was acquitted of charges of burning two copies of the Protestant Bible and several books be considered pestilential in Dublin.[147]

1857

English governors of India suppressed native newspapers as part of their stern military control. The Marquess of Wellesley, when governor, said printing presses in India were an evil of the first magnitude, useless to literature and to the public.[148]

Robert Dale Owen's *Moral Philosophy* written in 1835 became illegal in Great Britain in 1857 when new anti-obscenity laws made it obscene. [149]

1858

England prosecuted the publisher of *Tyrannicide: Is it Justifiable* by W.E. Adams because they considered it a libel of Napoleon III.

1859

John Stuart Mill, an English philosopher, said, "We can never be sure that the opinion we are endeavoring to stifle is a false opinion, and if we were sure, stifling it would be an evil still." [150]

John Stuart Mill said, "In an imperfect state of the human mind, the interests of the truth require a diversity of opinions." [151]

Mill defined some acts which were directly injurious only to the agents themselves, ought not to be legally interdicted, but which, if done publicly might rightfully be prohibited. These include offenses against decency. [152]

Mill's *On Liberty* utilitarianism contended the greatest good of the community cannot be separated from individual liberty. He said:
> Men are not more zealous for truth than they often are for error, and as sufficient applications of legal or even social penalties will generally succeed in stopping the propagation of either.
> If the opinion is right, they are deprived of the opportunity of exchanging error for truth, if wrong, they lose, what is almost as great a benefit, the clearer perception and livelier impression of truth, produced by its collision with error.

The whole strength and value, then of human judgment, depending on the one property that it can set right when it is wrong, reliance can be placed on it only when the means of setting it right are kept constantly at hand.

In the case of any person whose judgment is really deserving of confidence, how has it become so? Because he has kept his mind open to listen to all that could be said against him; to profit by as much of it as was just, and expound to himself, and upon occasion to others, the fallacy of what was fallacious. Because he has felt that the only way in which a human being can make some approach to knowing the whole of a subject is by hearing what can be said about it by persons of every variety of opinion, and studying all modes in which it can be looked at by every character of mind. No wise man ever acquired his wisdom in any mode but this; nor is it in the nature of human intellect to become wise in any other manner.

The beliefs which we have most warrant for have no safeguard to rest on but a standing invitation to the whole world to prove them unfounded. If the challenge is not accepted, or is accepted and the attempt fails, we are far enough from certainty still; but we have done the best that the existing state of human reason admits of; we have neglected nothing that could give the truth a chance of reaching us; if the lists are kept open we may hope that if there be a better truth it will be found when the human mind is capable of receiving it; and in the mean time we may rely on having attained such approach to truth as possible in our own day. This is the amount of certainty attainable by a fallible being and this the sole way of attaining it.

No argument, we may suppose, can now be needed against permitting a legislature, nor an executive, not identified in interest with the people, to prescribe opinions to them and determine what doctrines or what arguments they shall be allowed to hear.

The time, it is to be hoped, is gone by when any defense would be necessary of the "liberty of the press" as one of the securities against corrupt or tyrannical government. The greatest good of the community cannot be separated from individual liberty. The real advantage which truth has consists in this, that when an opinion is true, it may be extinguished once, twice, or many times, but in the course of ages there will generally be found persons to rediscover it, until some one of its reappearances falls in a time when from favorable circumstances it escapes persecution until it has made such a head as to withstand all subsequent attempts to suppress it. The peculiar evil of silencing the expression of an opinion is, that it is robbing the human race; posterity as well as the existing generation; those who dissent from the opinion still more than those who hold it. Wrong opinions and practices gradually yield to fact and argument: but facts and arguments, to produce any effect on the mind, must be brought before it. Very few facts are able to tell their own story without comments to bring out their meaning.

No one can be a great thinker who does not recognize as a thinker it is his first duty to follow his intellect to whatever conclusions it may lead. [153]

The Society for Suppression of Vice and Encouragement of Religion and Virtue reported 159 prosecutions. Convictions were won 154 times.

1860

The English press achieved freedom from government controls including general warrants, Parliamentary reporting, and seditious libel. Earlier in the Tudor-Stuart period, freedom of the press meant that the government was justified in controls to assure safety, stability, and the welfare of the state. Under the sovereign of the king concept, freedom of speech and press could be limited since they were only grants from the king. Later freedom of the press was considered part of natural law provided by God and not subject to any man-made powers. [154]

When the last warrant was served on George Holyoake for flouting the English newspaper tax, his total penalties amounted to $3,000,000. He spent six months in jail in 1860 for blasphemy. [155]

William Makepeace Thackery advised journalists, "Ah, ye knights of the pen! May honour be your shield, and truth tip your lances! Be gentle to all gentle people. Be modest to women. Be tender to children. As for Ogre Humbug, out sword, and have at him." He also said in describing newspapers:

There she is — the great engine — she never sleeps. She has her ambassador in every quarter of the world — her carriers upon every road. Her officers march along with armies, and her envoys walk into statesmen's cabinets. They are ubiquitious. [156]

1861

The stamp tax ended in 1855, advertising taxes ended in 1853, and paper duties ended in 1861. [157]

William Makepeace Thackery who edited a magazine called *The Cornhill* would not publish articles or poems he considered indecent. He rejected Elizabeth Barrett Browning's *Lord Walter's Wife* on this basis. He rejected many offerings by prominent authors. [158]

1867

Lord Chief Justice Alexander Cockburn in England decided in 1858 that *The*

Confessional Unmasked, an anti-Catholic pamphlet, was obscene. Obscenity was "whether the tendency of the matter charged as obscene is to deprave and corrupt those whose minds are open to such immoral influences and into those hands a publication of this sort may fall." This view became known as the Hicklin rule and was used in American courts until the 1950s. [159]

Max Muller, an English essayist, said, "He who keeps back the truth or withholds it from men is either a coward or a criminal, or both." [160]

1868

Richard Piggott, publisher of the *Irishman*, was given a year's sentence for reporting details of Finian Conspiracy activities seeking Irish independence. He was jailed in 1871 by the Dublin Commission Court for accusing the chief justice in an editorial of shameless lies and accepting perjury in a murder trial. [161]

Alexander Sullivan, publisher of the *Weekly News* in Ireland was sentenced to six months for seditious libel for articles criticizing a murder trial. [162]

1873

Sir James F. Stephen said John Stuart Mill was naive to urge toleration of a variety of opinion and free discussion, for such toleration would give rise to fanatics "who, when they get to power, will not tolerate the tolerant" [163]

1875

Benjamin Disraeli said, "The printing press is a political element unknown to classic or feudal times. It absorbs in a great degree the duties of the sovereign, the priest, the parliament; it controls, it educates, it discusses."

George Bernard Shaw called the suppression of literature "Comstockery."[164]

1876

Walter Bagehot, a British economist, said that writers, like teeth, are divided into incisors and grinders. [165]

Charles Bradlaugh and Annie Besant were indicted for blasphemy and obscenity for publishing Dr. Charles Knowlton's *The Fruits of Philosophy*, an American contraceptive manual. [166]

Thomas Henry Huxley, an English biologist, asked "If a little knowledge is dangerous, where is the man who has so much as to be out of danger?" [167]

1878

Edward Trulove was tried for obscenity in London. Moncure D. Conway a liberal British church minister, said, "They who menace man's freedom of thought and speech are tampering with something more powerful than gunpowder." [168]

1879

The Society for Suppression of Vice and the Encouragement of religion and Virtue had suppressed several cheap periodicals such as *Paul Pry, Polly Pree* and *Women in London.* They had seized 380,569 prints and 63,486 books by 1879. [169]

Robert Louis Stevenson, a Scottish novelist and poet, said, "It is only by trying to understand others that we can get our own hearts understood." [170]

1881

Robert Louis Stevenson, a Scottish author, said that books are good enough in their own way, but they are a mighty bloodless substitute for life. [171]

1882

Charles Bradlaugh said:
> My plea is, that modern heresy, from Spinoza to Mill, has given brain-strength and dignity to everyone it has permeated — that the popular propagandists of this heresy, from Bruno to Carlile, have been the true redeemers, the true educators of the people. And if today we write with higher hope, it is because the right to print has been partly freed from the fetters forged through long generations of intellectual prostration and almost entirely freed from the statuatory limitations, which under the pretense of checking blasphemy and sedition, have really gagged honest speech against Pope and Emperor, against church and throne.

George W. Foote was sent to prison for a 1882 issue of *The Freethinker* which was considered blasphemous for its Christmas materials. [172]

Sir Leslie Stephen said:
> Criminal laws should not be brought into play to punish people for outrages upon good taste, but only for directly inciting to violence. The fact that an opinion is offensive to a majority is so far a reason for leaving it to public opinion which in most cases is capable of taking care of itself; and we are certainly not impartial or really tolerant till we are equally anxious to punish one of the majority for insulting the minority. [173]

1883

The Freethinker was tried for blasphemy which was described by the chief justice as material including elements of reviling, promoting immorality, or the use of ribald language calculated to deprave public morality and to endanger the peace. George W. Foote, editor, was sentenced a year in prison for blasphemy. His printer, Mr. Kemp, got three months. W.J. Ramsey spent nine months in Holloway Jail in England for blasphemy for an article in *The Freethinker*. England's laws on blasphemy were repealed in 1884. [174]

1884

Novelist Henry James, in his very strong argument against censorship, said:
In the English novel more than in any other, there is a traditional difference between that which people know and that which they agree to admit they know, that which they see and that which they speak of, that which they feel to be a part of life and that which they allow to enter literature. There is the great difference, in short, between what they talk of in conversation and in print.

The essence of moral energy is to survey the whole field. To what degree a purpose in a work of art is a source of corruption I shall not attempt to inquire; the one that seems to me least dangerous is the purpose of making a perfect work. As for our novel as we find it in England today it strikes me as addressed in a large degree to young people, and that constitutes a presumption that it will be rather shy. [175]

1885

Henry S. Ashbee said, "More youths have become criminals through reading of deeds real or fictitious, of murders, pirates, highwaymen, forgers, burglars, etc., than have ever developed into libertines from the perusal of obscene novels.

1886

The Irish Law Times editorialized that "the newspaper as a watchdog of civilization does not believe in keeping silent because there is nothing to bark at; the law sometimes needs to let fly its bootjack to silence unnecessary howling."

England's National Vigilance Association for Repression of Criminal Vice and Public Morality took over the campaign against pornography. [176]

1887

Henry Fox Bourne said, "Sedition, blasphemy, scurrility, and immorality, if they have not been quite kept out of newspapers, have dwindled down and have lost all their force now that enlightened public opinion has substituted a new censorship for that of the old tyranny." [177]

1888

"Queen Mab," a privately-printed poem by Shelley, got Edward Moxon a heavy fine for publishing such blasphemous and seditious libel in Shelley's *Collected Works*. "Queen Mab" caused prosecutions of several booksellers. [178]

1889

Censorship is as antiquated as mail armour. [179]

Henry Vizetelly was jailed in England for publishing excerpts from *Nana* and *LaFerre*, novels by Emile Zola. He was prosecuted by William A. Coote, head of England's National Vigilance Association, an anti-indecent literature group. Parliament established an Indecent Advertising Act. [180]

1891

Oscar Wilde, a British dramatist, said, "In old days men had the rack; now they have the press." [181]

"There is no such thing as a moral or an immoral book. Books are well written, or badly written. That's all." [182]

1892

Israel Zangwill, an English writer, said that every dogma has its day, but ideals are eternal. [183]

1893

Auberon Herbert, an English political philosopher, said, "Of all the miserable, unprofitable, inglorious wars in the world is the war against words." [184]

Herbert Spencer said, "So long as he does not suggest the commission of crimes, each citizen is free to say what he pleases about any or all our institutions even to the advocacy of a form of government utterly different from that which exists, or the condemnation of all governments." [185]

M.E. Stone said, "There has never been an hour when the first aid to autocracy has not been the placing of the press in leash." [186]

1894

Oscar Wilde, the British dramatist, said, "In old days books were written by men of letters and read by the public. Nowadays books are written by the public and read by nobody." [187]

1895

Thomas Hardy's novel *Jude the Obscure* was banned as immoral. Hardy was so offended that he never wrote another novel. [188]

1898

George Bedborough was arrested in England for selling Havelook Ellis' *Studies in the Psychology of Sex*, his *The Adult* publication, and other books. He pled guilty, and later wrote a long apology to the Free Press Defence Committee entitled "George Bedborough, Coward." [189]

Lord Curzon, British politician, said, "I hesitate to say what the function of the modern journalist may be; but I imagine that they do not exclude the intelligent anticipation of facts even before they occur." [190]

Chapter 10

THE NINETEENTH-CENTURY CONFUSIONS
1800 Through 1899

1800

Louis Bonald, a French government official, said, "A censorship of the press is thus a necessity that power may have adequate protection. Only in this way can men of evil disposition be prevented from attacking every necessary institution of society.[1]

The Charter of Louis XVIII said that Frenchmen had the right of publishing and causing to be printed their opinions provided they conformed to the law. [2]

Pierre Dupont de Nemours said, "A large part of the nation reads the Bible, but all of it assidously peruses the newspapers. The fathers read them aloud to their children while the mothers are preparing breakfast."

Joseph Joubert, French essayist, said, "It is better to debate a question without settling it than to settle a question without debating it." [3]

Napoleon Bonaparte said, "A Constitution should be short and obscure." [4]

1802

Bizarre censorship was practiced under Napoleon; for example, a person could not use these words: *bourbon, usurper, tyrant, sovereign people, social compact,* or references to French defeats or unpleasant comments about Bonaparte family members. [5]

1803

Les Nouvelles Ecclesiastiques, a printed journal from 1728 to 1803, was a clandestine publication in France. The government spent millions trying to stop it.[6]

Napoleon said, "I want you to suppress completely the censorship of books (in Italy). This Country already has a narrow enough mind without straitening it any more. Of course, the publication of any work contrary to the government would be stopped." Smugglers brought forbidden publications into France in plaster busts of Napoleon, or in sealed boxes off the coast of Brittainy, or in hollowed-out lumps of coal. Spain got French Revolution propaganda in hat linings and clock part wrappings. [7]

1810

Napoleon said, "A journalist is a grumbler, a censurer, a giver of advice, a regent of sovereigns, a tutor of nations. Four hostile newspapers are more to be feared than a thousand bayonets." Napoleon allowed only one newspaper in each French province and four in Paris. He said to his press bureau, "I will not judge journalists for the wrong which they have done, but for the lack of good which they have done." He imposed government control and press limitations in all the territories he conquered. He said, "Newspapers say only what I wish." [8]

The Spanish Cortes declared freedom of the press in defiance of their French overlords. [9]

1812

Pierre Augustin Caron, in his satirical play, *The Marriage of Figaro*, described the French press thus, "They all tell me that if in my writings I mention neither the government, nor public worship, nor politics, nor morals, nor people in office, nor influential corporations, nor the opera, nor the other theatres, nor anyone who have aught to do with anything, I may print everything freely, subject to the approval of two or three censors."

1818

Ludwig Boerne, a German political writer, said, "Public opinion is a people's invincible armor." [10]

The Carlsbad decrees set up suppression and censorship of the German press for 30 years. The resolutions said:

> So long as this decree shall remain in force, no publication which appears in the form of daily issues or as a serial not exceeding 20 pages of printed matter shall go to press in any State of the Union without the previous knowledge and approval of the State officials. The Diet shall have the right to suppress on its own authority such writings included in whatever German State they may appear, as in the opinion of a commission appointed by it are inimical to the honor of the Union, the safety of individual states, or the maintenance of peace and quiet in Germany. There shall be no appeal from such decisions, and the

governments involved are bound to see that they are put into execution.[11]

In France, the printer was considered a part of the government obligated to restrain whatever was submitted to him for publication. Paris newspapers had to post a 10,000 franc good-behavior guarantee. The amount fluctuated up and down until finally the plan was abolished in 1881.

Frederich Gentz of Austria said, "As a preventive measure against the abuses of the press, absolutely nothing should be printed for years. With this as a rule, we should in a short time get back to God and the Truth."

Austrian Prime Minister Klemens von Metternich said, "The greatest and consequently most urgent evil now is the press." Ludwig Franke (in his memoirs of the Austrian Metternich era written later) said, "The self-esteem of those who wrote had fallen so low that they practiced a self-censorship of their own and destroyed every inborn thought as Chronas of Greek mythology did."

General Ramon Varvaez, Spanish dictator, said, "It is not enough to confiscate papers; to finish with bad newspapers you must kill all the journalists."

Lord Wellesley set up press censorship in India during the 1799 Revolutionary War, but Lord Hastings discontinued it in Bengal in 1818 as Lord Elphinstone did in Bombay. The press was really not free because the court still enforced controls.[12]

1819

The British regulation of the press in India forbade animadversions on the measures of English public authorities, or the local administrations, the members of Council, judges of the Supreme Court, the Lord Bishop of Calcutta, anything to excite alarm or suspicion among the natives concerning interference with their religion, private scandal, or personal remarks tending to excite dissension in society. [13]

1821

A German student said, "Man must always have an organ with which to express himself. If he is deprived of the Mouth and the Pen, he raises his arm and writes, instead of with the Pen, the sword, and instead of paper, on men's bodies."[14]

Heinrich Heine, German poet, said, "Whenever books are burned, men also in the end are burned." [15]

1823

The India Vernacular Press Act required Indian language newspapers obtain licenses. Lord Buckingham was sent home to England because British officials in India were displeased with his *Calcutta Journal.* [16]

1825

Governments censored books about birth control, and soon began censoring radical political works. This censorship continued into the mid-1950s. [17]

Karl Marx, 24, wrote for the *Rheinische Zeitung fur Politik, Handel, und Gewerbe* arguing for press freedom in 1825. Shortly afterward, the paper was closed down, and he edited German-language newspapers in Switzerland, Strasbourg, Paris, and London. [18]

1826

Francois Chateaubriand said, "Liberty of the Press is today the entire constitution. It consoles us for disgrace; it restrains oppressors through fear of the oppressed; it is the guardian of manners, the protector against injustice. Nothing is lost as long as it exists."

The Belgians declared their independence from the Dutch because Louis de Poiter and other editors defied stringent press controls established by William of Nassau when he assumed the Dutch Throne. [19]

The Belgian assembly declared the press to be free; it said, "The press is free; censorship may never be re-established and no surety bond may be extracted from authors, editors, or printers. In matters concerning the press, closed hearings may be held only with unanimous consent. Jury trial is required in all hearings of press offenses. [20]

1830

French typographers led demonstrations against Charles X reactionary government. The French bourgeoisie advocated freedom of the press. [21]

Zurich became the first Swiss Canton to remove press censorship as a result of a long campaign by the *Neue Zuricher Zeitung.* [22]

1832

King Louis Phillippe jailed Honore Daumier and Charles Philipon for exciting hatred and injury to the person of the king in cartoons and caricatures they published. The King censored images and prints from 1835 on. [23]

The French monarchy, by 1833 had prosecuted 411 newspapers, 143 newspapers were condemned, 65 years in prison terms had been assessed to journalists, and 350,000 francs in fines were collected. These practices continued for many years thereafter. [24]

The Church condemned *L'Avenir* which was a liberal Catholic publication urging separation of church and state in France. Louis Veuillot was imprisoned and his *L'Univers* suspended for opposition to liberal Catholicism. [25]

1832

An illustration of French officials raiding and destroying a printing establishment indicated they were displeased with the content of the printing. [26]

1835

The clash between Canadian authorities and Joseph Howe in Halifax led toward press freedom. Under the encouragement of the Roebuck pamphlets, a society for the abolition of the stamp tax was organized. [27]

Napoleon III provided nominal freedom of the press yet prosecuted 6,000 publishers during his reign. The French outlawed any attack against government or expressing the wish, hope, or threat of the destruction of the constitutional monarchial order. [28]

Alexis de Tocqueville, French historian, said: "The freedom of the press and universal suffrage are two things which are irreconcilably opposed by tyrannical governments." In *Democracy in America*, de Tocqueville said that liberty of the press was the only cure for the evils which equality might produce in a democracy. He said, "The more I consider the independence of the press in its principal consequences, the more I am convinced that in the modern world it is the chief and, so to speak, the constitutive element of liberty. A nation that is determined to remain free is therefore right in demanding, at any price, the exercise of this independence." [29]

de Tocqueville, said, "In order to enjoy the inestimable benefits that the liberty of the press ensures, it is necessary to submit to the inevitable evils that it creates." [30]

1842

Joseph Joubert, a French essayist, said, "Words, like eyeglasses, blur everything that they do not make clear." [31]

Samuel Lover, an Irish novelist, said, "When once the itch of literature comes over a man, nothing can cure it but the scratching of a pen." [32]

Karl Marx said:

> A free press is everywhere the open eye of the national spirit, the embodied confidence of the people in itself, the verbal bond that ties the individual to the state of the world, the incorporated culture which transforms material struggles into spiritual struggles and idealizes the crude materialized form. It is the heedless confession of a people before itself, and confession, as is known, has liberating power. It is the spiritual mirror in which the people observe themselves, and self-observation is the first condition of wisdom. It is the spirit of the state which can be carried into every hut, cheaper than material gas. It is versatile, the most modern and all knowing. It is the ideal world which always originates in the real world and flows into it again, giving life, as an ever richer spirit. Bear in mind that the advantages of freedom of the press cannot be enjoyed without toleration of its inconvenience. There are no roses without thorns.

He was expelled from Prussia in 1849 after his paper there, the *Neue Rheinische Zeitung,* was suppressed. He lived in poverty in London for the rest of his life, writing radical political materials, including *Das Kapital.* [33]

1844

An Irish publisher was convicted for seditious libel because the judge ruled that seditious libel could not be for any public benefit specified by Lord Campbell's act.

A monument to the First Martyrs of Political Liberty of Scotland was erected at Calton Hill to commemorate the lives and sacrifices of five men convicted of circulating seditious libel in 1793 and 1794.

1845

Austrian intellectuals protested that "The situation of the press with respect to the censor is, alas, one devoid of legality. The writer is judged by norms which be does not know and is condemned without being heard and without being able to defend himself."

1848

The concept of a wholly free press in France grew out of the Revolution of 1848 after the end of the Napoleonic era, and during the French second Republic. The French constitution of 1848 said that "the press can not in any case be subjected to censorship although absolute press freedom is not guaranteed." [34]

Press censorship was abolished in Hungary and Austria largely due to the leadership of Louis Kassuth who had opposed Klemens Metternich for years, even having been jailed for three years in defiance of Hapsburg censorship. [35]

1850

An African saying indicates that scandal is not like bread because there is never any shortage. [36]

An African proverb says, "Silence is also speech." [37]

Freedom of the press, freedom of education, freedom of associations, and freedom of public worship were memorialized in Brussels at the base of a tall column erected to commemorate establishment of Belgium. [38]

Hapsburg troops destroyed a revolution in Hungary, led by journalist Louis Kossuth who had been jailed for three years for articles in his *Diet Bulletin*. [39]

Victor Hugo, French writer, said, "A stand can be made against invasion by an army; no stand can be made against invasion by an idea." [40]

A Nigerian saying indicates, "Not to know is bad. Not to want to know is worse. Not to hope is unthinkable. Not to care is unforgivable." [41]

The Prussian constitution of 1850 said, "Censorship of the press may not be introduced; and no other restriction on the freedom of the press shall be imposed except by law. [42]

A Spanish proverb says, "It is better to appear in hell than in the newspapers." [43]

Otto von Bismarck-Shoenhausen, chancellor of Prussia, said, "Better pointed bullets than pointed speeches." [44]

1851

France used its army to defeat a rebellion of its citizens. Thereafter, the General Assembly passed the severest press censorship law in French history. In 1851, Louis Napoleon dragged opposition editors from their beds just before the "Massacre of the Boulevards." [45]

1852

Italy set up a law prohibiting editorial criticism of foreign rulers. [46]

Alexis de Tocqueville said:
> In the countries in which the doctrine of the sovereignty of the people ostensibly prevails, the censorship of the press is not only dangerous, but it is absurd. When the right of every citizen to cooperate in the government of society is acknowledged, every citizen must be presumed

to possess the power of discriminating between the different opinions of his contemporaries, and of appreciating the different facts from which inferences may be drawn.

1858

Edmund and Jules de Goncourt, French novelists, wrote, "That ephemeral sheet of paper, the newspaper, is the natural enemy of the book, as the whore is of the decent woman." [47]

1860

Karl Marx, German journalist and socialist, said, "The writer must earn money in order to live and to write, but he must by no means write for the purpose of making money." [48]

Marx said, "The daily press and the telegraph, which in a moment spreads inventions over the whole world, fabricate more myths in a day than could have formerly been done in a century." [49]

Press controls under Louis Napoleon were characterized by a journalist thus: Obstacles and pitfalls on all sides beset the newspaper and those who wrote for it. Self-censorship in the first instance, re-read and corrected with meticulous care by his editor, superintended in the last resort by the printer who was responsible before the law for everything that came off his press, stifled and hamstrung, attracting the thunderbolt and yet tied to the lightning-conductor, seated on the powder-barrel and condemned to strike the tinder-box, the journalist of 1866 was truly a victim tortured by the imperial regime.

1862

Newspapers in Germany had "sitting editors." These persons were the ones the newspapers handed up to prison sentences imposed by Chancellor Bismarck. The *Frankfurter Zeitung* had five such editors in jail at the same time. In 1878, more than 400 publications were suppressed for socialistic content. [50]

1863

The Crown Prince of Germany sternly criticized Chancellor Bismarck for having found no other means of coming to an understanding with public opinion than by imposing silence on it. [51]

Ferdinand Lassalle, a German socialist, said, "If a man makes money by publishing a newspaper, by poisoning the wells of information, he is the greatest criminal I can conceive." [52]

1864

When the Pope declared that opinions of Catholic writers were subject to the authority of the Roman congregations, Lord Acton a leading British Catholic publisher, promptly discontinued his *Review*. [53]

1865

Napoleon III permitted the publication of caricatures if the person pictured approved them. [54]

1866

Henri Rochefort quit the staff of *Figaro* in 1863 because officials disliked several of his articles. He started *La Lanterne* which was seized and he was fined and imprisoned; he fled to Belgium and smuggled copies back to France in hollow busts of imperial family members. [55]

1867

The Fundamental Law of Austria established press freedom. Act XXV for the regulation of printing press and newspapers in India became the basis of a registration and survelliance system. [56]

1868

France passed a press law which eliminated most of the controls put on the press by Louis Napoleon.

The penal code in India had provisions that added sedition prosecution and extended bureaucratic control of the press to cover class hatred and public mischief.

1869

Leo Tolstoy, in his novel *War and Peace,* said, "The most powerful weapon of ignorance — the diffusion of printed matter."

1870

Paul Gauguin, a French artist, said that art is either plagiarism or revolution.[57]

1874

An Irish civil court jury awarded one farthing to Rev. Robert O'Keefe, a parish priest, from Cardinal Paul Cullen, the Catholic Primate of Ireland, for libel committed against the priest by his ecclesiastical superior.

1875

During the 1870s, France, under command of General Begeaud, pacified Algeria with ferocity. The general said, "It may be that I shall be called a barbarian, but I consider myself as above the reproaches of the press." Benjamin Constant, a French painter, said, "With newspapers, there is sometimes disorder; without them there is always slavery."

1876

When the Meji government of Japan had been restored for eight years, at least 58 editors were imprisoned for utterances that were considered violations of the law. But by 1877 there were 225 newspapers and the total had increased to 470 by 1887. [58]

1877

Henrick Ibsen, playwight, said, "The spirit of truth and the spirit of freedom — they are the pillars of society." [59]

1878

Two attempts to kill the German Emperor caused Germany to repress the socialist press. During the year 127 periodicals and 278 other publications were suppressed in Germany for suspected socialistic leanings. In 1890, Bismarck had inflicted jail terms totaling 100 years on editors. He said, "Every country is held at some time to account for the windows broken by its press; the bill is presented, some day or other, in the shape of hostile sentiment in the other country."

The Vernacular Press Act placed heavy restrictions in the 170 native language newspapers of India until 1881. [60]

1880

Gustave Flaubert, French novelist, said, "What is beautiful is moral, that is all there is to it." [61]

1881

The French Republic provided press freedom. Freedom of the press had been suppressed in 1835, became a reality in 1848, was suppressed again in 1852 by Napoleon III. The National Assembly maintained censorship in 1871. The republicans won the Senate in 1879 and provided the 1881 press freedom law.

France prohibited anarchy and obscenity. Obscenity was defined as an offense against public and religious morality and good taste. The French also eliminated the press caution system of deposits to cover possible fines. The French press law of 1881 replaced 42 earlier laws containing a total of 235 control provisions.

Felicien Rops was tried several times for obscenity and Louis Legrand was sentenced for illustrations. [62]

1882

Henrick Ibsen, playwright, said, "A man should never put on his best trousers when he goes out to battle for freedom and truth." [63]

Bal Gangadhur Tilok used his Marathi language newspaper, *Kesari*, to oppose British rule in India. He was jailed for eighteen months for secition for his agitation which eventually led to India's escape from British domination. [54]

1883

William H. Crogman, a West Indian educator, said, "It is a grand and awful thing to be a free man." [65]

Karl Marx, German philosopher, said, "Last words are for fools who haven't said enough." [66]

Thomas Masaryk founded *The Athenaeum* review in which he exposed forged documents glorifying Bohemian culture, which he believed were the wrong basis for Czech freedom. [67]

1885

England suppressed *Bosphore Egyptian*, a newspaper critical of Great Britain, but relented to allow the Egyptian publication to resume publication. *Das Kapital's* second volume was approved by Russian censors because it was only comprehensible to specialists. [68]

Pope Leo XIII said, "The liberty of thinking and publishing whatsoever each one likes, without any hindrances, is not in itself an advantage over which society can wisely rejoice. [69]

1888

Anton Pavlovich Chekhov, a Russian author, said, "I would like to be a free artist and nothing else, and I regret God has not given me the strength to be one."

In Czechoslavakia, Masaryk founded a political weekly, *Cas*. [70]

Friedrich Nietzsche, German philosopher, advised, "Concerning great things one should either be silent or speak loftily." [71]

1889

Charles-Pierre Baudelaire's *Les Fleurs du Mal* poems were forbidden in France.[72]

1890

The German *index expurgatorius* contained the names of 13 periodicals, 83 newspapers, and 60 foreign publications. In response, socialist publications were smuggled into Germany by thousands every week from Switzerland and France. Otto Bismarck controlled the German government press; the opposition press was severely prosecuted. More than 600 "criticisms of the king" or "lese majesti" cases were prosecuted against German socialists. The German anti-socialist law was used to suppress 1,229 publications, including 104 newspapers and periodicals.

Thousands of copies of socialist publications were smuggled into Germany every week via state railways. These were printed in other countries after the German *index expurgatorius* had outlawed 13 German periodicals, 83 German newspapers, and 60 foreign journals. [73]

1896

Gustave Flaubert was charged with immorality and lasciviousness for publishing his novel *Madame Bovary* about the passions of a French woman in a provincial town. The novel became a best-seller when the court acquitted Flaubert. He refused to alter the novel for *La Revue de Paris* and said, "I'll do nothing more, not a correction, not a deletion, not a comma less, nothing, nothing. One can't whiten Negroes and one can't change the blood of a book; one can only impoverish it, that is all." [74]

Emile Zola, French novelist, was convicted of libel for publishing his famous *J'Accuse* letter which launched the exposure of French corruption in the Dreyfus affair. Zola fled to England to escape imprisonment.

Emile Zola said, "When truth is buried underground it grows, it chokes, it gathers such an explosive force that on the day it bursts out, it blows up everything with it."[75]

1899

The Empress Dowager of China issued this decree:
> As newspapers only serve to excite the masses to subvert the present order of things and the editors concerned are composed of the dregs of the literary classes, no good can be served by the continuation of such dangerous instruments, and we hereby command the entire suppression and sealing up of all newspapers published within the Empire, while the editors connected with them are to be arrested and punished with the utmost rigor of the law.

Among the victims of European press censorship in the nineteenth century were Jules Guesde and Paul Brouse, French socialists; Honore Daumier, French cartoonist; Prince Peter Kropotkin, an anarchist writer; Louis Kossuth, Hungarian nationalist; August Palm and Hjalmar Branting, Swedish socialists; Nicholas Pasic, Serbian radical leader; Victor Adler, Austrian socialist; William and Karl Lebknecht and Rosa Luxemburg, German socialists; and Michael Lemontov, Maxim Gorky, Leo Tolstcy, and Alexander Pushkin, Russian authors.

A Trindadian proverb said, "Conversation is food for the ears." [76]

Chapter 11

WARTIME CENSORSHIP
1900 Through 1924

1900

Anton Chekov, a Russian novelist, said:
> A literateur is not a confectioner, not a dealer in cosmetics, not an entertainer. He is just like ordinary people. What would you say if a newspaper reporter, because of his fastidiousness or from a wish to give pleasure to his readers, were to describe only honest mayors, high-minded ladies, and virtuous railroad conductors?

Spain confiscated liberal and republican newspapers for an anti-government campaign and prohibited news reports not authorized by officials. [1]

William Butler Yeats, Irish poet, said, "You might as well stay home and not even bother to vote because you've been lied to by the journalists and the statesman." [2]

1901

Australia set up federal censorship with its Customs Act. [3]

Bestnik Europy used this comparison of Russian Society to a crowded classroom:
> To breathe becomes ever more difficult. It is necessary to open a window, fling open the door, and give space for movement, free access to fresh air. In place of this, they intended to close the ventilators, to caulk up all the crevices. There remains for the multitude only to lose its breath or to leave the room in which it is assembled for important matters.

1902

Paul Fernando became a famed English pornographer using the pseudonym Charles Carrington.

Andre Gide, a French author, said, "To know how to free oneself is nothing; the arduous thing is to know what to do with one's freedom." [4]

1903

Police canceled a banquet to celebrate the founding of Russia's first newspaper because of several planned resolutions demanding freedom of the press. (More than 400 Russian journalists had been arrested by 1909.) [5]

George Bernard Shaw, an Irish dramatist, said, "Liberty means responsibility. That is why most men dread it." [6]

1904

Hungary suppressed newspapers of the Slovak and Rumanian minorities. *Narodine Noviny*, a Slovak paper, was prosecuted thirteen times in a 12-month period. [7]

1905

Lenin and Trotsky became newspaper editors as the Russian revolution was launched. There were 1,700 newspapers and periodicals in Russia. [8]

A jury found Sir Edward Russell and Alexander Jeans of the *Liverpool Daily Post and Mercury* not guilty of criminal libel for criticizing beerhall licensing. [9]

Russian censorship broke down as a result of the 1905 revolution. Nearly 1,700 newspapers and periodicals were operating as a liberalizing trend arrived in Russia. But in 1912, 317 papers were suppressed and even more in 1913; Russian censorship was extreme. The press could not use the words *authorities* or *bureaucracy*; it could not criticize the police, hospital administration, barracks sanitation, the number of schools, bribery, or use exclamation marks.

Oscar Wilde, English playwright, said, "All great ideas are dangerous." [10]

1907

The press in Imperial Germany was the most docile, well-drilled, and the most supine press in all international questions of any in the world, according to Austin Harrison writing for *The North American Review*. [11]

Karl Kraus, Austrian satirist, said, "How is the world ruled, and how do wars start? Diplomats tell lies to journalists, and they believe what they read." [12]

Russian dissidents developed extensive underground publications. In Baku by 1910 an operation produced more than a million copies in a plant which "expanded until it covered an area underground and contained a cutting machine, type in several languages, presses, binders, even a casting machine for using stereotype mats. In this plant underneath the houses of Tartar Baku, seven printers worked and lived. The plant was without heat or ventilation; windows leading to the street were sealed with brick and mortar. At night they took turns going up for air for three hour periods, according to Bertram Wolfe.

Spain set up tight press censorship because of problems with Moroccan tribesman. [13]

G.K. Chesterton, English author, said, "Journalism is popular but it is mainly popular as fiction. Life is one world, and life seen in the newspaper, another." [14]

1910

England enacted a press act to control the India press. Actions taken against Indian publications saw 1,121 items banned. There were 120 prosecutions, 15 security bond forfeitures, and 40 warnings to publications. Among Indian publications banned were *The Methods of the Indian Police in the 20th Century, British Rule in India, The Infamies of Liberal Rule, Sidelight of India, Choose, Oh Indian Princess, South African Horrors, The First Indian War of Independence*, and *Shabash*.

Stephen Leacock, a Canadian humorist, said, "Advertising may be described as the science of arresting human intelligence long enough to get money from it."[15]

Amanda McKittrick Rose, Irish novelist, said, "I don't believe in publishers. They love to keep the Sabbath and everything else they can lay their hands on."[16]

Between 1905 and 1910, Imperial Russia imposed 4,396 administrative penalties on periodicals and confiscated 1,000 newspapers. More than 400 journalists were arrested. [17]

New Zealand legislated an Indecent Publications Act. An international conference convened in France and developed an International Agreement for the Suppression of Obscene Publications. [18]

1912

T.H.S. Escott said:
> The journalist began by stirring up against himself Parliament's

persistent jealousy and scornful hate. He criticized or even observed its proceedings almost with a rope round his neck. He knew the ascent to the pillory as well as he did his own doorstep. In the near distance stood the common hangman, in one hand holding the whip which was to flog him at the cart-tail round the town, in the other displaying the shears that were to crop his ears before the day's programme was finished. A restless, unconscionable, irrepressible kind of being, he was, in the natural order of providence, suffered to spit his lies, libels, venom of all sorts abroad, and generally to infest the earth just as a like tolerance was granted to beasts, to birds of prey, and to other noisome creatures. Before the eighteenth century was out, the mightiest and most philosophical intellect in the Parliament of his day, Edmund Burke, had found out that this generally distrusted, detested, but inextinguishable person had laid the foundation of a Fourth Estate. [19]

1912

Vigilance committees in Ireland crusaded against immoral literature. The British Board of Film Censors was set up by motion picture makers and distributors. [20]

The library of Doncaster, England, banned *Tom Jones*.[21]

George Bernard Shaw, English dramatist, said, "A newspaper, not having to act on its descriptions and reports, but only to sell them to idly curious people, has nothing but honor to lose by inaccuracy and unveracity." [22]

Shaw said:
> All censorships exist to prevent anyone from challenging current conceptions and existing institutions. All progress is initiated by challenging current conceptions; consequently, the first condition of progress is the removal of censorship. [23]

1914

Austria suppressed 81 Serbian newspapers from being circulated by mail. Serbia suppressed all anti-Austrian publications at the request of the Austrian government.

Canada banned all seditious newspapers including the German *Fatherland*, four German newspapers published in Canada, and the Hearst newspapers from the United States. [24]

By 1914, prior censorship had been eliminated in European countries, but World War I produced drastic new censorship procedures. There were no prosecutions for sedition in England between the Reform Bill of 1832 and 1914. *The London Times* said that journalists were able to discuss the campaign in the West with far less freedom than its Russian contemporaries. "The Russian reports are far more full than ours and Russian comment is far more untrammeled and therefore illuminating." Irish papers were suppressed, and neither *The Irish World* nor *The Gaelic American* could be distributed in England. [25]

G.K. Chesterton, British essayist, said, "Journalism largely consists in saying 'Lord Jones Dead' to people who never knew Jones was alive." [26]

China laws prohibited publication of *In Camera* judicial proceedings, false charges against the government, attacks on the form of government, or importation of foreign publications. [27]

Both China and Japan imposed rigid preventive censorship laws throughout World War I. [28]

The Chinese government joined by Chinese bankers censored all reports about how bad conditions in the nation were so they could float a major loan. [29]

Georges Clemenceau, infuriated with French bungling, fought government censorship of his newspaper *L'Homme Libre*. When they closed him down, he started a second paper *L'Homme Enchaine!* When war became too severe, he eased his criticism. France reprimanded several newspapers, including the Paris edition of *The New York Herald* for scare headlines, interviews, and war reports. Paris journalists protested these actions; but suspensions and fines continued throughout the war. [30]

During World War I, France imposed heavy and confusing preventive censorship and prior restraints, even as the war ended officials didn't want any unfair reference made about President Wilson. [31]

During the German occupation, *La Libre Belgique* was a regular-irregular clandestine publication. Three newspapers were suspended in Bohemia. France suppressed newspapers for attacks on the government. [32]

An edition of *Munchener Zeitung* was confiscated when it advocated annexing Belgium, but later the censor allowed newspapers to agitate for annexations. The Bavarian Minister of War ordered Bavarian newspapers not to publish lists of war casualties. [33]

The Russian Council of Ministers produced a long list of subjects which could not appear in print. Eleven months before a *Press Yearbook* was issued, 340 Russian journals had been administratively censored or fined. Socialist Labor and Social Democrat papers were the hardest hit. One hundred and two papers had been prosecuted in Kiev, but anti-Jewish publications carried on heavy attacks on the Jews. *The New York Evening Post* reported that there were 1,634 cases of press repressions in Russia from 1906 through the first eleven months of 1913. One labor paper in

Russia had 67 of its 137 editions confiscated; it was suspended 17 times and finally suppressed. [34]

The evening edition of *Vossische Zeitung* was suppressed because it quoted the chancellor as saying that the German people would have to tighten their belts. The Kaiser suspended the leading German Catholic newspaper, *The Kolnische Volkszeitung*, for criticizing a note he had sent to President Woodrow Wilson. Germany set up an *Index Expurgatorians* which contained the names of 13 periodicals, 83 newspapers, and 60 foreign publications. Within eight months officials suppressed 127 periodicals and 278 other publications. [35]

President Yuan re-wrote the Chinese press freedom clause by adding "within the scope of laws and ordinances." His publication law containing 21 restrictions continued in force for many years.

1915

The Austrian press was ordered not to comment on relations with Italy. Austrian censorship was even tighter than German. In Vienna, the newspaper for Czech democracy was suppressed. Despite having an edition confiscated, *The Lokal Amzeiger* commented on relations with the United States; when its second evening edition came out, it attacked President Woodrow Wilson.

The *English Review* complained that the British Lion was fighting the war in blinkers because of military censorship. [36]

· Italy, angered by reports of naval disasters, held editors personally responsible for publishing any facts not made public by the government. The press had to present the Dutch government's attitude of what was said at an international meeting of women at the Hague.

La Libre Belgique was a very successful underground newspaper published irregularly during German occupation. The Germans could not destroy it. [37]

The London Globe reported Lord Kitchener had resigned despite official denials; the newspaper was suspended for more than two weeks. Austin Harrison of England said, "A democracy which does not trust itself, that is to say, its press, is a poor thing. Only the press can arouse the people to see the war as it is and take the proud steps essential to victory." Scotland Yard suppressed Jefferson Jones' *The Fall of Tsingtua* because it offended the Japanese government and kept it suppressed even into World War II.[38]

The *London Truth* said:
> One thing which the country will have to make up its mind about very
> speedily is whether it is going to be governed by newspapers.

British police seized every copy of *The Labour Leader* and *The Socialist Review* and hundreds of pamphlets about war-time labor problems. British officials seized the printing plant of *The London Globe*. [39]

William Somerset Maugham, English novelist, said, "There are two good things in life, freedom of thought and freedom of action." [40]

Mexico decreed that fines of 50 to 500 pesos or imprisonment from one to eleven months would apply to slander, libel, or false or distorted statements. [41]

Otto Bismarck carried "a bundle of printed forms containing formal charges requiring merely the mention of the name of the offender, or of the paper or papers in which the offense had been committed." He would send several of the completed strips each day to the states attorney. [42]

In Bohemia textbooks in French were considered disloyal to the Austrian monarchy. [43]

A cartoon of an intoxicated soldier brought fines against the editor and the cartoonist of *The Bystander* in England. British officials would not allow *The Manchester Labour Leader*, *The Cambridge Magazine*, and *Common Sense* mailed outside England. France created a film *comison de controle*. Police seized a Scotland newspaper for publishing an unapproved account of a conference between Glasgow Union Officials and the British prime minister. Police seized *Forwards*, a Scotish Socialist newspaper. Two women were prosecuted in England for publishing a leaflet containing an article printed in an 1813 edition of the *Edinborough Review*, and an article written in 1902 by the home secretary of the British Cabinet. Bertrand Russell was fined 100 pounds for violating English wartime conscription laws by circulating a leaflet defending Ernest Everett who had been sentenced to two years hard labor for refusing military service. *The London Times* complained that the British people found themselves waging an impersonal war of asterisks in a chilling darkness. [44]

In England critics of the government were punished for having a pamphlet of Scripture quotations. Two ladies were prosecuted for having passages taken from the 1813 *Edinborough Review*, and from 1902 written by the Home Secretary. [45]

German officials banished the editorial staff of *Leipziger Volkszeitung* to internment in Switzerland and discontinued the newspaper because it was dangerous to the state. *The Berliner Tageblatt* was suspended for an editorial about food problems and war aims. German officials closed down *The Berliner Tageszeitung* for reporting Count von Reventlow's assertion that international law did not apply to submarine war. Maximillan Harden said of German Censorship that "right and left the foe is listening but nowhere can he detect the voice of the German people. Censorship attempts to show the enemy that 67 million human beings have the same opinion as big and little matters and contrary views must not be allowed to come to the surface."

The Berliner Post, The Lokal Amzeiger, and *Vorwarts* were all suppressed for articles displeasing military and other government officials. In Bohemia, French books were banned because they seemingly expressed sentiments displeasing to the Austrian monarchy. Chief Editor Marx pointed out, at the annual meeting of the National Association of the German Press, that press discussion of war aims could be harmful, but that forbidding that discussion was more harmful since the usefulness of the press is only possible with full freedom of the press. [46]

The printing machinery and plant of the *Nubarer,* and *Kerryman,* and the *Liberator* in Ireland were seized by government officials. [47]

1917

Two Athens newspapers were suspended for exposing King Constantine's pro-German intrigues. [48]

The Bolsheviks restored press censorship two days after taking over the Russian government.

The Bull, a strident Irish publication, lost its mailing privileges for opposing wartime cooperation with the British. [49]

Dutch journalists and professors protested strongly the suppression of Dutch newspapers for anti-German content: military officials punished publications for articles which displeased them. [50]

French journalists ridiculed government censorship of newspapers, novels, or other literature and found many ways to evade that censorship, sometimes renaming their newspapers. [51]

Germany issued the *Official Censorship Book for the German Press* which proscribed many forbidden subjects. Austria had even more severe restrictions. [52]

For a little while German officials eased up on censorship, but soon stronger controls were placed on political newspapers. *The Straalsburger Zeitung,* an anti-Semitic paper, and *The Weekly World,* a radical one, were both suppressed. [53]

The Goerlitzer Volkszeitung was taken over by the German government when its editors refused to publish a government article. The officials published the article and made the paper pay for the edition. *The Breslau Volkswacht* was suppressed for objecting to air raids which had killed women and children. A German city freed by the allies instructed its newspapers not to criticize the United States. In Bohemia all German newspapers were suspended in anticipation of May Day. [54]

William MacDonald said, "No reputable correspondent needs a censorship, no official ought to be shielded by it, no secret diplomatic intrigue ought to be fostered by it. Most of all should it find tolerance in a war which is being fought by democracies for the safeguarding of democracy. [55]

Mexico prohibited malicious expressions exciting hatred by the authorities, the army, the national guard, fundamental institutions, or the public good. [56]

Maxmillian Harden, editor of the *Die Zukunft*, was drafted to be a military clerk, and his paper suspended for the remainder of the war because he criticized a government newspaper. When the war began, every newspaper in Germany had to use all the articles provided by the Wolff News Agency without any changes, or use none at all. Germany used its 1917 *Official Censorship Book for the German Press*. [57]

Russian censorship eliminated all news coming out of Russia. Nikolai Lenin said, "The capitalists define freedom of the press as the suppression of the censor and the power for every part to publish newspapers as they please. In reality that is not freedom of the press but freedom for the rich, for the burgeoisie to deceive the oppressed and exploited masses of the people. State monopoly of newspaper advertising is the only solution." [58]

Spain imposed censorship on the press, partly because of German protests, and threatened the propagators of false news with severe punishment. [59]

Lord Sumner told the House of Lords that the phrase "Christianity is part of the law of England" was really not law, but only rhetoric. Blasphemy had to have elements of contumely and ribaldry. The British Venereal Disease Act forbade advertising or giving information about treatments.

1918

The Arbeiter Zeitung sarcastically observed how free the press of Austria had become with whole columns left blank by the German censors. In Germany, newspapers attacking Pan-Germans were severely punished and censorship of all content was severe. [60]

Rosa Luxenburg, a German revolutionary writer, said, "Freedom is always and exclusively freedom for the one who thinks differently." [61]

The editor of the *Athens Chronos* was sentenced to eight years in prison, fined $2,000, and had to suspend his paper for three months for publishing militarily prohibited articles. [62]

Fifty-five provincial newspapers were suppressed in Austria because they reported on food conditions. [63]

Seven conservative Berlin newspapers were suppressed for reporting on a trial of an Independent Socialist deputy. *Vorwarts* and the *Berliner Tageblatt* were suppressed for printing news from Vienna. [64]

The commander-in-chief of the Berlin district forbade the appearance of the *Berliner Neueste Nachrichten*. The majority parties forming the new German government demanded modification of law to protect personal liberty, freedom of the press, and limitation of censorship about articles about foreign governments and military matters. Chancellor von Hertling's changes would see the dismantling of the German system but press regulations forbade all adverse comment on occupied area conditions. When the editors of *Liberal Korrespondenz* revealed that the Fatherland party was a front for the Conservative party, they were fined and threatened with jail. [65]

Repressive Chinese officials suspended the *Pekin Gazette* when Japan complained about several of its articles. [66]

Georges Clemenceau, France's Premier, let news of the record battle of the Maine be freely published. [67]

Georges Clemenceau abolished censorship of political publications in France, but he quickly reversed this action to prevent unfavorable references being made about President Woodrow Wilson and the peace conference. [68]

Petrograd's *Dien* changed from being a liberal publication to a moderate socialist one, but was suspended by Trotsky. It reappeared under a new name — *Notch (Night)*. *Russkaye Slovo*, a Russian newspaper, said, "The freedom of speech and of the press is guaranteed only for the extreme left, and the remainder of the press is exposed to the rigor of military censorship." At least 17 newspapers had been suppressed. [69]

Field Marshall Paul von Hindenberg of Germany begged the Kaiser to forbid circulation of the *Frankfurter Zeitung*, the *Berliner Tageblatt*, and *Vorwarts* on the western front. [70]

Thomas Masaryk had a Paris newspaper called *La Nation Tcheque* and in Italy he had the *Czeckoslovak Samonstatnost*. When he became its first president, Czechoslovakia established a free press. [71]

Noel Pemberton Billing, an ultra-conservative member of Parliament, won acquittal in a libel trial based on his *Vigilants* newspaper demanding vigorous prosecution of the war and a return to imperialism. He claimed 47,000 British subjects — many in high places — were homosexuals who had been blackmailed by the Germans into not waging a fierce war. The English Defense of the Realm Act gave great arrest powers to the government. For example, the *Weekly World* was fined $500 for an article about the Versailles conference based on reports in several other publications. [72]

The Pope suspended the Roman Catholic *Corriere Fuli* after it printed the Pope's speech releasing Italians from serving in Italy's military forces. [73]

The *Russkaye Slovo*, liberal Moscow newspaper, reported as the Revolution took over:

> The freedom of speech and of the press is guaranteed for the extreme "Left," and the remainder of the press is exposed to the right of a "military" censorship. We are citing a list of seventeen daily newspapers of important provincial towns with republican tendencies which were suppressed by an arbitrary censorship.[74]

Swiss officials threatened to suspend the *Gazette de Lausanne* if it continued to print criticism of Germany. [75]

Crown Prince Wilhelm telegraphed, "I beg you to forbid the circulation of the three newspapers — *Frankfurter Zeitung, Berliner Tageblatt*, and *Vorwarts* on the western front. The damage which these three have done during the recent months to sentiment among our men is lamentable" [76]

1919

When the Allies took over the Rhine valley, they suppressed German newspapers in Treves and Coblenz. Robert Herrick pointed out that the curse of propaganda spread like a pestilence throughout every corner of the world because of four years of German effort, and showed no sign of abatement. [77]

The Chinese government banned publications critical of the Japanese in an effort to make relations between China and Japan friendly. [78]

The Cork (Ireland) *Examiner* was suspended and raided and its machinery dismantled without explanation. Later it and other Irish newspapers appeared, believing the fuss was based upon support for a Sinn Finn loan.[79]

Anatole France, a French novelist said, "Burn, burn all the books which teach hatred." [80]

In Imperial Germany the press was the most docile, well-drilled and controlled, the most supine press in all international questions. [81]

A member of the House of Lords complained the most serious thing of all was that ever since the war began the expression of honest and reasonable criticism and the publication of accurate news had been made very difficult by the stupid and ill-conceived pressure of the censorship. Facts had been suppressed or ignored, and untrue conclusions fostered in the supposed interests of the nation. Bruce Rogers was convicted of the crime of having published "to be an American patriot willing to die in defense of the trade supremacy of the British empire and her subjugation of India and Ireland." The English Rowlett Act continued the censorship of Indian newspapers following World War I.[82]

Japan suppressed 30 newspapers for articles about the high price of rice. [83]

Benito Mussolini, editor of *il Popolo d'Italio*, met with 100 followers to launch Italian fascism. One of their first acts was to burn down the Socialist paper, *Avanti*. Italian newspapers strongly opposed Mussolini and the fascists. *The Idea Nazionale* was seized by Italian police because an article in it was hostile to France. [84]

1920

Arnold Bennett, British novelist, said, "Journalists say a thing that they know isn't true, in the hope that if they keep on saying it long enough it will be true." [85]

The British Defense of the Realm Act prohibited distribution of leaflets and pamphlets without permission from the censor. [86]

The Dublin *Freeman's Journal* was suppressed for six weeks because of charges it made against the government. [87]

In England's national Red scare, 2,700 Communists, anarchists, and other radicals were arrested.

J.W. Gott was jailed nine months in England for publishing critical material to anyone in sympathy with the Christian religion. George Bernard Shaw said, "The extreme form of censorship may not be assassination."

Adolf Hitler became owner of a weekly anti-semitic weekly, *The Voelkischer Beobachter*, by becoming chairman of the board and owner of a corporation. This business ultimately owned all the German press; Hitler was a canny publisher. [88]

Nikolai Lenin, Russian revolutionary, said:
> Why should freedom of speech and freedom of the press be allowed? Why should a government which is doing what it believes is right allow itself to be criticized? It would not allow opposition by lethal weapons. Ideas are much more fatal things than guns. Why should any man be allowed to buy a printing press and disseminate pernicious opinion calculated to embarrass the government? [89]

Paul Valery, a French philosopher, said, "If some great catastrophe is not announced every morning, we feel a certain void. Nothing in the paper today; we sigh." [90]

1921

H.A.L. Fisher, a British historian, said:
> It is easier for eight or nine elderly men to feel their way towards unanimity, if they are not compelled to conduct their converging maneuvers under the microscope and telescope of the Press, but are permitted to shuffle about a little in slippers. [91]

V.I. Lenin, Russian revolutionist, said, "The freedom of the press is the freedom to buy up papers, the freedom to buy writers, to buy and manufacture public opinion in the interest of the capitalists." [92]

1922

John Galsworthy, British novelist, said, "Public opinion's always in advance of the law." [93]

Mahatma Gandhi was arrested because of seditious articles which appeared in *Young India*, a newspaper he edited. He pleaded guilty and was sentenced to six years in prison, but was released in two years because of appendicitis. [94]

Katherine Mansfield, a New Zealand author, said, "Risk! Risk anything! Care no more for the opinion of others, for those voices. Do the hardest thing on earth for you. Act for yourself. Face the truth." [95]

1923

England ratified the International Convention for the Suppression of the Circulation of and the Traffic in Obscene Publications. Members of the League of Nations signed a convention to suppress the circulation of and the trafficking in obscene publications. [96]

Joseph Paul Goebbels, Nazi propaganda minister, said, "It is the absolute right of the State to supervise the formation of public opinion." [97]

Adolf Hitler said, "The greater the lie, the greater the chance that it will be believed." [98]

Italy adopted a regulation prohibiting the printing of news of a false or biased nature, with the intent of hampering the government in its regulations with foreign powers, or damaging national credit at home or abroad. Police could suspend newspapers that they believed violated this regulation. [99]

Rudyard Kipling, the English author, said, "Words are, of course, the most powerful drug used by mankind." [100]

Parliamentary theory in England believed that reporting debates in the House of Commons was a breach of privilege and newspapers were forbidden to report anything said or done in Parliament, but this prohibition was completely ignored.

Joseph Stalin, Russian dictator, said, "Print is the sharpest and the strongest weapon of our party." [101]

1924

Thomas Mann, German novelist, said, "Speech is civilization itself. The word, even the most contradictious word, preserves contact — it is silence which isolates."[102]

Mann said, "Opinions cannot survive if one has no chance to fight for them." [103]

Benito Mussolini placed all newspaper managers under the control of local prefects to end press freedom and non-fascist newspapers. [104]

Clennell Wilkinson pointed out in *The Outlook*, a London periodical, that the notion that movies were more dangerous than the old penny dreadfuls remained to be proved. [105]

Chapter 12

NEW TYRANNIES
1925 Through 1959

1925

Mussolini decreed all Italian newspapers had to submit to a government director and all journalists had to carry a Fascist Party card to be journalists. Mussolini said, "I consider Fascist journalism as my orchestra." [1]

Alfred North Whitehead, English mathematician, said, "In formal logic, a contradiction is the signal of a defeat: but in the evolution of real knowledge it marks the first step in progress towards a victory. This is one great reason for the utmost toleration of variety in opinion." [2]

1926

John Galsworthy, English novelist, said:
> It has often been remarked that the breakfast-tables of people who avow themselves indifferent to what the Press may say of them are garnished by all the newspapers on the morning when there is anything to say.[3]

An Inter-American Press Association was organized by 550 western hemisphere publications and people to guard freedom of the press.[4]

Ireland enacted a Censorship of Publications law. Poet William Butler Yeats vigorously opposed an Irish censorship bill while serving as a senator in the Dail Eiream. He said it would create "an instrument of tyranny and place control over the substance of our thoughts in the hands of one man, the Minister of Justice." [5]

D.H. Lawrence had his novel, *Lady Chatterley's Lover*, printed in Italy but it was confiscated by custom agents both in the United States and England. [6]

Rebecca West, British novelist and journalist, said, "God forbid that any book should be banned. The practice is as indefensible as infanticide." [7]

1929

Michel de Ghelderode, a Belgian dramatist, said:
> A serious and profitable occupation, reading the newspapers. It teaches
> you to reason as well as the next person. It gives you irrefutable and
> generally admitted opinions on all events. [8]

D.H. Lawrence, British novelist, said, "What is pornography to one man is the
laughter of genius to another." [9]

1930

Aldous Huxley, British novelist, said:
> The remedy against pornography is in the heads of everyone who
> chooses to use it. If you do not like a book, all you have to do is not read
> it. Let every man be his own censor. [10]

D.H. Lawrence said, "Freedom is a very great reality. But it means, above all
things, freedom from lies." [11]

The London County Council censored several Russian films including *Mother*,
Ten Days That Shook the World, *The Fall of St. Petersburg*, and *The General Line*. [12]

1931

Scotland Yard seized the manuscript of D.H. Lawrence's *Pansies*, and the
English government wouldn't let it be published unless some poems were omitted.

George Bernard Shaw, British playwright, said, "Newspapers are unable,
seemingly, to discriminate between a bicycle accident and the collapse of
civilization." [13]

1932

Berthold Brecht said:
> The radio must be transformed from a means of distribution into a
> medium of communication. Radio might be the most wonderful medium
> of communication imaginable for the public, a vast, close-meshed
> network. This it could become if it was not only to receive but also to
> transmit, a means given to the listener, not only to listen but also to
> speak, a means of putting him in touch rather than isolating him.

Maxim Gorky, Russian playwright, said:
> It is no exaggeration to say that the press of Europe and America busies
> itself assiduously and almost exclusively with the task of lowering the

cultural level of its readers, a level which is already sufficiently low. [14]

1933

Under the German editors law devised by Paul Joseph Goebbels, all journalists had to negotiate with the state. The chief editors became state officials publishing only Goebbels approved materials. By 1936 the Nazis owned more than 100 newspapers and Goebbels banned criticism by newspapers. [15]

Jean Geraudeux, French playwright, said, "When humankind ceased any longer to heed the words of the seers and prophets, Science lovingly brought forth the Radio Commentator." [16]

Dr. Campbell West-Watson, speaking for the New Zealand University Teachers Association, said:
> I confess that I regard with dismay the desire to inhibit our teachers from political expression. If there is one problem which faces us squarely, and the shirking of which threatens utter disaster, it is the problem of living together socially and internationally. If our leaders of thought are to be forbidden to express opinions of these matters we are depriving ourselves deliberately of one of our most hopeful spring of help. I should myself be sorry to see our university leaders enter the arena of party politics, for I should feel that they had sacrificed something of their independence of judgment. But if we look on them as men who are responsible to truth, surely it is unwise to try to prevent them from speaking what they feel.

1934

Joanna Field, a British psychologist, pointed out that the growth of understanding follows an ascending spiral rather than a straight line. [17]

D.H. Lawrence, in *Dirty Words*, supposedly said, "There are no dirty words. There are only dirty minds and tongues. And these have imported a foul odor what originally were mere descriptive terms for quite common experiences."[18]

1935

John A. Spender, said in *The Spectator*:
> The really important freedom is not that of dancing on the edge of Campbell's Act, but freedom to write fearlessly on matters of public importance, freedom, above all, to express unpopular opinions — opinions which the established authorities may think dangerous. A free and courageous press is needed to prevent conservatism from slipping into fascism and radicalism into revolution. [19]

1936

C.S. Lewis, English critic and author, said, "Truth is an unruly subject and, once admitted, comes crowding in on us faster than we wish." [20]

1937

American book publishers refused to attend the International Publishers Congress in Leipzig as a protest of German censorship. [21]

The newspaper *Asahi* had its presses and editorial offices wrecked. From then on, no one dared oppose the military. [22]

W.H. Auden said, "Owners of the press hire clever writers to produce liberal articles and opinions." [23]

Britain censored a *March of Time* film [24]

Stephen Brown contended that "some sort of censorship over the printed word is not only the right but the duty of Governments such as Ireland; in the case of pornography few would question that right." [25]

1938

Antonin Artaud, a French actor and director, said, "All writing is garbage. People who come out of nowhere to try to put into words any part of what goes on in their minds are pigs." [26]

Cyril Connally, British critic, said, "Literature is the art of writing something that will be read twice; journalism what will be grasped at once." [27]

Adolf Hitler said," Our law concerning the press is that divergencies of opinion between members of the government are no longer an occasion for public exhibitions, which are not the newspapers' business." [28]

Jawaharlal Nehru founded the *National Herald* in Luchnow when he was released from prison in an effort to promote the cause of Indian freedom. [29]

George Orwell, British novelist, said, "Freedom is the right to tell people what they do not want to hear." [30]

1939

The Canadian Supreme Court invalidated the Alberta Press Act which gave the government complete control over the press to suppress communist doctrines.[31]

Paul Joseph Goebbels said, "News policy is a weapon of war. Its purpose is to wage war and not to give out information." [32]

1940

Winston Churchill, English statesman, said, "A free press is the unsleeping guardian of every other right that free men prize; it is the most dangerous foe of tyranny." [33]

Mahatma Gandhi, at one time, said:
>I am a journalist myself and shall appeal to fellow journalists to realize their responsibility and to carry on their work with no idea other than that of upholding the truth.

Sir Hugh Walpole said:
>For many centuries now the Englishman has enjoyed perfect freedom in the reading of any kind of literature. So the freedom of books is indestructible and the men and women of our country, with all their faults and lacks, are made of this freedom. No government is tolerable to them for a moment that tries to prevent their right to think for themselves, often studying all the evidence, past and present. That trust in their independence is their right, owned through years of conflict, and never again to any power on this earth will they surrender it. [34]

H.G. Wells said:
>The cause of the decline and fall of the Roman Empire lay in the fact that there were no newspapers in that day. Because there were no newspapers there was no way by which the dwellers in the far-flung nation and the empire could find out what was going on at the center.

Virginia Woolf, a British author, said, "We are a free people fighting to defend freedom. With a roof to cover us and a gas mask handy, it is our business to puncture gas bags and discover the seeds of truth." [35]

She said, "To make ideas effective, we must be able to fire them off." [36]

1941

George Bernard Shaw, British dramatist, said, "No American newspaper will print anything contrary to its own interests." [37]

Alfred G. Stephen of Australia said, "Indecency, or even obscenity, simply cannot enter into the artistic question. A picture of a saint has no more artistic merit than a vile Pompeian fresco, and it may have less." He believed a community could control who could see indecent works. [38]

1942

Jose Marti, a Cuban political activist, said, "The dagger plunged in the name of Freedom is plunged into the breast of Freedom." [39]

1943

The Australian Senate refused to punish Professor John Anderson for condemning religious doctrines being imposed on children.

Winston Churchill, English statesman, said: "Everyone is in favor of free speech. Hardly a day passes without its being extolled, but some people's idea of it is that they are free to say what they like, but if anyone says anything back, that is an outrage." [40]

1945

George Orwell, British novelist, said, "To write in plain, vigorous language, one has to think fearlessly; one cannot be politically orthodox." [41]

Orwell said:
> The controversy over freedom of speech and of the press is at the bottom of a controversy over the desirability, or otherwise, of telling lies. What is really at issue is the right to report contemporary events truthfully. Intellectual freedom is under attack on the one hand by apologists of totalitarianism and, on the other, by the drift toward monopoly and bureaucracy. [42]

1946

Ireland had the Irish Censorship of Publications Act and used a register of Prohibited Publications to suppress literature. [43]

1947

The Constitution of the Republic of China again promised freedom of the press but provided the press could be controlled. There were nearly 4,000 works banned for India, or for the British museum, or for the India Office Library.

Sir Harold Nicolson, British politician and writer, said, "The gift of broadcasting is, without question, the lowest human capacity to which any man could attain." [44]

1948

Gandhi, Indian leader, said, "Truth never damages a cause that is just." [45]

Tehyi Hsieh, a Chinese writer, said, "if the world knew how to use freedom without abusing it, tyranny would not exist." [46]

1949

The Chinese Communists took over and revised yearly press control measures thereafter.

Publications in areas of China controlled by the Communists were totally regulated. The KMT government engaged in heavy press repressions with arrests, kidnapping, killing, and bribery. Nevertheless, constant demands for a free press occurred daily on a widespread basis. [47]

A Royal Commission on the English Press, formed in response to a request from the National Union of Journalists who were fearful of newspaper monopoly, recommended that a General Council of the Press be established to admonish the press for its sins. [48]

The report of the English Royal Commission on the Press said:
A newspaper is one of the most remarkable products of modern society. To gather news from five continents; to print and distribute it so fast that what happens at dawn in India may be read before breakfast in England; to perform the feat afresh every twenty-four hours, and to sell the product for less than the price of a box of matches — this, were it not so familiar, would be recognized as an astonishing achievement. [49]

Jean Anouilh, a French playwright, said, "Have you noticed that life, real honest-to-goodness life, with murders and catastrophes and fabulous inheritances, happens almost exclusively in the newspapers?" [50]

Winston Churchill said:
A free press is the unsleeping guardian of every other right that freemen prize; it is the most dangerous foe of tyranny. Under dictatorship the press is bound to languish, and the loudspeaker and the film to become more important. But when free institutions are indigenous to the soil, and men have the habit of liberty, the press will continue to be the Fourth Estate, the vigilant guardian of the rights of the ordinary citizen. [51]

Winston Churchill also said, "I am always in favor of the press but sometimes they say quite nasty things."

Ilya Ehrenburg's *The Thaw* and Boris Pasternak's *Dr. Zhivago* opened a new phase of Russian literary courage despite heavy government controls. [52]

The Indian Constitution guaranteed freedom of the press in 1950. In 1951 the government controlled newsprint supply and punished the publication of material which was likely to undermine the government, interfere with necessary services, or seduce military persons from completing their duties. [53]

Stanley Kauffman's *The Philanderer* was judged not guilty of obscene libel in England. [54]

Thomas Mann wrote, "Speech is civilization itself. The word, even the most contradictory word, preserves contact. It is silence which isolates." [55]

Mao-Tse-Tung stated that "the role of the press in China would be to organize, to stimulate or encourage, to agitate, to criticize, and to propel. The press must be a collective propagandist, collective agitator, and a collective organizer." All published and broadcast material had to be channeled through a high party bureau. [55]

Juan Peron took over *La Prensa* and made that newspaper a government mouthpiece. But Peron was finally driven from power in 1955, and *La Prensa* was again edited by Gainza Paz. [57]

The state of Queensland in Australia had an Objectionable Literature Act. [58]

The most banned book in Quebec was entitled the *Awful Disclosures of Maria Monk; As Exhibited in a Narrative of Her Sufferings During a Residence of Five Years as a Novice, and Two Years as a Black Nun, in the Hotel Dieu Nunnery at Montreal.*

Antoine de Saint-Exupery, a French writer, said, "I know but one freedom and that is freedom of the mind." [59]

Humbert Wolfe wrote, "You really don't need to bribe British journalists who write whatever the boss says." [60]

Lionel Trilling, an English critic, said, "Literature is the human activity that takes the fullest and most precise account of variousness, possibility, complexity, and difficulty." [61]

1952

American occupation administrators fired hundreds of Japanese journalists who had supported the Japanese war, but they soon returned to their jobs. The Americans fired 700 pro-Communist journalists. American restrictions on the Japanese press did not end until the San Francisco Peace Treaty.

Fulgencio Batista imposed strict censorship in Cuba.

K.R. Srinvasa Iyengar of India said:
> Literature can present sex or vice or perversion, and yet remain literature, so long as these are imaginatively seized and fully consumed in the whole design. Literature that boldly and purposefully describes those aspects of human experience over which polite society feels compelled to throw a blanket of silence is a kind of strong meat which may conceivably injure weak or diseased stomachs, but these risks of indigestion are the necessary concomitants of all good things.

France prosecuted Henry Miller's *Sexus* and Boris Vian's *I'll Spit on Your Grave*. South Africa's Suppression of Communism Act and Sabotage Act forbade publications by listed authors considered communistic.

Pedro Segura y Saenz, archbishop of Seville in Spain, complained that the universal aspiration of the present time may be summed up in one magical word, which has succeeded in reducing people — liberty. [62]

1953

British publishers set up a voluntary press council. The Ministry of Cinematography was the Chief Directorate of the Cinema as part of the Russian Ministry of Culture. Soviet citizens were instructed to cut out the pages about Lavrenti Beria in the *Large Soviet Encyclopedia* after he had been executed. [63]

Francisco Franco, Spanish dictator, said, "We are for liberty, but liberty with order, the kind of liberty which will not threaten the basic principles of our nation, nor threaten its faith and unity." [64]

William Nathan Oatis, an Associated Press correspondent, was jailed in Czechoslovakia for activities hostile to the state. He was sentenced to ten years after being held incommunicado for 72 days. In 1953 he was released, but not cleared of guilt until eighteen years later after a Czechoslovakian action which admitted the whole thing was rigged. [65]

Marguerite Yourcenar, a French novelist, said, "Any truth creates a scandal." [66]

1955

James Baldwin, an American novelist, said, "I love America more than any other country in the world, and exactly for this reason, I insist on the right to criticize her perpetually." [67]

1956

Claude Cockburn, a British writer, said, "A newspaper is always a weapon in somebody's hands." [68]

Aldous Huxley, British novelist, said, "Thanks to words, we have been able to rise above the brutes; and thanks to words, we have often sunk to the level of the demons." [69]

Mao-Tse-Tung, Chinese dictator, said, "Let a hundred flowers bloom. Let a hundred schools of thought contend." [70]

1957

Author Albert Camus said, "A free press can of course be good or bad, but most certainly without freedom the press will never be anything but bad. Freedom is nothing else but a chance to be better, whereas enslavement is certainty of the worse." [71]

A Standing Committee on Television Viewing was established in England as a voluntary agency to evaluate commercial and government television.

Rebecca West, a British journalist, described journalism as an ability to meet the challenge of filling space. [72]

Gainza Paz resumed control of *La Prensa* of Argentina after President Peron was arrested. Peron had suppressed the newspaper in many ways and had the government take it over in 1951. [73]

Leopold Senghor, president of Senegal, said, "All change, all production and generation are effected through the word." [74]

Jean Cocteau, a French poet, said, "The instinct of nearly all societies is to lock up anybody who is truly free." [75]

Nikita S. Khrushchev, Soviet premier, said, "The press is our chief ideological weapon." [76]

Khrushchev, also said, "Just as an army cannot fight without arms, so the Party cannot do ideological work successfully without such a sharp and militant weapon as the press." [77]

J.B. Priestly, English novelist, said, "Already we viewers, when not viewing have begun to whisper to one another that the more we elaborate our means of communication, the less we communicate." [78]

Mao-Tse-Tung, the Chinese leader, said:
> The only way to settle questions of an ideological nature of controversial issues among the people is by the democratic method, the method of discussion, criticism, persuasion and education, and not by the method of coercion or repression." [79]

Chapter 13

FREEDOM OF EXPRESSION STRUGGLES ON
1960 Through 1979

1960

Brendan Behan, an Irish dramatist, said, "Critics are like eunuchs in a harem. They know how it's done; they've seen it done every day, but they're unable to do it themselves." [1]

Aneurin Bevan, British Labour leader, said, "I read the newspapers avidly. It is my one form of continuous fiction." [2]

Dr. William Bland was convicted of seditious libel in Australia for criticizing Governor Macquarie. [3]

Jorge Luis Borges, an Argentine author, said, "I have always imagined that Paradise will be a kind of library." [4]

Allbert Camus, French philosopher, said, "A free press can of course be good or bad, but, most certainly, without freedom it will never be anything but bad." [5]

Camus said, "Freedom is nothing else but a chance to be better, whereas enslavement is a certainty of the worse." [6]

Camus said, "Freedom of the press is perhaps the freedom that has suffered the most from the gradual degradation of the idea of liberty." [7]

An English Court ruled that *Lady Chatterley's Lover* was not obscene. The publisher subsequently dedicated the next three editions to the trial jury. [8]

Maurice Giradias said, "I accept the title of pornographer with joy and pride. I enjoy annoying people I dislike deeply, the bourgeois class which is in power everywhere. I think it is very healthy to shock them. Censorship is absurd, inefficient, and without justifiable function in a society which claims to be an adult and civilized democracy." [9]

Gabriel Garcia Marquez, a Columbian author, said, "Ultimately literature is nothing but carpentry. With both you are working with reality, a material just as hard as wood." [10]

Peter B. Medawar, a British zoologist, said, "The human mind treats a new idea the way a body treats a strange protein; it rejects it." [11]

Statesman Jawaharlal Nehru said, "Never do anything in secret or anything that you wish to hide. For the desire to hide anything means that you are afraid, and fear is a bad thing, and unworthy of you. Privacy, of course, we may have and should have, but that is a very different thing from secrecy."

Kwame Nkrumah, a Ghanian politician, contended it is far better to be free to govern or misgovern yourself than to be governed by anybody else. [12]

1961

James Baldwin, author, said that freedom is the fire which burns away illusions.[13]

New Zealand set up censorship with the Cinemaograph Films Act. [14]

Vita Sackville-West, a British writer and poet, said that writing is the most egotistic of occupations and the most gratifying while it lasts. [15]

1962

Stanislav Lem, a Polish poet, said, "The window of the world can be covered by a newspaper." [16]

Marshall McLuhan, Canadian media scholar, said, "Gutenberg made everybody a reader. Xerox made every one a publisher." [17]

Anthony Sampson, an English biographer, said, "In America journalism is apt to be regarded as an extension of history; in Britain, as an extension of conversation." [18]

Mao-Tse-Tung, China's leader, said, "Let other people speak out. The heavens will not fall and you will not be thrown out. If you do not let others speak, then the day will surely come when you will be thrown out." [19]

1963

Daniel George, a British author, said, "Oh, Freedom, what liberties are taken in thy name." [20]

Lord Longford, a British politician, said, "On the whole, I would not say that our

Press is obscene. I would say that it trembles on the brink of obscenity." [21]

Fanny Hill was judged obscene by an English Court. The Obscene Publications Act made it illegal to have an obscene article for publication or gain. [22]

Maurice Girodias was arrested and convicted in France for the publication of six English language books by his Olympia Press of Paris. In 1962 he said, "To corrupt and deprave is my business. It is my business to publish those forbidden books, those outrageous obscenities." Girodias, as a result of French government raids and actions, acquired 100 banned books, orders not to publish anything for 80 years, six years of jail sentences, and 29,000 pounds in fines. But he only was in jail for two days. [23]

J. Krishnamury, an Indian mystic, said, "Freedom is really a state of mind in which there is no fear or compulsion, no urge to be secure." [24]

Marshall McLuhan, Canadian media evaluator, said, "The medium is the message." [25]

Nelson Mandela, South Africa's president, said, "I have cherished the ideal of a democratic and free society in which all persons live together in harmony and equal opportunity." [26]

New Zealand's Indecent Publications Tribunal declared James Baldwin's *Another Country* was not indecent. [27]

1965

Peter Fryer poked fun at the British Museum for its shielding practices that kept its 5,000 cupboard books of erotica away from both mulitators and serious scholars [28]

Anthony Grey, a Reuters man, was imprisoned 26 months in Peking in retaliation for England's imprisonment of several Chinese journalists after the Hong Kong Communists riots. [29]

Malcolm Muggeridge, an English critic, said, "Surely the glory of journalism is its transcience." [30]

The Soviet Supreme Court sentenced Andrei Sinyavsky for *On Socialist Realism* to seven years and Yuli Daniel for *Moscow Calling* to five years. The books were published outside Russia. Censorship was officially ended in Russia, but the prosecution of journalists continued with cruel regularity under various sections of the penal code. [31]

1967

Patrick Campbell, British editor and humorist, said, "Journalism is the only job that requires no degrees, no diplomas, and no specialized knowledge of any kind." [32]

Finland tried a plan giving government subsidies to political parties for their newspapers. Sweden and Norway tried similar plans, but none of these really insured continuation of the newspapers. [33]

The Irish 1967 Censorship Bill removed bans on 110 books, some of them twentieth century masterpieces. But thousands more were still banned. [34]

Christos Lambrakis, wrote, "In Greece today, the press is not simply being censored or dictated. It is being violated. Experience shows that when freedom of the press vanishes, the press vanishes with it." [35]

Jonathan Miller, a British writer and physician, said, "Censorship is nothing more than a legal corollary of public modesty." [36]

Last Exit to Brooklyn by Hubert Selby, Jr., was tried for obscenity in London under provisions of the British Obscene Publications Act of 1959.[37]

Aleksandr Solzhenitsyn told the Russian Union of Writers that the "Now intolerable oppression, in the form of censorship, which our literature has endured for decades, the Union of Writers can no longer accept." [38]

1968

Czechs used a scheme of underground replicas of regular newspapers and clandestine radio and even television broadcasts. When Alexander Dubcek announced new controls on the press, the Czechs no longer accepted his leadership. In summing up, a journalist said:
> The Czechoslovakian people learned during that time that freedom of the press is the groundstone of all our liberties. The Soviets were so afraid of that freedom that they sent soldiers with guns and tanks to suppress it. The muzzling of the free press and the re-introduction of censorship was a result of their criminal adventure. The world is not going to forget that.[39]

1969

The Beatles believed everyone has to be free.[40]

Arthur Dobson, a Bradford bookseller publisher, was fined 1,000 pounds and sent to jail with a two-year sentence for selling *My Secret Life*, an anonymous parade of sexual escapades.

Dr. Tricis Menders was sentenced to five years for libeling Russia when he submitted a manuscript to an American historian about the Latvian revolution.

William H. Orchard, an Australian psychiatrist said, "Censorship is an institutional form of childlike denial designed to preserve equanimity at the expense of realty." [41]

The Ryazan unit of the Soviet Writers Union expelled Aleksander Solzhenitsyn. [42]

Nicholas Tomalin, British journalist, said, "The only qualities essential for real success in journalism are rat-like cunning, a plausible manner, and a little literary ability." [43]

1970

Dictator Juan Alvardo of Peru decreed fines and jail for any journalist he decided had insulted his government. [44]

The government of Kenya declared that the local press is expected to identify itself with the aspirations of the country. [45]

Oriana Fallaci, an Italian writer and journalist, describes an author as, "When a book is done, he has his own life and you forget about him. He goes and lives alone; he takes an apartment." [46]

Argentine President Juan Carlos Ongania suspended civil liberties and gagged the press. [47]

Revolt Pimenov was jailed for six years for protests about the Russian invasion of Hungary and another five years for protests about Czechoslovakia. Mikkail Makarenko was jailed eight years for promoting hidden facts. [48]

Rhodesia and South Africa expelled foreign correspondents and disciplined the foreign press. [49]

1971

Steve Biko, a South African activist, said, "The most potent weapon in the hands of the oppressor is the mind of the oppressed." [50]

Lord Diplock, a British attorney, said, "Censorship is about stopping people reading or seeing what we do not want to read or see ourselves." [51]

Violette Leduc, French writer, said, "To write is to inform against others." [52]

Mary Whitehouse crusaded for many years against obscene literature in England. The Pope praised her for such efforts. [53]

1972

Bukovsky, a Russian citizen, was jailed eight years for slander in reports to the west and for trying to smuggle a printing press into Russia. [54]

Germaine Greer was fined $40 for saying *shit* in Aukland, N.Z., but was acquitted of obscenity for saying *bullshit*.

Aleksandr I. Solzhenitsyn in his Nobel prize lecture said:
> Woe to that nation whose literature is disturbed by the intervention of power. Because that is not just a violation against "freedom of print." It is a closing down of the heart of a nation, a slashing to pieces of its memory. [55]

Tony Smythe, a British civil historian, said, "Censorship is more depraving and corrupting than anything pornography can produce." [56]

Tom Stoppard, British playwright, said, "The media. It sounds like a convention of spiritualist." [57]

1973

Margaret Laurence, a Canadian novelist, said, "When I say 'work' I only mean writing. Everything else is just odd jobs." [58]

George Orwell of England described a pamphlet as being:
> A one man show, one has complete freedom of expression, including the freedom, if one chooses, the freedom to be scurrilous, abusive, and seditious, or, on the other hand, to be more detailed, serious, and high brow, than is ever possible in a newspaper or in most kinds of periodicals. At the same time, since the pamphlet is always short and unbound, it can be produced much more quickly than a book, and in principle, at any rate can reach a bigger public. Above all, a pamphlet does not have to follow any prescribed pattern. It can be in prose or in verse, it can consist largely of maps or attributions or quotations; it can take the form of a story, a fable, a letter, an essay, a dialogue, or a piece of reportage. All that is required of it is that it shall be topical, polemical, and short.

Raids to confiscate pornography saw the London West End porno team pick up 40 tons of material and arrest the nine principal pornographers.

George Orwell said, "In this country (England) intellectual cowardice is the worst enemy a writer or a journalist has to face. Anyone who challenges the prevailing orthodoxy finds himself silenced with surprising effectiveness."

Police seized 10,000 copies of 238 different magazines in a raid on Johnson's Central News Agency in Bath, England; 146 were ruled obscene. Customs officials seized 324,000 copies of *Men Only*, a Dutch magazine specializing in female masturbation photos. Two thousand policemen arrested 40 pornographers in the Soho District of London. Officials also picked up 100,000 copies of books and magazines at Cobham farm, including soft pornography as well as hard pornography in the eighteen ton lot.

1974

Alexander Cockburn, a British journalist, said, "The First Law of Journalism: to confirm existing prejudice, rather than to contradict it." [59]

1975

John Birt, British television executive, said, "There is a bias in television journalism. It is not against any particularly party or point of view — it is a bias against understanding." [60]

1976

Indira Gandhi said, "We want to hear Africans on events in Africa. You should similarly be able to get an Indian explanation of events in India. It is astonishing that we know so little about leading poets, novelists, historians, and editors of various Asian, African, and Latin American countries while we are familiar with minor authors and columnists of Europe and America."

1977

Chief Constable James Anderton ordered 286 raids, confiscated 160,000 obscene articles, and won convictions in all his cases designed to rid Greater Manchester of pornography. Private actions against pornography had to have the approval of the English attorney-general to proceed. English courts refused to accept any therapeutic value for pornography. Margaret Thatcher, prime minister, and Mary Whitehouse joined forces in England to urge Parliament to outlaw kiddie porn.

Mary Stewart, English novelist, said, "It is harder to kill a whisper than even a shouted calumny." [61]

1978

Stefan Loran, Hungarian photojournalist, said, "The camera should be like the notebook of a trained reporter: to record events as they happen, without trying to stop them to make a picture." [62]

1979

A Frankfort School of Critical Theorists believed that media have caused the decline of mass politics and discourse because economic constraints have eroded media used to create a truly democratic society. The democratic socialist theory of the press believes that the press should not be an instrument for private owners; instead, the press should be instruments of the people, operating as public utilities through which the people's aspirations, ideas, and criticism of the state and society would be disseminated since people would have positive access to place their views in the press, which would be considerably subsidized by the government.

The British Adult Publications Association would not sell publications showing erect penile penetrations.

James Cameron, a British journalist, said, "The press can only be a mirror — albeit a distorting mirror, according to its politics or the smallness of its purpose — but it rarely lies because it dare not." [63]

Chapter 14

A CENTURY ENDS—
A CENTURY BEGINS
1980 Through 1994

1980

Indira Gandhi said, "When there are no newspapers there is no agitation. That is why we imposed censorship."

Germaine Greer, an Australian author, said, "Freedom is fragile and must be protected. To sacrifice it, even as a temporary measure, is to betray it." [1]

Graham Greene, a British novelist, said, "Media is a word that has come to mean bad journalism." [2]

Princess Diana of Britain said, "I know it's just a job journalists have to do, but sometimes I do wish they wouldn't." [3]

Wei Jinsheng, a Chinese dissident, said, "The reason why America is ahead in everything is that Americans have free speech, even the freedom to say things that are wrong." [4]

Margaret Thatcher, British prime minister, said, "I love argument. I love debate. I don't expect anyone just to sit there and agree with me, that's not their job." [5]

1982

Charles Njonjo, Kenyan broadcaster, said, "I think we're incorrect and naive to assume our people swallow everything we dish out on the radio." [6]

1984

Marguerite Duras, a French author, said, "Journalism without a moral position is impossible. Every journalist is a moralist. It's absolutely unavoidable." [7]

Nadine Gordimer, a South African author, said, "Art is on the side of the oppressed for it is freedom of the spirit, how can it exist within the oppressors?"[8]

1985

Under strict provisions of its Official Secrets Act, inherited from the British, Malaya arrested one reporter for disclosing that the government planned to buy United States AWACS planes. Earlier a reporter was jailed for articles about Malaysian-Chinese relations.

All newspapers in Israel are licensed by the government. *Alef Yad*, a West Bank settlers' newspaper was shut down because the government believed it was initiating rebellion.

Complete government control of the press existed in Nicaragua, Chile, Cuba, Guyana, Suriname, and Paraguay. Journalists in Costa Rica, the Dominican Republic, Columbia, Venezuela, Honduras, Panama, Ecuador, and Peru could only work if authorized by a journalists' collegium or by government license. Freedom of the press possibilities were improved in Argentina, Brazil, Uruguay, and Guatemala.

Andrei D. Sakharov, a Russian political dissident, said, "As long as a country has no civil liberty and freedom of information and no independent press, then there exists no effective body of public opinion to control the conduct of government." [9]

1986

Princess Anne of Britain said, "The media are a pest, by the very nature of that camera in their hands." [10]

1987

Lifang Zhou, Chinese journalism dean, said:
> A Chinese journalist must always contemplate what kind of consequences his writing will have. If critical reporting results in something positive, that's fine. But revealing information which might have a negative effect on society is useless, maybe even harmful. [11]

Nikita S. Khrushchev, Soviet premier, said that just as an enemy cannot fight without arms, so the Party cannot do ideological work successfully without such a sharp and militant weapon as the press. The press is our chief ideological weapon. [12]

Russian officials rejected Boris Pasternak's *Dr. Zhivago* and said:
> We were both alarmed and distressed. The thing that disturbs us about your novel is something that neither the editors nor the author can alter by cuts or revisions. We mean the spirit of the novel, its general tenor, the author's view of life, the real one or not, but whose collective opinion you have no reason to regard as biased, so that it would be reasonable, at least, to hear it out. The spirit of your novel is that of non-acceptance of the socialist revolution. The general tenor of your novel is that the October Revolution, the Civil War, and the social transformation involved brought the people nothing but suffering, and destroyed the Russian Intelligentsia, physically or morally.

He was expelled from the Soviet Union of Writers and future publishing; he was pressured into not accepting the Nobel Prize for literature.

J.B. Priestley, an English novelist, said, "Already we viewers, when not viewing, have begun to whisper to one another that the more we elaborate our means of communication, the less we communicate." [13]

Bertrand Russell, philosopher, said:
> The invention of printing is a doubtful blessing if it is not accompanied by the safeguarding of freedom of discussion. For falsehood is printed just as easily as truth, and just as easily spread. It avails a man precious little to be able to read if the material put in front of him must be accepted without question. Only when there is freedom of speech and criticism does the wide circulation of the printed word enhance inquiry. Without this freedom it would be better if we were illiterate. In our time this problem has become more acute, because printing is no longer the only powerful medium for mass communication. Since the invention of wireless telegraphy and television it has become even more important to exercise that eternal vigilance without which freedom in general begins to languish. [14]

Tom Stoppard, a British playwright, said, "If your aim is to change the world, journalism is a more immediate short-term weapon." [15]

1989

Mohandas Gandhi, Hindu nationalist leader, said, "Freedom is not worth having if it does not connote freedom to err." [16]

Princess Grace of Monaco said that the freedom of the press works in such a way that there is not much freedom from it. [17]

Gunter Grass, a German writer, said, "Even bad books are books and therefore sacred." [18]

Rupert Murdoch, an Australian media executive, said, "A lot of American publishers say, well, we leave a lot to our editors. I don't agree with it. I think that with the person, the chief executive, the owner, whoever it is, the buck stops on his desk."[19]

Christabel Pankhurst, a British militant suffragist, said, "Never lose your temper with the Press or the public is a major rule of political life." [20]

1990

Vaclav Havel, Czech president, said, "Falsefiers of history do not safeguard freedom but imperil it."[21]

Onora O'Neill, a British professor, said, "Censorship destroys communicative powers and possibilities even when not 100 per cent effective." [22]

1991

Alexander, crown prince of Yugoslavia, said, "My country needs a real free media." [23]

Slevenka Drakulic, Yugoslav writer, said:
> I am free to love my country in the best way I can as an individual — a writer and novelist who cherishes her language most of all. But if I am forced to "love" it in a way others define that love, then I am a prisoner in my country. [24]

David Fanning, a South African documentary producer, said that he came to the United States "for something called the First Amendment." [25]

Carlos Fuentes, a Mexican novelist, said, "A society that demands unanimity and disguises it as 'patriotism' has lost its bearings." [26]

Cesar Gaviria, president of Colombia, said, "Press freedom in the Americans is threatened now not by the authoritarian repression of dictatorship but by organized crime." [27]

Nikolai Ignatovich, a Soviet commissioner, said, "Where secrecy begins, justice ends." [28]

Frederico Mayor, UNESCO president, said, "A future predicated on the free flow of information is the only way that the global village we seek can come about." [29]

Mukende Wa Mulumba, a Zairian commentator, said, "We don't think freedom to speak is something the government should even be allowed to give or take away."[30]

Boris Notkin, a Soviet TV anchor, said, "We journalists are free to say what's on our minds. But how to tell the people the truth without making them despair is very important." [31]

Mikhail Poltoranin, Soviet press minister, said, "Glasnost means nothing unless it is supported by supplies of printing paper. Otherwise it is like music for the deaf."[32]

Vladimir Pozner, Soviet commentator, said, "Freedom and responsibility go hand in hand and, in the Soviet Union, I don't think enough attention is really being given to that equation." [33]

Zoltan Szabo, Hungarian journalist, said, "Freedom of the press is relative. For journalists, it depends on whether their publishers want to hear what they say." [34]

Melos Venawi, president of Ethiopia, said, "One thing that is very important to me is that people can be free to talk without looking back over their shoulders."[35]

Marites Vitug, a Filipino reporter, said, "Those who have been offended by the pen use the gun to silence criticism."[36]

Lech Walesa, president of Poland, said, "Our entire revolution was created by a free press and free thought." [37]

1992

Natalya Yermilina, a Soviet photo editor, said, "Now it's a very good time to communicate, and to know how people live. Our people have been living so many years in isolation." [38]

Yassen Zassoursky, a Russian journalism educator, said, "There is no freedom without speech."[39]

Sully Abu, a Nigerian editor, said, "The complexity of the country makes it difficult to box the press in. The government can try to muzzle the press, but the press always wins in the end." [40]

Assen Agov, a Bulgarian TV news editor, said, "I do not believe that free press and free speech could have been successful in Eastern Europe without those who encouraged us in times of doubt." [41]

Ludmila Blumova of Russia said, "We are not the same people. Through glasnost we have learned too much." [42]

Sir Paul Fox, a former managing director of the British Broadcasting Corporation, said, "We have a long, long way before we have the freedom that you have — not all of them I approve of by the way." [43]

Peter Galliner, director of the International Press Institute, said, "Political suppression is not only suppression against the press, but against human rights."[44]

Igor Golemblovsky, a Russian editor, said, "The Russian press has no greater enemy than the government." [45]

Lkev Guschin, a Russian editor, said, "This society cannot be considered free. People are devoid of property. The press is not free because it is devoid of property."[46]

Pavel Gusev, a Russian editor, said "Glasnost was what Gorbachev wanted to hear most. Freedom of the press is what we wanted most. So we went our separate ways. We're still afloat. Gorby is not." [47]

Vaclav Havel, president of Czechoslovakia, said, "Our papers write stupid things, but of course this is the price of freedom."[48]

Journalists in Indonesia have a worse lot than murderers according to Mochtar Lubis, an Indonesian journalist who said 'Murderers are presumed innocent and can make their own defense. We don't get that opportunity. For us the government is both prosecutor and judge." [49]

Alexei Izyumov, a correspondent for the *Mexico News*, said, "Helping to assure the survival of the free media against the challenges of the market is absolutely essential to the survival of the young Russian democracy." [50]

Oleg Kuzin, a Russian editor, said, "Today freedom of the press is related to freedom of the economy. " [51]

Nelson Mandela, president of South Africa, said, "The sign of freedom looming on the horizon should encourage us to redouble our efforts." [52]

Lord McGregor, British statesman, said, "The press enables electorates to make informed choices, and there one set of troubles starts." [53]

Milan Panic, premier of Yugoslavia, said, "Whatever is against free speech, against free press, is against me." [54]

Carlos Ramirez, editor and publisher of *El Diario/La Presna*, said that he wasn't concerned about all the death threats he had received, but "I'm worried more about the ones I haven't got." [55]

Joseph Verner Reed, United Nations undersecretary general, said:

Whenever freedom has been regained, wherever human rights have been restored, whenever the rule of law has been maintained, that is also where the men and women of a free press have been present in full force. [56]

Salman Rushdie, Iranian author, said:
Free societies are societies in motion, and with motion comes tension, dissent, friction. Free people strike sparks, and those sparks are the best evidence of freedom's existence. [57]

Khazbulat Shamsutdinov, a Russian editor, said, "To get the truth, we should get opinions of all sides." [58]

1993

Sheik Omar Abdel-Rahman, a Muslim cleric, said that freedom in America allows us to explain our cause. [59]

Evgueno V. Sabov, Russian editor, said, "The people believe the printed word. The press could really be a tool for making public opinion." [60]

Thelma McCormack, a Canadian college professor, said, "We have an opportunity to redefine what we mean by freedom of expression and civil liberties in a feminist context. One cannot separate equality from freedom."

Nelson Mandela, president of the African National Congress, said, "One has to accept that democracy cannot function without the media." [61]

Sheila Nalarajan, Malaysian journalist, said, "We're aware if there's bad news and we don't report it, people will suffer. But if it may cause a riot, we must assess the situation." [62]

Borhanoddin Rabbani, president of Afghanistan, said:
As the freedom of the press is a principle, the decency of what is being said and obligation to the ethics of writing is an important matter. Everything should not be said. No one's prestige and honor shall be attacked. I am sure that when the press is based on Islamic culture in a country, no one will fill restrictions, and no one will be insulted.

Salman Rushdie, an Iranian author, said, "When you allow limits on freedom of the press, you think you are giving away one per cent of your freedom and you still have 99 per cent left, but it's amazing how quickly you lose that other 99 per cent." [63]

Lech Walesa, president of Poland, said, "Information is like a knife. In the hand of a surgeon, it can save a life. In the hand of a criminal, it can end a life." [64]

1994

Razia Bhatti, Pakistani journalist, said, "The only side that journalists should take is the side of truth." [65]

Razia Bhatti, a Pakistani journalist, said, "Journalists must seek and speak the truth, for we are the voice of the voiceless millions." [66]

Dina Ezzat, an Egyptian reporter, said, "I would still prefer to work in an environment where a reporter spends most of his time trying to find the news rather than calling up his sources to receive the news." [67]

Jose Maria Figueres, president of Costa Rica, said, "The role of the press can be very disruptive if the name of the game is to put more wood into the fire and help groups confront each other and clash instead of finding the logical boundaries and working our possible solutions." [68]

Aristides Katoppo, Indonesian newspaper editor, said, "Sometimes journalists cannot afford the luxury of taking the concept of news and being indifferent to the plight of many." [69]

F.W. de Klerk, president of South Africa, said:
Society undoubtedly needs the media to play a dynamic watchdog role. Nevertheless, watchdogs sometimes bay at the moon and disturb the neighborhood; strew garbage over the front lawn; can be obsessed by the scent of sex; invade the privacy of the neighbor's garden and, alas, they have been known to bite. [70]

Cheng Yip Seng, a Singapore newspaper editor, said, "There is no such thing as total freedom of the press." [71]

Margaret Thatcher, British politician, said, "History has taught us that freedom cannot long survive unless it is based on moral foundations." [72]

Chapter 15

BUT TYRANNY RULES
1995 to 1998

1995-1998

An African proverb points out that silence is also speech. [1]

Isaias Afwerki, president of Eritrea, said, "If man is thinking animal, the psychological urge to communicate his views, visions, fears, hopes, and anxieties to his fellow human beings, cannot, in the end, be regulated by a body of legal interfaces, provisions or restrictions." [2]

Oscar Arias, a Costa Rican statesman, said, "Dissension demands strength, devotion and sacrifice. Dissension is not only disagreement, it is the effective attempt to question the status quo." [3]

David Frost, a British columnist and television producer, said, "Television is an invention whereby you can be entertained in your living room by people you wouldn't have in your house." [4]

Veronica Guerin, an Irish journalist, said, "I know this will sound so pious, but I really do think that as journalists we are serving a purpose." [5] (She was slain in 1996.)

John Honderich, a Canadian editor, said, "In the United States, journalists believe the law doesn't apply to them. In Canada, journalists believe we have no special rights. We're like everyone else; we respect the law." [6]

Douglas Hurd, British foreign secretary, said, "Public debate is not run by the events themselves but by the coverage of those events" [7]

Slobodanka Jovanovska, a Macedonian journalist, said, "Without press freedom, journalism is an instrument of politics, regardless of whether it is good politics or not."[8]

Hiroshi Kume, a Japanese journalist, said, "If television news can be talking about the tragic loss of life in one breath and switch in the next breath to a commercial for cockroach traps, what kind of intrinsic decorum does television really have, anyhow."[9]

Aristides Katoppo, an Indonesian editor, said, "The role of the press in developing countries is also to provide hope. By excessive criticism we might be self-defeating." [10]

Carlos Saul Menem, president of Argentina, said, "When the freedom of the press is used as a sort of stepladder to pry into the intimate and the personal lives of people, then the freedom of the press will become a dictatorship of the press."[11]

Talyana Merzlyakova, a Russian editor, said, "Advertising is not just another form of information. It is form of prostitution." [12]

Alexander Lebed, Russian politician, said, "Those who experience battle and death inevitably learn to speak plainly. If you don't tell the truth, you can end up with a pile of bodies in a sea of blood." [13]

Maria Luisa MacKay, an Argentina journalist, said, "The media gain prestige whenever they are able to put the political establishment in the culprit's seat. We journalists are understandably addicted to such reporting." [14]

Nelson Mandela, president of South Africa, said, "The press is to be used as a mirror in which public figures can see whether they are on the right track." [15]

Christopher F. Patton, governor of Hong Kong, said, "Freedom through the press. It's a good phrase. How can a society claim to be free if it is not possible to tell freely what is going on in that society." [16]

Pope John Paul III said, "We must guard the truth that is the condition of authentic freedom especially in view of the challenges posed by a materialistic culture and by a permissive mentality that reduced freedom to license." [17]

Javier Perez de Ceullar, a Peruvian statesman, said:
> A press can be independent, rebellious, inquisitive, unruly, and almost insolent toward democratic rulers, but prudent — extraordinarily prudent — toward autocratic leaders. This may be freedom of the press but it is not freedom of information.[18]

Lillyanne Pierre-Paul, a Haitian rail executive, said, "Democracy is one little candle with a lot of wind trying to blow." [19]

Horria Saihi, an Algerian journalist, said, "If you speak, you are dead. If you keep silent you are dead. So speak and die." [20]

Ken Saro-Wiwa, a Nigerian playwright, said, "Lord, take my soul, but the struggle continues." [21]

Sheikh Saud Nasser al-Saud al-Sabah, Kuwait information minister, said, "There is no doubt open media and open information is the most effective way you can communicate with the world. The more you close your country the more you become isolated."
Saud al Sabah, a Kuwaiti official, said, "People are talking about the media revolution or the cultural revolution. The best way to confront it is to provide a better alternative. It has to be left to the family. It should not come from the state."[22]

Norodom Sihanouk, a Cambodian prince, said, "It is futile to fight against hostile journalists. They were always the winners and I was the big loser, even if my cause was right." [23]

Leszek Spolinski, a Polish presidential spokesman, said, "The president should not be present in the media everyday. But when he is, his voice should sound like a bell." [24]

Paisel Sricharatchanya, a Thai journalist, said, "We have been told time and again by government leaders that freedom has to be accompanied by responsibility. Who defines responsibility? The public is probably the best judge." [25]

Vadim Pehehkov, a Russian reporter, said, "Dependence upon readership is the best option for the independent press." [26]

Elana Urumova, a Bulgarian editor, said, "There is no such thing as tips from readers in my newspaper. Reporters and editors in Bulgaria think probably that they are more intelligent and educated than their readers." [27]

Bong Jin Yang, a Korean editor, said, "Freedom of speech shines when it is tested by the dark hands of control." [28]

The Writers and Scholars International organization of Lancaster House in England monitors the status of free expression and free press throughout the world. Every two months the organization publishes a journal titled *Index on Censorship*. From the journal's general articles and summary "Index Index," 1995 presents a gloomy picture of free press and free speech across the world. Here are 1995 reports arranged nation by nation. Knowing about the work of the organization and having its publication available would be of great assistance and significance for persons concerned about free press and free speech as the Twentieth Century ends. The Writers and Scholars International is a not-for-profit corporation supported primarily by donations.

Afghanistan

All movie theaters were closed because officials wanted to stop the spread of immoral films. The government shut down all centers of cultural corruption. [29]

Albania

Albanian press law requires the press to verify the truthfulness, content, and source of news. [30]

The Tirana, Albania, mayor would permit newspapers to be sold in 20 state-owned places. [31]

Gjergio Zefi, a former editor of *Lajmentari* was forbidden from writing for a year or from holding public office because of two articles considered defamatory. But one was published before the press law was established. [32]

Algeria

The Algerian government shut down or hampered *La Nation* and *Al-Wajh Al Akhar, El Khatar, Le Soir d'Algerie, Le Matin, La Tribune* and *El Watan*. Journalists killed in Algeria included Abdelhamed Yahiloui, Nasser Ouari, Djamel Ziatar, and Mohammed Hassaine. [33]

At least seven more journalists were killed in Algeria, and several publications were suspended. [34]

Ten national papers in Algeria stopped publishing for three days to protest the murders of journalists in the nation's civil war. [35]

A statement by the Armed Islamic Group of Algeria threatened all broadcast journalists and said, "Those who fight us by the pen shall be fought by the sword."[36]

Angola

In Angola, 18 journalists had been killed since UNITA rejected 1992 election results. [37]

Armenia

Armenian officials closed down a dozen newspapers of the rival Armenian Revolutionary Federation. [38]

Opposition newspapers of the Dachnaksourtoien party were closed down. [39]

Australia

The Australian government ignored a 1984 law freeing films from censorship and banned a Spanish movie, *Tias El Cristal*, because its sadism offended "community standards." [40]

The Senate Select Committee on Community Standards believed that no sexually explicit or violent material should be shown on television before 10:30 p.m. [41]

Australia considered increasing sanctions against journalists who expose illegal activity by state agencies. [42]

Belarus

President Lukasenka of Belarus denied he was censoring the press, but he said the state-owned media was obliged to do everything for the benefit of our state. [43]

Poetry by Janka Kupala and others was banned by the Russian Ministry of Culture which denied subsidies to the books in Belarusian. [44]

President Lukansenka deplored the lack of objectivity, true, and constructive materials in the media and warned that the ministries of justice, culture, and of the press could not be tolerant of some media. [45]

Bulgaria

The ruling Socialist party replaced television executives because the national television had eroded national values with cheap foreign products. [46]

The Constitution of Bulgaria guarantees media independence and forbids censorship. But Bulgarian national television canceled a beauty contest and a casino program to protect public morals and threatened to take off others. Twenty members of an organization were arrested for distributing leaflets for a separatist organization. No wonder the president and the prosecutor-general wanted press laws liberalized. [47]

The Bulgarian Constitutional Court ruled that Parliament could not approve regulations, structures, financing, programming, or management of the state radio and television or of the Bulgarian News Agency. [48]

Burma

As many as ten writers languished in prisons, some with sentences as long as 20 years. [49]

Burundi

In Burundi, journalists claim they were prevented by police and the army from investigating scenes of Tutsi massacres of Hutus. [50]

Cambodia

Although the National Assembly of Cambodia substituted civil sanctions for proposed criminal penalties in a draft press law, journalists still would be punished for degrading or humiliating public authorities. [51]

A new press law provides criminal sanctions for spreading news affecting political stability. [52]

Cameroon

A satirical supplement of Cameroon's *Le Message* was seized because of a front cover picture of the wife of the head of state. [53]

Government seizure of copies of *Le Message* on three days were designed to bankrupt the newspaper; police beat up a dozen workers and arrested the editor of *Le Nouvel Independent* for articles critical of the government. [54]

Canada

The Supreme Court of Canada ruled that the Tobacco Control Act banning cigarette advertising and promotion violated tobacco company rights to free expression. [55]

Central African Republic

An editor of a newspaper, *Le Rassemblement*, was arrested for attacking the dignity and honor of the republic's president. [56]

Chad

The president said a raid on *N'Ojamina Hebdo* weekly's headquarters was a mistake. Workers were beaten and two editors were arrested. [57]

China

Chinese officials seized two million illegal publications in Jiangsu province. They contended 676 posed serious political problems, closed down were 82 printing plants and 366 unlicensed book outlets. Forty-seven criminals were sentenced. Publisher Lu Ping was sentenced to life for publishing 600,000 copies of books since 1990. [58]

Rupert Murdoch proposed to Chinese officials that he would provide smart-card technology for his satellite transmissions to control television programming in his effort to expand his Star network in China. [59]

Gu Jeishu was executed in China for publishing obscenity and selling pornographic books; seven other persons were jailed for such activities. [60]

The Chinese Film Administration agreed to import the ten most popular films annually, providing they were in line with the Chinese situation and laws. [61]

A Chinese Foreign Ministry spokesman said that jailed dissident Wei Jinsheng was a criminal and that he did not deserve to be nominated for the Nobel Peace prize. [62]

China's Central Committee's propaganda department had a seminar for editors to tell them how to guide the people with correct opinions. [63]

Translators at the World Conference on Women were not permitted to translate references to Tibet. China said it could deny visas to delegates to protect its security despite an earlier agreement not to do so. [64]

Colombia

The government set stiff penalties for any broadcast media violating censorship emergency rules. [65]

Colombian President Samper declared his commitment to freedom of the press, and promised an investigation of threats to journalists. The Cali drug cartel denied any involvement in threatening journalists. [66]

The Colombian Senate passed a law to prevent journalists from reporting about legal actions against public officials and setting restrictions on access to public documents. [67]

A state of internal commotion allows Colombian officials to suppress constitutional rights. [68]

Congo

A National Assembly law listed 46 penalty provisions for press violations including five years in prison. Journalists working for state media have to be loyal to the government. [69]

Officials fired the editor of the state radio stations because he released embargoed reports about salary cuts of public employees even though the information had appeared in other media. [70]

Costa Rico

The Costa Rican Supreme Court ruled that licensing journalists was unconstitutional. [71]

Cote d'Ivoire

Dembele Fousseni, Kema Brohama, Abiou Cisse, and De Be Kwasi, journalists in Cote d'Ivoire, were imprisoned for articles in their newspapers. [72]

Two journalists were sentenced to a year in prison and fined two million francs for insulting the president. Their newspapers was suspended for three months. [73]

Croatia

A Croatian Statehood campaign accused media of being anti-Croatian and of falsifying Croatian history. Meanwhile Catholic media complained that the government was trying to use Catholicism as part of a state ideology. [74]

Czech Republic

A draft law presented in the Czech legislature would require media to publish unedited government statements. [75]

Egypt

In Egypt, the *Jerusalem Post* was suspended because of an article by Yehudi Blum, a former Israeli ambassador. [76]

President Mubarak said, "I am with freedom of the press and not the freedom to offend. The amended law [on libel] will not affect those who write honourably and with trust." [77]

Ethiopia

Reports from Ethiopia indicate many journalists have been arrested and served prison terms before some of them have been released. [78]

At least 24 journalists were jailed in Ethiopia. [79]

European Union

The Consultative Commission on Racism and Xenophobia of the European Union wanted legal sanctions against media breaches of ethical guidelines. [80]

France

The Paris High Court in France banned distribution of the Christian Communities Bible, a simplified version, because two passages were considered anti-Semitic. [81]

Germany

The German interior ministry closed down several Kurdish organizations after the request of Turkey to ban such groups. [82]

Guatemala

Catholic bishops established a Truth Commission to recover historic memory and break the silence imposed by fear. They were frustrated by a brief investigation planned by a Truth Commission of the U.N. [83]

India

Fifteen journalists were injured by Indian police in Jammu when the police broke up a peaceful protest against police attacks on reporters. [84]

Indonesia

W.S. Rendra, an Indonesian poet, refused to participate in a West Java reading of twelve of his poems because the government ordered him not to read four of the twelve. [85]

Dranoedya Ananto Toer's book *Silent Song of a Dumb Man* was banned by order of the Indonesia attorney-general because its circulation might cause unrest and disturb public order. [86]

Two members of the Alliance of Independent Journalists were tried for sowing hatred against the government, insulting President Suharto, and violating the Press Act. Another was charged with expressing hatred against the state and the president. [87]

Two members of the Indonesian Alliance of Independent Journalists were imprisoned 32 months for sowing hatred against the government and for publishing an unlicensed paper. [88]

Iran

A foreign ministry spokesman of Iran said that Muslim nations consider support for the apostate Rushdie as an act of support for slander and an insult against the sacred nations of Islam. [89]

In Iran, the government banned a magazine, *Takapoo*, after it published an article and open letter about freedom of expression signed by 134 writers.

Iran banned satellite dishes. [90]

The weekly student magazine *Payam-e Danesghu* was suppressed for habitual defamation and sensational writing contrary to the principles of Islamic journalism.[91]

Ireland

Ireland has a Censorship of Publications Board which banned two books in 1995 as well as *Playboy* magazines, but the ban on *Playboy* was soon lifted. [92]

Israel

Israel closed the Al Arab Press Office in East Jerusalem, claiming it was being used by the Palestinian Broadcasting Company. [93]

Several journalists were attacked by Israel soldiers following car bombings in Gaza. [94]

Kenya

Plans were announced for a law to set up a commission to investigate journalistic ethics, media licensing, and newspaper registration. Opposition leaders were frequently jailed and beaten. [95]

Kazakstan

In Kazakstan, the newspaper *Kazakhssbyaya Pravda* was shut down because it was anti-Semitic and invited ethnic hatred. [96]

Kyrgyzstan

President Askar Akayev of Kyrgyzstan rejected new laws on media because they were an attempt to reinstate censorship. He asked media to be balanced in criticism of the country's leadership. [97]

Lebanon

Muslims and Christians joined to encourage the publisher of three books by Al-Sadeqal-Nayhaum to appeal the Lebanon seizure requested by a Sunni cleric who considered them offensive as provided by law. [98]

Macedonia

About 300 private radio and television stations were operating in Macedonia without permits; the government closed down forty of these. [99]

Malaysia

The information minister of Malaysia directed the three TV channels not to show scenes of sex and violence. [100]

The Ministry of Information delayed broadcast of foreign television for one hour so it could censor out pornography and negative content. Malaysians could use dishes only large enough to receive government transmissions. [101]

Mauritius

The Interior Ministry of Mauritius banned an international seminar organized by the Study and Research Group in Democracy and Economic and Social Development.[102]

Mexico

The Mexico Federal Public Security Secretariat established an operation to protect journalists in the mass media from attacks by the Zaptista National Liberation Army.[103]

Nigeria

General Abacha of Nigeria extended for six months a ban on the independent Guardian newspaper group. [104]

Oman

The director general of Oman set up a censor's office at the baggage counter of Serb Airport to control video cassettes from abroad. [105]

Pakistan

Two Pakistani Catholics had blasphemy charges dismissed; otherwise, they would have been executed. [106]

Palestine

Yasser Arafat lifted a three-month suspension early on al-Vatan, a Palestinian newspaper, inspired by a State Security court. [107]

Papua

The senior media adviser canceled a talk-back radio program planning to discuss the local government system or to present information contrary to the majority view expressed by Parliament. [108]

Poland

The Polish Supreme Court ruled that journalists must reveal their information sources if required by a judge or prosecutor. [109]

Poland will make files from the Communist secret police archives available to historians. Journalists, however, would have to apply to the interior ministry for permission to see the files. [110]

Poland proposed a press law to place journalists under government regulations with educational prerequisites, registration, a government financial press council, and requirements for editors. [111]

Russia

The Russian Duma adopted a resolution to outlaw fascist propaganda, pageantry, international contacts and paramilitary organizations. [112]

Subscriptions to Russian publications dropped from 220 million in 1990 to only about 21 million in 1994. [113]

Rwanda

Rwandan journalists decided to shun ethnic hatred and to rebuild their country and profession. They wanted the government to review press laws and give licenses to private radio stations. [114]

Slovakia

The Slovakia Cabinet appointed a 20-member media council to be an advisory agency without decision making power. More than 100,000 people signed petitions protecting cancellation of three satirical programs. [115]

More than 7,000 persons in Slovakia marched in Bratslavia organized by the Christian Democratic Movement to protect government attacks on free speech and to demand return of popular television satirical programs. [116]

The Slovakian Petition Committee for the Preservation of Freedom of Speech wanted the director of state television to resign because of lies strongly antidemocratic activities. In June the government planned for a new Slovak Information Agency to promote the nation abroad. [117]

South Africa

In South Africa, legislators considered exempting theatrical, art, literature from censorship controls and blasphemy would be eliminated from the legal code. [118]

South Korea

South Korea was very hard on citizens who discussed North Korea. Kim Mu-Yong, a history lecturer at Bangsong Tongshin University, was arrested for writings about the Korean guerrilla movement of 1948-53. March Ki Sehmoon and Lee Kyurg Ryol were arrested for printing a pamphlet they intended to distribute at a funeral for a captured North Korean soldier. [119]

Sri Lanka

President Kumaratunga of Sri Lanka said that the press has a wild ass's freedom and that there is utterly irresponsible journalism going on. [120]

The Federation of Buddhist Organizations in Sri Lanka insisted that the Vatican withdraw statements in the Pope's book saying Buddhism is an atheistic system with a negative doctrine of salvation. [121]

Sinha Ratungo of Sri Lanka was charged with criminally defaming President Kumaratunga in the *Sunday Times* which he edited. [122]

President Kumaratunga told reporters when threatening stouter censorship that, "We will not kill journalists and drop them by air on the beaches, but they must be responsible in their reports." [123]

Sudan

Anyone practicing journalism without a license could be fined and jailed according to the journalists' Committee of the National Council for Press and Publication. [124]

Swaziland

Seven supporters of the People's United Democratic Movement of Swaziland were found guilty of sedition for participating in a peaceful demonstration without proper police permission. [125]

Swaziland developed a media law designed to fight intimidation by government officials. [126]

Taiwan

There had been a long series of raids in Taiwan to shut down several radio stations in 1994 and 1995. [127]

Tanzania

Press suppression in Tanzania include establishment of an Information Service, prevention of contact between the press and officials, proposals to license journalists, requirement of a university degree to be a journalist, and pressures connected with newsprint shortages. [128]

Eleven media workers in Tanzania faced criminal charges as the government increased pressure on independent media before elections. [129]

Tibet

Tibet's official People's Broadcasting Station reported that authorities have seized thousands of reactionary propaganda materials. [130]

Toga

Martin Gbenouaga had his five-year sentence canceled after he had written that Toga president Eyadema held power by force of arms, distortions, lies, and tribalism. [131]

Turkey

Ali Baransel, head of the radio and television council in Turkey, warned broadcasters who aired separatist propaganda that they were being monitored and faced being closed down. Turkish authorities frequently arrested journalists, and many were given long prison terms. [132]

In Turkey, 65 per cent of the 1,774 trials held by the Istanbul Security Court concerned press offenses involving 2,098 journalists and editors. At the end of 1994, there were at least 74 Turkish journalists in jail. [133]

Publishers of *Freedom of Thought and Turkey* were supported by 99 intellectuals, 1,080 artists, writers, journalists, trade union officials, and 50,000 other petition signers when the Istanbul State Security Court produced indictments of the real publishers. [134]

Uganda

Uganda law required editors to have a degree in journalism. Only three did. [135]

United Kingdom

The English Conservative Party closed down a satirical magazine, *Scallywag*, by issuing libel writs against companies that distribute it. One of its articles reported that the Conservatives were planning a dirty tricks campaign against the Labour Party. [136]

More than 4,000 comic books published by Savoy Books of England were seized, and Savoy was accused of violating the Obscene Publications Act. [137]

New media ownership rules allowed newspaper groups owning less than 20 percent of the national circulation to control 15 percent of the television market. No groups can control more than 10 percent of the total media including radio, television, and press. [138]

The government white paper on the press favored self-regulation by the press itself; however, it wanted to tighten provisions of the Press Complaints Commission regulations about privacy. [139]

BBC set up an administrative unit to monitor intimidatory and abusive behavior by politicians to influence news in the general election. And the Prince of Wales obtained a worldwide ban of a book written about him by his housekeeper. Her *Dairy of a Housekeeper* was filled with intimate details of the royal household. [140]

United Nations

Authors of articles planned for the U.N. book *Vision of Hope* withdrew their names to protest elimination of articles by the Dalai Lama and non-governmental human rights organizations. [141]

Vanuaty

The prime minister banned information about the French nuclear treaty including local and foreign broadcasts and demonstrations. [142]

Vietnam

The Voices of Vietnam radio said customs officials had confiscated 253 reactionary magazines mailed from the United States, Canada, and France. [143]

Zambia

Zambia's Parliamentary and Ministerial Code provides jailing anyone making a false allegation against a political leader. [144]

The High Court of Zambia prevented the government from passing media legislation which would have given responsibilities to regulate the press to the government instead of to the Press Association of Zambia. [145]

Writers and Scholars International of London publishes six issues of its *Index on Censorship* each year. The issues produced in 1996, 1997, and 1998 all reflect a gloomy picture of any progress in the extension of freedom of speech or of the press in the repressive nations of this century. Ruling echelons continue their autocracy and tyrannical control of publications, radio, television, motion pictures and internet. Algeria and Turkey continue to be the most repressive nations in the world with censorship and executions.

Another source of what people believe about freedom of expression is the Freedom Forum Calendar of the Freedom Forum which has been located for several years in Arlington, Va. The Forum is contemplating a move soon; copies of the calendar are made available at a modest cost. Here are several recent comments.

1995

"Every generation of Americans needs to know that freedom consists not in doing what we like, but having the right to do what we ought." — Pope John Paul. [146]

"I know what awaits me in the end is a bullet in my head, but what kills me more is censorship." — Horria Saihi, Algerian journalist. [147]

"To the government, the press is something to be feared, to be regarded as an enemy, to be crushed." — Ahmed Taufik, Indonesian journalist. [148]

1996

"We are not journalists but war correspondents in our own country." — Marcia Jimena Duzan, Colombian journalist. [149]

"It matters what we journalists do. If I didn't think my work made a difference, I'd probably give it up." — Veronica Guerin, an Irish journalist slain in 1996. [150]

"When you report about things as they are, that's when the trouble starts." — Jusuf Jameel, Indian journalist. [151]

"Information is the raw material in the construction of freedom." — Alejandro Junco de la Vega, Mexican newspaper publisher. [152]

"History has shown that presidential onslaughts in the media are generally the precursors of legislative restrictions, which, in turn, set the scene for a slide into authoritarian rule." — Raymond Louro, South African journalist. [153]

"Freedom is like gas. It has a natural tendency to expand." — Monsignor Diarmuld Martin, Vatican official. [154]

"Our political leaders, concerned primarily about popularity, public approval, and winning votes, might not realise it is in the country's, and indeed their own, interest that we have a vigorous, independent, and critical press." — Kaiser Nyatsumba, South African journalist. [155]

"It seems to me that we live in an increasingly censorious age. By this I mean that the broad, indeed international, acceptance of First Amendment principles is being steadily eroded." — Salmam Rushdie, exiled Iranian novelist. [156]

"Every despot thinks that by confiscating books, banning articles, imprisoning people who seem too independent, he can blot out dissent and dissatisfaction." — Edward Said, Palestinian writer. [157]

"The media have an incredible calling (they were the midwife of democracy). Now you must be the watchdog to ensure that this beautiful thing is not corrupted." — Desmond Tutu, South African religious leader. [158]

"If the press does not tell the people what is happening, who will?" — Hennie van Deventer, South African newspaper executive. [159]

1997

"In newspapers, you print the message, not mail it with Semtex explosive." — Baghida Dergham, Middle Eastern journalist. [150]

"Press freedom remains vulnerable because dictators know something we sometimes forget; dictatorship thrives in an information vacuum, and weakens in the face of unfettered news flow." — Marilyn Greene, World Press Freedom Committee executive director. [161]

"It's time to return to the core values of journalism, to reform, to entertain, to advise, to shed light in dark places." — Bruce Guthrie, Australian newspaper editor.[162]

"Our press has to much freedom." — Nasri Lahoud, Lebanese judge. [163]

"When freedom dies, it never dies alone." — Goenawen Mahamad, Indonesian journalist. [164]

"The difference betwen an actor and a journalist is that an actor's career is over if he is booed on the stage. A journalist's career is over if he is never booed." — Adam Michnik, Polish editor. [165]

"In Mali, we think the American press system pays too much attention to politicians private lives." — Adam Ouologuem, Malian journalist. [166]

"Self-censorship is like celibacy: nobody can tell if you actually practice it." — Tsang Tak-sing, Hong Kong newspaper editor. [167]

The Khordad Foundation, a state agency of Iran, raised the bounty the nation was offering to $2,500,000 in 1997 for Salmon Rushdie, a novelist the Iranian government hates. In 1998, the Foundation plans to raise the bounty amount once again. [168]
Within a few days, Mohammad Javad Zarit, an Iranian deputy foreign minister, told the United Nations it would not carry out the death sentence on Rushdie, but it could not set it aside.

In March, 1998, Rushdie was awarded an honorary doctorate by the University of Tromsoe for his continuing struggle for free speech, which has forced him to be a writer in hiding. The Norwegian University also presented an honorary doctorate to William Nygaard, a Norwegian publisher who produced *The Satanic Verses* in Norway.

Fred H. Cate, law professor at Indiana University, in a 1998 review of early international efforts to regulate expression, reported that France and Spain agreed to postal treaties in 1601 and France and England entered such agreements in 1670. The Universal Postal Union was established by a Postal Congress in Berne in 1874. The General Agreement on Tariffs and Trade of 1848 led to both domestic and international postal regulations. By 1849 agreements were made to regulate telegraph communications. Napoleon III set up a Paris Conference in 1865 which established the International Telecommunications Union, which included the Radiotelegraph Union. When telephones became available in 1876 the structure for controls existed. So far, regulation of the Internet is handled by national regulation.[169] Other international communications control efforts are discussed in Chapter 16.

When Princess Diana of England was killed in an automobile accident in Paris, the press of Great Britain generally succumbed to overwhelming tabloidization and sensational coverage and unsubstantiated spectulation. The press of France and the United States joined in that frenzy. As a result, calls for greater press controls surfaced many places, even in the United States Congress. One aspect of coverage included quasi-legal discussions on English and American television. The participants generally ignored the great differences between English regulation and American laws concerning both privacy and defamation. This, of course, was a great disservice to American viewers who soon became quite confused about the legally protected rights of the press in its operations. The performance of elements of the press in both nations was reprehensible in many situations. This led to an all out blitz of bad journalism in subsequent high profile trials or accusations in the United States throughout 1997 and 1998 and promised to last well into the twenty-first century.

In February 1998 a news report indicated that maybe a car driven by a photographer might have contributed to the accident but French police indicated this car was not involved.

In May 1998, the International Press Institute reported that more than 200 journalists had been killed in Central and South America between 1988 and 1998 by drug cartels and criminal clans.

Chapter 16

THE FUTURE OF THE WORLD'S FREEDOM OF EXPRESSION

The desire for a free press was a main principle of the revolutions in the Western world for a forty-year period beginning in 1800.

In 1886, the Berne Convention set up international copyright agreements.

1927

A Japanese delegation to the League of Nations Conference of Journalists demanded the prevention of news reports harmful to world peace. This was a reflection of the press struggle within Japan. [1]

The League of Nations passed resolutions to improve international telecommunications, facilitate the distribution of newspapers between countries, limit censorship, and provide international freedom for journalists. [2]

World War I ended international efforts to expand free press concepts generally, but the end of the war saw many efforts that continued for the rest of the century.

1946

The American Society of Newspaper Editors Committee on World Freedom of Information proposed that World War II treaties provide that there would be no censorship, no use of the press as an instrument of government, and to allow the free flow of information. [3]

1947

The U.N. Charter, The UNESCO Constitution, and the Universal Declaration of Human Rights all said, "Everyone has the right to freedom of opinion and expression; this right includes freedom to hold opinions, and to seek, receive, and impart information and ideas through any media and regardless of frontiers." The Mass Communications Division of UNESCO set up a section on the free flow of information and, at the request of the American delegation, a subcommission on freedom of information and of the press. The General Assembly of the United Nations resolved that "freedom of information is a fundamental human right, and is a touchstone of all the freedom to which the United Nations is consecrated."

The principle of free expression was at least given world-wide moral status in the United Nations Universal Declaration of Human Rights in Article 19.

The United States delegation to the United Nations Conference of Freedom of Information said: "It is the hope of the six of us that this Conference helped to turn the tide that has been running against freedom throughout much of the world. It is our conviction that in the future conduct of our foreign policy, the United States should continue to take vigorous action in this field of freedom of thought and expression."

The Conference on Freedom of Information adopted the United States view of the free flow of information but weakened the impact by having only two signatures appear on the document. UNESCO sent the document to the United Nations General Assembly where no action was taken.

1948

The American Society of Newspaper Editors sent a delegation to 22 cities and eleven nations to carry the message of an international free press into every friendly capital of the world.

The Mexico City Inter-American Conference on Problems of War and Peace accepted the United States proposal for free access to information, A free flow of information was a paramount consideration in forming the constitution of UNESCO.

The United Nations Economic and Social Council passed sixteen resolutions pertaining to freedom of information and freedom of the press based upon a 1948 conference on freedom of information. The United Nations also updated and adopted the old 1910 agreement for suppressing obscene publications.

The principle of free expression was again proclaimed in the United Nations Universal Declaration of Human Rights. [4]

1950

The United Nations established a committee for the Peaceful Uses of Outer Space, including communications satellites.

1952

The International Press Institute noted that most news flowed from the developed to the underdeveloped nations. The Universal Convention eased international copyright restrictions.

1963

The Thompson Foundation of Great Britain provided training for Third World journalists. The British Press Council was revitalized and became an effective organization from both readers' and journalists' viewpoints.

1964

The subcommittee of science and technology of the United Nations Committee on the Peaceful Uses of Outer Space pointed out that "direct broadcast satellites able to transmit programs direct to television sets is likely to take place by 1974 or so."

1970

The Council of Europe issued a Declaration on Mass Communications Media and Human Rights urging the end to censorship, the independence of the press and other mass media, the responsibility of such agencies, and the protection of individual rights to privacy.

The InterAmerican Press Association reported that press freedom had declined greatly in Latin America. [5]

The International Press Institute reported "newspapers in Africa are at best tolerated and generally endure harrassment or suppression and at worst are propaganda organs aimed at telling the people what the government wishes them to know." [6]

Something of a crisis in international news occurred in the 1970s between industrialized nations and developing nations. This crisis led to combining a New International Order and a New International Communications Order. UNESCO turned its attention on the content of news and the role of the media in society.

The Universal Postal Convention allowed member countries the option of granting a maximum 50 percent reduction in the tariff applicable to printed materials for newspapers, periodicals, books, and pamphlets.

1971

UNESCO revised the Universal Convention Copyright Provisions and made them more permissive. The International Telecommunications Union held the World Administrative Radio Conference for Space Telecommunications in Geneva to set up provisions for registering broadcast frequencies.

1972

The Report of the InterAmerican Press Association said, "At this moment there is hardly a country where the press is not subject either to a frontal onslaught by its many enemies or to severe tensions and threats even if practically every one of our constitutional guarantees of freedom of speech, written as well as oral, secrecy, and news management, and sometimes even prior restraints as well as open censorship are the order of the day."

The United Nations General Assembly voted that it was necessary that states, taking into account the principle of freedom of information, reach arrangements concerning direct satellite broadcasting to the population of countries other than the country of origin of the transmission. The United States cast the only vote against the idea. Frank Stanton said it ignored "the rights which form the frame work of our constitution, the principles asserted in the Universal Declaration of Human Rights, and the basic principles of the free movement of ideas."

1973

The Algiers Non-aligned Summit Meeting issued a statement on communicating issues to increase communications and communications media. The meeting in Algiers said national media had to be strengthened to eliminate the harmful consequences of the colonial era.

Finland's President Urho Kekkonen told the Helsinki Conference of Security and Cooperation in Europe that "a mere liberalistic freedom of communications is not in everyday reality a neutral idea, but a way in which an enterprise with many resources at its disposal has greater opportunities than weaker brethren to make its own hegemony accepted."

1975

Participants in the Dag Hammarskjold Seminar for Third World Journalists stated that their national government should share information media experiences.

The Information Act of the Helsinki Conference on Security and Cooperation in Europe urged greater access, circulation, and exchange of information between governments, and improved working conditions for journalists.

A regional conference on information imbalance in Asia was held in Kandy, Sri Lanka, under the auspices of the Asian Mass Communication Research and Information Center.

1976

The Council of Europe called a conference to draft an international treaty for data protection.

The declaration of San Jose issued by the UNESCO intergovernmental conferences in Costa Rica urged that communications policies contribute to greater knowledge and understanding of peoples. Twenty-one Latin American nations demanded balanced North-South reporting.

At a summit meeting of 84 non-aligned countries, the participating heads of state said that a new international order in the fields of information and mass communications was vital to a new international economic order.

Ministers from 58 non-aligned nations meeting in New Delhi planned a Third World news pool.

Soviet Russia sponsored a draft resolution at the Nairobi UNESCO conference which said, "States are responsible for the activities in the international sphere of all mass media under their jurisdiction." UNESCO adopted it. The United States contended that the Soviet proposed draft on mass media would reduce freedom of the press.

The Western press kept telling Third World leaders what they didn't want to know.

UNESCO in its Nineteenth General Assembly in Nairobi formed the International Commission for the Study of Communication Problems.

1978

The Declaration on the Mass Media was adopted by consensus at the 20th UNESCO General Conference in Paris in 1978. The Organization for Economic Cooperation and Development set up a group of experts to provide guidelines for trans-border data flow was planned for 1980. The UNESCO declaration emphasized human rights, diversity of news, free flow of information, and the journalist's right of access to news.

Sean MacBride, UNESCO official, said:

> It is obvious that communication in the world today, in all forms and at all levels, is vital to building a more humane, more just, and more prosperous world tomorrow. Hence I firmly believe the news agencies and media bear a heavy responsibility to inform the peoples of the world about the urgency and magnitude of the problems facing humanity.

The Stockholm seminar specified a right of access to government sources and to the entire spectrum of opinion within all countries. UNESCO issued a mass media declaration in Paris concerning the contributions of mass media to strengthen peace and understanding.

1979

The European Court ruled that England could modify free trade of the Treaty of Rome in cases involving pornography.

The World Administrative Radio Conference for broadcasting satellites set up an *a priori* plan for all areas of the world except the Western Hemisphere.

1980

Sean MacBride said, "Surely it is time to draw up national and international standards on journalistic practices, not only to protect journalists on perilous assignments, but to guarantee their freedom in carrying out professional tasks."

UNESCO issued its 1980 report of its International Commission for the Study of Communications Problems, otherwise known as the MacBride Commission, in a book entitled *Many Voices, One World: Communication and Society Today and Tomorrow*; it said:

> Such values as truthfulness, accuracy, respect for human rights are not universally applied at present. Higher professional standards and responsibility cannot be imposed by decree, nor do they depend solely on the goodwill of individual journalists, who are employed by institutions which can improve or handicap their professional performance. Voluntary measures can do much to influence media performance. Nevertheless it appears necessary to develop further effective ways by which the right to assess mass media performance can be exercised by the public. All those working in the mass media should contribute to the fulfillment of human rights. The media could contribute to promoting the just cause of peoples struggling for freedom and independence and their right to live in peace and equality without foreign interference. Censorship or arbitrary control of information should be abolished.

The conference set up a formal International Program for the Development of Communication.

1981

All of the recommendations of the study groups of the Conference Toward an American Agenda for a New World Order of Communication reflected historical values that have permeated American communication practices.

The International Commission for the Study of Communications Problems completed its work at the 21st General Conference UNESCO in Belgrade.

Primary areas of concern of world wide communications covered news flow, mass culture, technology transfer, national sovereignty, and communications rights.

A seminar on the Future for Books in the Electronics Era speculated that the future would see:
1. A book would be a bubble-wrapped package containing a dust jacket and a computer chip from which the text is printed out at home.
2. Publishers will print out books when ordered and not stock them.
3. Information will be in computerized data books, but literature and poetry may still be in books.
4. Language usage may change to staccato TV-talk..
5. Electronic technology may create an isolated living room culture.

The conference report was prepared by J. Robert Maskin, senior editor for the Aspen Institute which co-sponsored the Jerusalem seminar with the Jerusalem International Book Fair.

1983

Each year the International Press Institute of London and Zurich took inventory throughout the world. The conclusion for 1983 indicated journalists generally were living in an age of severe repression which had become worse worldwide year by year. The institute estimated that only 24 of 86 covered nations, mostly in the West had a press free enough to criticize governments or publish opposition news. In 1983 it made 65 formal protests to governments for press repression. Turkey had the worst record with its fining and jailing of editors and reporters. South Africa had convicted or threatened 15 editors and 24 newspapers for failure to support the government's pro-white racist view. Reporters had been threatened with death in eastern bloc nations, Asia, Latin America, and Africa.

The annual general assembly of the International Press Institute passed resolutions condemning harassment and persecution of the press in South Africa. It criticized Argentina, Brazil, Uruguay, and Nicaragua. Committee on Freedom of the Press and Information of the InterAmerican Press Association said, "Governments continue to close and harass newspapers, censor news, imprison journalists, and conspire to restrict the flow of news." Garcia Lavin of Mexico reported that the InterAmerican Press Association sent 36 protests about press violations to 23 countries in his year as president of the organization.

Senegal and Cuba defended UNESCO proposals for restraints on information under the New World Order of Information and Communication.

A Western Hemisphere conference of the World Administrative Radio Conference worked on a Western Hemisphere broadcast satellite plan.

1984

In its 1984 report of a Comparative Survey of Freedom created by Freedom House for its January Map of Freedom. 52 nations were depicted as maintaining freedom for the press. There were 56 nations providing partial freedom of the press. All other nations practiced severe press repression and control. Repression appeared mostly in Asia, eastern Europe, Arabian areas, and in Africa.

1985

The InterAmerican Press Association reported that in El Salvador, staff members of *El Diario* were intimidated by the government which also used placement of advertising and foreign exchange allocation needed to purchase newsprint to pressure newspapers and taxes to do the same for radio and television.

The Space Planning World Administrative Radio Conference determined world wide satellite broadcasting arrangements.

At the end of 1985, the United Kingdom withdrew from UNESCO in protest of its new information order or press control.

Even after the United States withdrew from UNESCO in 1985, press organizations in the United States continued efforts to keep UNESCO from approving press control by government regulation.

1986

Soviet Russia planned to join Intelsat of the International Telecommunications Satellite Organization consortium sponsored by 109 other nations.

1989

At least 19 major international conferences were planned between 1980 and 1989 to study and decide how the electromagnetic spectrum, the basic building blocks of communication, would be allocated among the nations.

1992

The world probably had 523 million main telephone stations in operation by 1991 according to a telecommunications study.

1994

Freedom House, a watchdog agency that evaluates the level of a free press in nation's around the world found that the level of press freedom had declined in 31 countries in 1994. Many of these, surprisingly, were in western Europe.

Jesse Helms had the Senate Foreign Relations Committee table consideration of a United Nations treaty pertaining to children's rights. Article 12 of the treaty grants children the right to express views freely in all matters.

The International Federation of Journalists reported 1994 was the bloodiest year ever recorded as 115 correspondents were killed by various governments. [7]

The Committee to Protect Journalists had to report that 1994 was one of the worst years on record for attacks on the press.

At a Brussels meeting in Belgium, the G7 industrialized countries established principles for the Global Information Infrastructure. Nine human rights organizations said that G7 did not promote the free exchange of ideas and information.

F.M. Zargoza, director general of UNESCO, upon signing the Chapultepec declaration in Paris, said, "The fundamental democratic principles are justice, freedom of expression, equality, and solidarity."

Although Freedom House was able to report that freedom of the press had arrived in more nations by 1995, there still remained serious restraints in a majority of the world's nations.

Boutros-Ghali, United Nations secretary, said, "Press attention is like a beam of light; it illuminates where it shines but leaves all else in obscurity." [8]

In Algeria 19 journalists were assassinated by extremists and Turkey jailed 74 journalists trying to report the Turkish military action against Kurdish dissidents. Altogether, 72 journalists were killed and 173 were imprisoned. Nations where journalists lost their lives included Rwanda, Somalia, Chechnya, South Africa, Angola, Tajikistan, and Cambodia.

1995

Reporters Without Borders reported that 51 journalists had been killed and more than an additional 100 had been jailed around the world in 1995. Journalists find Algeria, Cuba, China, Burma, Iran, Iraq, and Russia to be most risky. Romania and Egypt allow their criminal justice systems to curtail press freedom. [9]

Reporters Without Borders, an organization concerned with what happens to journalists around the world, reported that 50 or more journalists were killed in 1995, compared to the 103 killed in 1994. In an eight year span, the organization indicated that 498 journalists had been killed while covering news events and conflicts. Algeria was the most dangerous place in 1995 where 22 journalists were killed. [10]

A ceremony on May 21, 1996, dedicated a monument honoring 934 journalists who were killed while on the job. The memorial is in a park in Arlington, Va., and became part of the Newseum being built by The Freedom Forum.

The list was necessarily incomplete because several additional names have been suggested and research is continuing to make the memorial as accurate as possible.

Journalists were once given safe passage by both sides in warfare, but contemporary guerrilla and religious conflicts often target journalists.

Between 1981 and 1985, 52 died each in Algeria and the Philippines, 48 in Colombia, 30 in Peru, 28 in Tajikstan, 27 in Guatemala, 25 in Croatia and El Salvador, 22 in Turkey, 21 in Russia, 20 in Bosnia-Herzegovina, 19 in India, 16 in Mexico, Japan and Rwanda, 15 in Brazil, 14 in Thailand, 12 in the United States, 11 in Afghanistan, and 10 in Somalia and Lebanon. [11]

The World Press Freedom Committee of Reston, VA, and journalists from 34 countries devised a Charter for a Free Press in 1987. Joining in this effort were the International Federation of Newspaper Publishers, the International Press Institute, InterAmerican Press Association, the North American National Broadcasters Association and the International Federation of the Periodical Press. Other journalistic organizations in the United States and around the world have supported it.

Here is the Charter for a Free Press:

A free press means a free people. To this end, the following principles, basic to an unfettered flow of news and information both within and across national borders, deserve the support of all those pledged to advance and protect democratic institutions.

1. Censorship, direct or indirect, is unacceptable; thus laws and practices restricting the right of the news media freely to gather and distribute information must be abolished, and government authorities, national or local, must not interfere with the content of print or broadcast news, or restrict access to any news source.

2. Independent news media, both print and broadcast, must be allowed to emerge and operate freely in all countries.

3. There must be no discrimination by governments in their treatment,

economic or otherwise, of the news media have to all material and facilities necessary to their publishing or broadcasting operations.

4. States must not restrict access to newsprint, printing facilities and distribution systems, operation of news agencies, and availability of broadcast frequencies and facilities.

5. Legal, technical and tariff practices by communications authorities which inhibit the distribution of news and restrict the flow of information are condemned.

6. Government media must enjoy editorial independence and be open to a diversity of viewpoints. This should be affirmed in both law and practice.

7. There should be unrestricted access by the print and broadcast media within a country to outside news and information services, and the public should enjoy similar freedom to receive foreign publications and foreign broadcasts without interference.

8. National frontiers must be open to foreign journalists. Quotas must not apply, and applications for visas, press credentials and other documentation requisite for their work should be allowed to travel freely within a country and have access to both official and unofficial news sources, and be allowed to import and export freely all necessary professional materials and equipment.

9. Restrictions on the free entry to the field of journalism or over its practice, through licensing or other certification procedures, must be eliminated.

10. Journalists, like all citizens, must be secure in their persons and be given full protection of law. Journalists working in war zones are recognized as civilians enjoying all rights and immunities accorded to other civilians.

William Orme, executive director of the Committee to Protect Journalists, in its most recent *Survey of World Press Freedom* issued in 1998. Said that a precondition of democracy is a free press. In the 117 countries the Committee found that some improvements existed because fewer persons were in jail. The C-Span program of March 27 indicated that governments used libel and litigation threats, seditious libel and treason charges, censorship, murders, executions, imprisonment, harrassment, capitalization requirements, confuscations, and suspicion to control their presses. [12]

The new century will pose a great challenge to American journalists and diplomats even on a day to day basis in their endeavors to inform or negotiate a better world. The best export that could provide that world are the provisions proclaimed in America's First Amendment.

Nonetheless, International Freedom of the Press Day is observed every May 3rd.

NOTES

Chapter 1

1. Associated Press Report in 1995.
2. Grendlar, Paul F. "The Advent of Printing" *Censorship: 500 Years of Conflict*. New York Public Library, 1984. p. 24.
3. *Freedom Forum Calendar*. November 6, 1993.
4. Hohenberg, John. *Free Press/ Free People*. The Free Press, 1973.
5. *The New Encyclopedia Britannica*. Volume 4. *Encyclopedia Britannica*. 1993. p. 292.
6. *The New Encyclopedia Britannica*. Volume 3. *Encyclopedia Britannica*. 1995. p. 784.
7. *Freedom Forum Calender*, June 25, 1996.
8. *Freedom Forum Calendar*. June 14, 1994.
9. Russell, Bertrand. *Wisdom of the West*. Rathbone. 1959. p. 11.
10. *Freedom Forum Calender*. February 21, 1994.
11. *Freedom Forum Calendar*. August 18, 1992.
12. *Freedom Forum Calendar*. March 30, 1994.
13. *Freedom Forum Calendar*. March 18, 1994.
14. Gillett, Charles Ripley. *Burned Books*. Columbia University Press. 1923. Vol I. p. 4.
15. *Freedom Forum Calendar*. July 24, 1992.
16. *Freedom Forum Calendar*. February 4, 1995.
17. Hohenberg, John. *Op. cit.*
18. *Freedom Forum Calendar*. November 8, 1992.
19. Salmon, Lucy Maynard. *The Newspaper and Authority*. Oxford University Press. 1923. p. 250.
20. *Freedom Forum Calendar*. April 16, 1994.
21. Schlesinger, Arthur, Jr. "Preface." *Censorship: 500 Years of Conflict*. New York Public Library. 1984. p. 7.
22. Hohenburg, John. *Op. cit.*

23. *The New Encyclopedia Britannica.* Volume 2. *Encyclopedia Britannica.* 1995. pp. 749, 750.
24. Mayle, Walter. *An Essay Upon the Constitution of the Roman Government.* 1726.
25. Gilbert, Charles Ripley. *Burned Books.* Columbia University Press, 1923. Vol I. p. 5.
26. *Freedom Forum Calendar.* January 4, 1996.
27. *Freedom Forum Calendar.* January 5, 1994.
28. *The New Encyclopedia Britannica.* Volume 3. *Encyclopedia Britannica.* 1995. pp. 314, 315.
29. *Freedom Forum Calendar.* February 25, 1994.
30. Hohenburg, John. *Op. cit.*
31. *Freedom Forum Calendar.* September 24, 1993.
32. *Freedom Forum Calendar.* December 25, 1995.
33. *Freedom Forum Calendar.* March 8, 1994.
34. *Freedom Forum Calendar.* February 22. 1992.
35. *Freedom Forum Calendar.* April 20, 1992.
36. Grendler, Paul F. "The Advent of Printing." *Censorship: 500 Years of Conflict.* New York Public Library. 1984. p. 24.
37. *Freedom Forum Calendar.* October 18, 1997.
38. *Freedom Forum Calendar.* April 2, 1994.
39. *Freedom Forum Calendar.* January 5, 1992.
40. *Freedom Forum Calendar.* February 23, 1993.
41. *The New Encyclopedia Britannica.* Volume I. *Encyclopedia Britannica.* 1995. pp. 556, 557.
42. *Ibid.* p. 251.
43. Hohenburg, John. *Op. cit.* pp. 10, 11.
44. *Freedom Forum Calendar.* April 1, 1995.
45. *Freedom Forum Calendar.* November 3, 1992.
46. Edwards, Mike. "The Great Khana." *National Geographic.* Vol. 191, No. 2. February 1997. p. 25.
47. *Freedom Forum Calendar.* February 23, 1992.
48. Siebert, Frederick Seaton. *Freedom of the Press in England* 1476-1776. University of Illinois Press. 1852. pp. 118, 119.
49. Russell, Bertrand. *Op. cit.* p. 165.
50. *Freedom Forum Calendar.* August 5, 1995.
51. Russell, Bertrand. *Op. cit.* p. 167.
52. Hohenburg, John. *Op. cit.* p. 11.
53. *Ibid.* p. 12.
54. Alter, Ann Ilan. "An Introduction to the Exhibit." *Censorship: 500 Years of Conflict.* New York Public Library. 1984. P. 16.
55. Hohenburg, John. *Op. cit.* p. 13.
56. *Ibid.* p. 13.
57. Andersson, Christianne. "Polemic Prints During the Reformation." *Censorship: 500 Years of Conflict.* New York Public Library. 1984. P. 37.

Chapter 2

1. Davis, G.R.C. *Magna Carta.* The British Library, 1977. pp. 9,10.
2. *Ibid.*
3. Gillet, Charles Ripley. *Burned Books.* Columbia University Press. 1923. Vol. I. p. 15.

4. *Freedom Forum Calendar*. March 18, 1992.
5. Brown, Louis F. "On the Burning of Books." *Vassar Medieval Studies*. Yale University Press. 1923. pp. 249-271.
6. Hohenburg, John. *Free Press/ Free People*. The Free Press. 1973. p. 14.
7. Siebert, Frederick Seaton. *Freedom of the Press in England, 1476-1776*. University of Illinois Press. 1952. p. 24.
8. Gillet, Charles Ripley. *Op. cit.* p. 17.
9. Siebert, Frederick Seaton. *Op. cit.* 22-24.
10. *Ibid.* p. 44.
11. *Ibid.* p. 30.
12. *Ibid.* p. 29.
13. Ransom, Harry. *The First Copyright Statute*. University of Texas Press. 1956. p. 145.
14. Siebert, Frederick Seaton. *Op. cit.* p. 45.
15. Foxe, John. *Acts and Monuments of John Foxe*. Seeley and Burnside. 1837-1841. Vol. 4. pp. 557-704.
16. Gillet, Charles Ripley. *Op. cit.* Volume II. p. 19.
17. Siebert, Frederick Seaton. *Op. cit.* p. 42.
18. Gillet, Charles Ripley. *Op. cit.* Volume II. p. 19.
19. Siebert, Frederick Seaton. *Op. cit.* pp. 43,44.
20. *Ibid.* p. 2.
21. Demaus, Robert. *William Tyndale: A Biography. A Constitution to the Early History of the English Bible*. Religious Toact Society. 1886. P. 468.
22. Siebert, Frederick Seaton. *Op. cit.* p. 43.
23. *Ibid.* p. 44.
24. Gillet, Charles Ripley. *Op. cit.* Volume I. p. 20.
25. Siebert, Frederick Seaton. *Op. cit.* p. 44.
26. *Ibid.* p. 44.
27. *Ibid.* p. 31.
28. *Ibid.* p. 45.
29. *Ibid.* p. 2.
30. Hohenburg, John. *Op. cit.* p. 19.
31. Siebert, Fredrick Seaton. *Op. cit.* p. 45.
32. Hohenburg, John. *Op. cit.* p. 19.
33. Devereux, E.J. "Elizabeth Barton and Tudor Censorship." *Bulletin of the John Rylands Library, Manchester*. Autumn 1966. pp. 91-106.
34. New York Public Library. *Censorship: 500 Years of Conflict*. New York Public Library. 1984.
35. Siebert, Frederick Seaton. *Op. cit.* p. 15.
36. *Ibid.* p. 32.
37. *Ibid.* p. 15.
38. *Ibid.* p. 48.
39. *Ibid.* p. 15.
40. Gillet, Charles Ripley. *Op. cit.* Volume II. pp. 20,21.
41. Siebert, Frederick Seaton. *Op. cit.* p. 66.
42. *Ibid.*
43. *Ibid.* pp. 38,39.
44. Grendler, Paul F. "The Advent of Printing." *Censorship: 500 Years of Conflict*. New York Public Library. 1984. pp. 31-33.
45. Siebert, Frederick Seaton. *Op. cit.* p. 51.

46. *Ibid.* p. 50.

47. *Ibid.* p. 51.

48. Gillet, Charles Ripley. *Op. cit.* Volume II. p. 23.

49. Siebert, Frederick Seaton. *Op. cit.* p. 50.

50. *Ibid.* p. 51.

51. *Ibid.* p. 52.

52. *Ibid.* p. 51.

53. Salmon, Lucy Maynard. *The Newspaper and Authority.* Oxford University Press. 1923. p. 48.

54. Siebert, Fredrick Seaton. *Op. cit.* p. 15.

55. *Ibid.* p. 55.

56. *Ibid.* p. 15.

57. *Ibid.* p. 120.

58. Gillet, Charles Ripley. *Op. cit.* Volume II. p. 30.

59. *Ibid.* Volume I. p. 28.

60. Salmon, Lucy Maynard. *Op. cit.* p. 50.

61. Gillet, Charles Ripley. *Op. cit.* Volume I. p. 35.

62. Siebert, Fredrick Seaton. *Op. cit.* pp. 2, 15, 57, 58.

63. *Ibid.* pp. 69, 83.

64. *Ibid.* p. 83.

65. *Ibid.* p. 139.

66. Hohenburg, John. *Op. cit.* pp. 19, 20.

67. Siebert, Fredrick Seaton. *Op. cit.* pp. 33, 97, 98.

68. Gillet, Charles Ripley. *Op. cit.* Volume I. p. 66.

69. *Ibid.* Volume I. P. 63.

70. Siebert, Fredrick Seaton. *Op. cit.* pp. 101, 102, 104.

71. *Ibid.* p. 84.

72. Grendlar, Paul F. "The Advent of Printing." *Censorship: 500 Years of Conflict.* New York Public Library. 1984. P. 33.

73. Siebert, Fredrick Seaton. *Op. cit.* p. 92.

74. *Ibid.* p. 103.

75. Gillet, Charles Ripley. *Op. cit.* Volume II. p. 53.

76. *Ibid.* Volume II. p. 62.

77. *Ibid.* Volume II. p. 62.

78. Siebert, Frederick Seaton. *Op. cit.* p. 90.

79. *Ibid.* p. 50.

80. *Ibid.* pp. 15, 62, 85.

81. Gillet, Charles Ripley. *Op. cit.* Volume II. p. 65.

82. *Ibid.* Volume II. p. 67.

83. *Ibid.* p. 76.

84. Siebert, Frederick Seaton. *Op. cit.* p. 102.

85. Gillet, Charles Ripley. *Op. cit.* Volume II. p. 51.

86. Siebert, Frederick Seaton. *Op. cit.* p. 100.

87. *Freedom Forum Calendar.* September 7, 1997.

88. Gillet, Charles Ripley. *Op. cit.* Volume I. p. 76.

89. Bacon, Francis. "Of Sedition and Troubles" *Essays or Counsels Civill and Morell.* See *Selected Writings of Francis Bacon.* Modern Library. 1955. pp. 38-44.

90. Gillet, Charles Ripley. *Op. cit.* Volume II. p. 91.

91. Siebert, Frederick Seaton. *Op. cit.* p. 63.

92. *Ibid.* pp. 73, 74.

Chapter 3

1. *Freedom Forum Calendar.* September 19, 1990.
2. *Freedom Forum Calendar.* April 5, 1992.
3. Hohenburg, John. *Free Press/ Free People.* The Free Press. 1973. p. 13.
4. Salmon, Lucy Maynard. *The Newspaper and Authority.* Oxford University Press. 1923. p. 15.
5. Hohenburg, John. *Op. cit.* p. 13.
6. *Ibid.* p. 17.
7. Siebert, Frederick Seaton. *Freedom of the Press in England, 1476-1776.* University of Illinois Press. 1952. p. 14.
8. Grendlar, Paul F. "The Advent of Printing." *Censorship: 500 Years of Conflict* New York Public Library. 1984. p. 25.
9. *Ibid.* p. 35.
10. Anderson, Christianne. "Polemic Prints during the Reformation." *Censorship: 500 Years of Conflict.* New York City Public Library. 1984. pp. 35, 39.
11. Grendlar, Paul F. *Op. cit.* pp. 26, 27.
12. *Freedom Forum Calendar.* November 18, 1994.
13. Baruch Van Isaac. "Sefer ha-Terumoh." *Censorship: 500 Years of Conflict.* New York City Public Library. 1984. pp. 8, 9.
14. Grendlar, Paul F. *Op. cit.* p. 32.
15. Anderson, Christianne. *Op. cit.* p. 37.
16. Grendlar, Paul F. *Op. cit.* p. 27.
17. Hohenberg, John. *Op. cit.* p. 28.
18. Jacob, Margaret C. "A New Consensus, 1600-1700." *Censorship: 500 Years of Conflict.* New York City Public Library. 1984. P. 58.
19. Grendlar, Paul F. *Op. cit.* p. 32.
20. *Ibid.* p. 29.
21. *Ibid.* p. 30.
22. *Ibid.* p. 30.
23. Anderson, Christianne. *Op. cit.* p. 38.
24. Alter, Ann Ilan. "An Introduction to the Exhibit." *Censorship: 500 Years of Conflict.* New York City Public Library. 1984. P. 16.
25. *Freedom Forum Calendar.* December 9, 1992.
26. Alter Ann Ilan. *Op. cit.* p. 16-19.
27. *Freedom Forum Calendar.* May 23, 1993.
28. P.E. Corbett. "Introduction." *The Law of War and Peace.* By Hugo Grotius. Walter J. Black, Inc. 1949. pp. xi-xxv.
29. Jacob, Margaret C. *Op. cit.* p. 52.
30. *Freedom Forum Calendar.* June 14, 1996.
31. *Freedom Forum Calendar.* April 28, 1992, and June 30, 1993.
32. Jacob, Margaret C. *Op. cit.* p. 63.
33. Hugo Grotius. *The Law of War and Peace.* Walter J. Black, Inc. 1949. pp. 3-16.
34. Hohenberg, John. *Op. cit.* p. 28.
35. *Ibid.* p. 17.
36. Jacob, Margaret C. *Op. cit.* p. 56.

37. Herrick, R. "The Paper War." *Dial*. February 8, 1919. pp. 113, 114.
38. *Freedom Forum Calendar*. December 3, 1992.
39. *Freedom Forum Calendar*. September 10, 1993.
40. *Freedom Forum Calendar*. March 30, 1993.
41. Salmon, Lucy Maynard. *Op. cit.* p. 243.
42. *Ibid.* pp. 240, 241.

Chapter 4

1. Gillett, Charles Ripley. *Burned Books*. Columbia University Press. 1932. Vol. I. p. 8.
2. Neilson, William A. "The Theory of Censorship." *Atlantic Monthly*. January 1930. pp. 13-16.
3. Gillett, Charles Ripley. *Op cit.* Vol.ume I. p. 87-89.
4. Siebert, Frederick Seaton. *Freedom of the Press in England, 1476-1776*. University of Illinois Press. 1952. p. 92.
5. Gillett, Charles Ripley. *Op cit.* Volume I. p. 9.
6. Siebert, Frederick Seaton. *Op cit.* p. 33.
7. Hohenberg, John. *Free Press/ Free People*. The Free Press. 1972. p. 19.
8. *Freedom Forum Calendar*. April 22, 1996.
9. Siebert, Frederick Seaton. *Op cit.* pp. 119, 120.
10. Jones, John. *De Libellis Famosis*. Rosseau. 1812. p. 73.
11. *Freedom Forum Calendar*. January 17, 1997.
12. Gillett, Charles Ripley. *Op cit.* Volume I. p. 19.
13. *Freedom Forum Calendar*. April 6, 1994.
14. Legate, Bartholomew, and Edward Wightman. "Cases Against Bartholomew Legate and Edward Wightman for Heresy. 1612." *State Trials*. Volume 3. pp. 727-742.
15. Busher, Leonard. *Religion's Peace*. John Sweeting. 1646. p. 38.
16. Gillett, Charles Ripley. *Op cit.* Volume II. p. 388.
17. M., R. B. "Censorship in 1615." *Devon and Cornwall Notes and Queries*. October 1928. pp. 181, 182.
18. Gillett, Charles Ripley. *Op cit.* Volume I. p. 105.
19. Herd, Harold. *The March of Journalism*. George Allen and Unwin. 1952. pp. 12, 13.
20. Siebert, Frederick Seaton. *Op cit.* p. 152.
21. *Ibid.* p. 15.
22. *Ibid.* p. 146.
23. *Ibid.* p. 153.
24. *Ibid.* pp. 113, 114, 153.
25. Hohenberg, John. *Op cit.* p. 20.
26. Siebert, Frederick Seaton. *Op cit.* p. 115.
27. Gillett, Charles Ripley. *Op cit.* p. 232.
28. Siebert, Frederick Seaton. *Op cit.* p. 154.
29. *Ibid.* p. 154.
30. *Ibid.* p. 155.
31. *Ibid.* p. 133.
32. Gillett, Charles Ripley. *Op cit.* Volume I. p. 144.
33. Siebert, Frederick Seaton. *Op cit.* pp. 114, 115.
34. Gillett, Charles Ripley. *Op cit.* Volume I. p. 144.

35. Putnam, George H. *Books and Their Makers during the Middle Ages.* Putnam's. 1907. Volumes.
36. Siebert, Frederick Seaton. *Op cit.* p. 113.
37. Gillett, Charles Ripley. *Op cit.* Volume I. p. 125.
38. Siebert, Frederick Seaton. *Op cit.* p. 111.
39. *Ibid.* pp. 139-141.
40. Siebert, Frederick Seaton. *Op cit.* p. 155.
41. *Ibid.* p. 122.
42. *Ibid.* p. 138.
43. Bael, William. *A Brief Treatise Concerning the Regulation of Printing.* London, 1651. P. 16.
44. Gillett, Charles Ripley. *Op cit.* Volume I. pp. 150-158.
45. Hohenberg, John. *Op cit.* p. 22.
46. Siebert, Frederick Seaton. *Op cit.* p. 156.
47. *Ibid.* p. 156.
48. *Ibid.* p. 136.
49. *Freedom Forum Calendar.* September 4, 1993.
50. Siebert, Frederick Seaton. *Op cit.* p. 15.
51. Salmon, Lucy Maynard. *The Newspaper and Authority.* Oxford University Press. 1923. p. 50.
52. Siebert, Frederick Seaton. *Op cit.* p. 125.
53. Gillett, Charles Ripley. *Op cit.* Volume I. pp. 158-168.
54. *Ibid.* Volume I. pp. 271-314.
55. Siebert, Frederick Seaton. *Op cit.* p. 142.
56. *Ibid.* pp. 3, 15.
57. Gillett, Charles Ripley. *Op cit.* pp. 172-174.
58. Lilburne, John. *A Christian Man's Trial.* Edited by William Larner. 1641. p. 39.
59. Siebert, Frederick Seaton. *Op cit.* pp. 127, 142, 156-160.
60. *Freedom Forum Calendar.* November 12, 1997.
61. Siebert, Frederick Seaton. *Op cit.* pp. 156-160.
62. Gibb, Mildred A. *John Lilburne, The Leveler, A Christian Democrat.* Drummond, 1947. P. 359.
63. Gillett, Charles Ripley. *Op cit.* Volume II. p. 364.
64. Siebert, Frederick Seaton. *Op cit.* p. 192.
65. *Ibid.* p. 174.
66. Gillett, Charles Ripley. *Op cit.* p. 186.
67. Sparke, Michael. *Scintilla, or a Light Broken into Darke Warehouses.* Sparke. 1641.
68. Herd, Harold. *Op cit.* p. 15.
69. Gillett, Charles Ripley. *Op cit.* Volume II. p. 361.
70. Siebert, Frederick Seaton. *Op cit.* p. 171.
71. *Freedom Forum Calendar.* April 19, 1992.
72. Gillett, Charles Ripley. *Op cit.* Volume II. p. 378.
73. *Ibid.* Volume II. p. 371.
74. Siebert, Frederick Seaton. *Op cit.* p. 181.
75. Gillett, Charles Ripley. *Op cit.* Volume II. pp. 365-368.
76. *Ibid.* Volume II. pp. 373-375.
77. *Ibid.* Volume II. pp. 376, 377.
78. *Ibid.* Volume II. p. 376.
79. Siebert, Frederick Seaton. *Op cit.* p. 175.

80. Salmon, Lucy. *The Newspaper and the Historian.* Oxford University Press. 1923. p. 115.
81. *Freedom Forum Calendar.* January 4, 1994.
82. Gillett, Charles Ripley. *Op cit.* Volume II. p. 369.
83. Hohenberg, John. *Op cit.* p. 22.
84. Herd, Harold. *Op cit.* p. 27.
85. Gillett, Charles Ripley. *Op cit.* Volume II. p. 370.
86. Herd, Harold. *Op cit.* p. 19.
87. Hohenberg, John. *Op cit.* p. 23.
88. Siebert, Frederick Seaton. *Op cit.* p. 183.
89. Gillett, Charles Ripley. *Op cit.* Volume I. p. 188.
90. Siebert, Frederick Seaton. *Op cit.* p. 177.
91. Gillett, Charles Ripley. *Op cit.* Volume II. p. 381.
92. Siebert, Frederick Seaton. *Op cit.* p. 207.
93. *Ibid.* pp. 207-209.
94. Gillett, Charles Ripley. *Op cit.* Volume II. p. 382.
95. Herd, Harold. *Op cit.* p. 15.
96. Siebert, Frederick Seaton. *Op cit.* pp. 185, 186.
97. Robinson, Henry. *Liberty of Conscience.* 1643. p. 62. (See Haller. *Tracts on Liberty in the Puritan Revolution.* Volume 3. pp. 107-178.)

Chapter 5

1. Herd, Harold. *The March of Journalism.* George Allen and Unwin, 1952. p. 21, 97.
2. *Freedom Forum Calendar.* July 9, 1992.
3. Milton, John. *Areopagitica.* London, 1644. Facsimile edition, Douglas. 1927.
4. *Freedom Forum Calendar.* July 9, 1996.
5. Gillett, Charles Ripley. *Burned Books.* Columbia University Press. 1932. Volume I. pp 158-181.
6. Laud, William. *The History of the Troubles and Tryal of William Laud.* Ri Chiswell. 1695. 616 pp.
7. Siebert, Frederick Seaton. *Freedom of the Press in England, 1476-1776.* University of Illinois Press. 1952. pp. 199.
8. Herd, Harold. *Op. cit.* pp. 199-21, 27, 28.
9. Gillett, Charles Ripley. *Op. cit.* Volume I. pp. 199, 201, 314, 316.
10. *Ibid.* Volume I. p. 195.
11. Siebert, Frederick Seaton. *Op. cit.* pp. 192-194.
12. Gillett, Charles Ripley. *Op. cit.* Volume I. p. 9.
13. Siebert, Frederick Seaton. *Op. cit.* p. 210.
14. Gillett, Charles Ripley. *Op. cit.* Volume II. p. 255.
15. Siebert, Frederick Seaton. *Op. cit.* p. 221.
16. Overton, Richard. *A Remonstrance of Many Thousand Citizens.* 1646. Reproduced in *Tracts on Liberty and the Puritan Revolution.* Haller. Vol. 3. pp. 353-370.
17. Gillett, Charles Ripley. *Op. cit.* Volume II. p. 391.
18. *Ibid.* Volume II. p. 382, 383.
19. Siebert, Frederick Seaton. *Op. cit.* p. 177, 178.
20. Gillett, Charles Ripley. *Op. cit.* Volume I. pp. 389-391.
21. Siebert, Frederick Seaton. *Op. cit.* p. 188.
22. *Ibid.* pp. 194, 195.
23. Herd, Harold. *Op. cit.* p. 17.

24. Gillett, Charles Ripley. *Op. cit.* Volume II. p. 383.
25. Siebert, Frederick Seaton. *Op. cit.* p. 193.
26. March, John. *Actions for Slaunder.* M. Walbank and R. Best. 1647. 241 pp.
27. Siebert, Frederick Seaton. *Op. cit.* pp. 202, 217.
28. Gillett, Charles Ripley. *Op. cit.* Volume I. p. 393.
29. Siebert, Frederick Seaton. *Op. cit.* p. 3.
30. Gillett, Charles Ripley. *Op. cit.* Volume I. pp. 344, 345.
31. *Ibid.* Volume II. p. 420.
32. Petty, Sir William. *The Advice of W.P. to Mr. Samuel Hortlib.* 1648. 34 pp. See also *The Harllian Miscellany.* Volume 6. pp. 141-157.
33. Gillett, Charles Ripley. *Op. cit.* Volume II. P. 297.
34. *Ibid.* Volume II. p. 326-356.
35. Siebert, Frederick Seaton. *Op. cit.* p. 216.
36. Gillett, Charles Ripley. *Op. cit.* Volume II. p. 267-293.
37. *Ibid.* Volume I. p. 271, 300, 317.
38. Siebert, Frederick Seaton. *Op. cit.* p. 221.
39. *Ibid.* p. 3.
40. *Ibid.* p. 101.
41. *Ibid.* p. 225.
42. Jacob, Margaret C. "A New Consensus 1600 1700." *Censorship: 500 Years of Conflict.* New York. Public Library. 1984. P. 57.
43. Gillett, Charles Ripley. *Op. cit.* Volume I. p. 25.
44. *Ibid.* Volume II. pp. 344-345.
45. *Ibid.* Volume I. p. 25.
46. Siebert, Frederick Seaton. *Op. cit.* p. 224.
47. Gillett, Charles Ripley. *Op. cit.* Volume II. pp. 256-262.
48. Jacob, Margaret C. *Op. cit.* p. 56.
49. *Freedom Forum Calendar.* November 10, 1992.
50. Gillett, Charles Ripley. *Op. cit.* Volume I. p. 307
51. Herd, Harold. *Op. cit.* p. 21.
52. Gillett, Charles Ripley. *Op. cit.* Volume II. pp. 405-415.
53. Siebert, Frederick Seaton. *Op. cit.* p. 228.
54. Norwood, Robert. *A Brief Discourse Made by Capt. Robert Norwood.* London. 1652. 6 pp.
55. Siebert, Frederick Seaton. *Op. cit.* p. 221, 225.
56. Chidley, Samuel. *The Dissembling Scot.* London. 1652.
57. Siebert, Frederick Seaton. *Op. cit.* pp. 226, 227.
58. Gillett, Charles Ripley. *Op. cit.* Volume II. pp. 446-449.
59. *Ibid.* Volume I. pp. 267-293.
60. Siebert, Frederick Seaton. *Op. cit.* pp. 3, 16.
61. *Ibid.* p. 227.
62. *Ibid.* pp. 230, 231.
63. *Ibid.* p. 222.
64. Gillett, Charles Ripley. *Op. cit.* Volume II. p. 500.
65. Brailsford, Mabel R. *A Quaker from Cromwell's Army James Nayler.* Macmillan, 1927. 240 pp.
66. Gillett, Charles Ripley. *Op. cit.* Volume II. p. 513.
67. *Ibid.* Volume I. p. 327.
68. Croope, John. *Conscience — Oppression.* London. 1657. 56 pp.

69. Gillett, Charles Ripley. *Op. cit.* Volume II. p. 428.

70. *Ibid.* Volume II. p. 416.

71. *The London Printer, His Lamentation; or the Press Oppressed, or Overpressed. Harlecan Miscellany.* Volume 7. pp. 104-111.

72. Siebert, Frederick Seaton. *Op. cit.* p. 291.

73. *Ibid.* p. 16.

74. Gillett, Charles Ripley. *Op. cit.* Volume II. pp. 423, 428.

75. Herd, Harold. *Op. cit.* p. 27.

76. Gillett, Charles Ripley. *Op. cit.* Volume II. p. 436.

77. Siebert, Frederick Seaton. *Op. cit.* p. 243.

78. *Ibid.* p. 238.

79. Hanson, Laurence. *Government and the Press 1695-1763.* Oxford University Press. 1967. P. 29.

80. Gillett, Charles Ripley. *Op. cit.* Volume II. p. 427.

81. Salmon, Lucy Maynard. *The Newspaper and Authority.* Oxford University Press. 1923. P. 51.

82. Salmon, Lucy Maynard. *Op. cit.* p. 51.

83. Walker, J. "The Censorship of the Press During the Reign of Charles II." *History.* October 1950. pp. 219-238.

84. Gillett, Charles Ripley. *Op. cit.* Volume II. p. 567.

85. Siebert, Frederick Seaton. *Op. cit.* p. 16.

86. Gillett, Charles Ripley. *Op. cit.* Volume II. p. 389

87. *Ibid.* Volume II. p. 442.

88. *Ibid.* Volume II. p. 443-445.

89. Herd, Harold. *Op. cit.* p. 31.

90. Gillett, Charles Ripley. *Op. cit.* Volume II. p. 443.

91. Herd, Harold. *Op. cit.* p. 27.

92. Hobbes, Thomas. *An Historical Narration Concerning Heresies, and the Punishment Thereof.* London. 1680. 18 pp.

93. Gillett, Charles Ripley. *Op. cit.* Volume II. p. 457.

94. Siebert, Frederick Seaton. *Op. cit.* p. 253.

95. *Ibid.* p. 251.

96. *Ibid.* p. 4.

97. Gillett, Charles Ripley. *Op. cit.* Volume I. p. 4, 5.

98. Siebert, Frederick Seaton. *Op. cit.* p. 296.

99. *Ibid.* p. 243, 244.

100. Gillett, Charles Ripley. *Op. cit.* Volume II. p. 490.

101. *Ibid.* Volume I. p. 476-498.

102. *Ibid.* Volume I. p. 214.

103. See *Harleian Miscellany.* Volume 8. pp. 290-300.

104. Siebert, Frederick Seaton. *Op. cit.* p. 272.

105. Hanson, Laurence. *Op. cit.* pp. 15, 31.

106. Siebert, Frederick Seaton. *Op. cit.* p. 297

107. Hanson, Laurence. *Op. cit.* p. 15.

108. *Freedom Forum Calendar.* February 10, 1992.

109. Siebert, Frederick Seaton. *Op. cit.* p. 16.

110. *Ibid.* p. 272, 273.

111. Gillett, Charles Ripley. *Op. cit.* Volume I. p. 490.

112. Siebert, Frederick Seaton. *Op. cit.* p. 269.

113. *Ibid.* p. 269.
114. Colledge, Stephen. *The Arraignment Tryal and Condemnation of Stephen Colledge.* Bassett and Fish. 1981. 102 pp.
115. Denton, William. *An Apology for the Liberty of the Press.* London. 1681. 9 pp.
116. Fitz-Harris, Edward. *The Arraignment and Plea of Edw. Fitz-Harris, Esq.* Tyton and Basset. 1681. 66 pp.
117. Hickeingill, Edmund. *The Late Famous Tryal of Mr. Hickeingill.* F. Smith. 1681. 14 pp.
118. Hindmarsh, Joseph. *The Tryal and Condemnation of Several Notorious Malefactors.* London. 1681. 2 pp.
119. Thompson, Nathaniel. *Tryal of Nathaniel Thompson et al.* T. Simmons. 1682. 53 pp.
120. Gillett, Charles Ripley. *Op. cit.* Volume I. p. 470.
121. *Ibid.* Volume II. pp. 685-702.
122. *Ibid.* Volume II. pp. 449-451.
123. Sidney, Algernon. *Discourse Concerning Government.* A. Miller. 1763. pp. 46, 198, 496.
124. Siebert, Frederick Seaton. *Op. cit.* p. 299.
125. Gillett, Charles Ripley. *Op. cit.* Volume I. p. 42.
126. *Ibid.* Volume II. p. 468.
127. *Ibid.* Volume I. p. 412.
128. *Ibid.* Volume II. p. 412.
129. *Ibid.* Volume I. p. 48.
130. *Ibid.* Volume II. p. 475.
131. *Ibid.* Volume II. p. 476.
132. *Ibid.* Volume II. p. 507.
133. *Ibid.* Volume II. pp. 516-520.
134. *Ibid.* Volume I. p. 50.
135. Siebert, Frederick Seaton. *Op. cit.* pp. 269-271.
136. Gillett, Charles Ripley. *Op. cit.* Volume II. p. 496.
137. *Ibid.* Volume II. pp. 496-502.
138. Jacob, Margaret C. *Op. cit.* p. 61.
139. Hanson, Laurence. *Op. cit.* p. 21.
140. Gillett, Charles Ripley. *Op. cit.* Volume II. p. 491.
141. Erskine, Thomas E. *The Rights of Juries Vindicated.* Erskine's *Works.* Ridgway edition. Volume I. pp. 151-393.
142. Gillett, Charles Ripley. *Op. cit.* Volume II. p. 412.
143. Siebert, Frederick Seaton. *Op. cit.* p. 275.
144. *Ibid.* p. 281.
145. Locke, John. *Essay Concerning Toleration.* In *Works of John Locke.* Eleventh edition. 1812.
146. Salmon, Lucy Maynard. *Op. cit.* p. 281.
147. Siebert, Frederick Seaton. *Op. cit.* pp. 284-286.
148. Gillett, Charles Ripley. *Op. cit.* Volume I. p. 45.
149. *Ibid.* Volume II. p. 533.
150. *Freedom Forum Calendar.* April 2, 1993.
151. *Freedom Forum Calendar.* August 25, 1992.
152. Blount, Charles. *Reasons Humbly Offered for the Liberty of Unlicensed Printing.* London. 1693. 32 pp.
153. Gillett, Charles Ripley. *Op. cit.* Volume II. p. 557.
154. Thomas, Donald. "Vice Society." *Censorship.* Winter 1967. pp. 34-40.
155. Siebert, Frederick Seaton. *Op. cit.* p. 244.

156. *Ibid.* p. 28.
157. Bourne, H.R. Fox. *English Newspapers*. Chatto and Windus. 1887. 2 volumes.
158. Locke, John. *Works of John Locke*. Eleventh edition. Volume 6. 1812.
159. Hanson, Laurence. *Op. cit.* pp. 1, 7, 29.
160. Siebert, Frederick Seaton. *Op. cit.* p. 4.
161. Hanson, Laurence. *Op. cit.* p. 8.
162. Siebert, Frederick Seaton. *Op. cit.* p. 16.
163. Jacob, Margaret C. *Op. cit.* p. 52.
164. Siebert, Frederick Seaton. *Op. cit.* pp. 16, 17, 107.
165. *Ibid.* p. 280.
166. Gillett, Charles Ripley. *Op. cit.* Volume II. pp. 538-540.
167. Siebert, Frederick Seaton. *Op. cit.* p. 280.
168. *Ibid.* p. 287.
169. Collier, Jeremy. *A Short View of the Professors and Immorality of the English Stage.* Kable, Sare and Hindmash. 1699. 139 pp.
170. Gregory, Francis. *A Modest Plea for the Due Regulation of the Press.* R. Sare. 1698. 46 pp.
171. Defoe, Daniel. *An Essay on the Regulation of the Press.* Lutrell Society. 1948. 29 pp.

Chapter 6

1. Salmon, Lucy Maynard. *The Newspaper and Authority.* Oxford University Press. 1923. p. 285.
2. Jacob, Margaret C. "A New Consensus, 1600-1700," *Censorship: 500 Years of Conflict..* New York Public Library. 1984. pp. 63, 64
3. Siebert, Frederick Seaton. *Freedom of the Press in England, 1476-1776.* University of Illinois Press. 1952. pp. 330, 335.
4. *Ibid.* p. 331.
5. Gillett, Charles Ripley. *Burned Books.* Columbia University Press. 1932. Volume II. p 540.
6. Hanson, Laurence. *Government and the Press 1695-1763.* Oxford University Press. 1967. p. 9.
7. Siebert, Frederick Seaton. *Op. cit.* p. 325.
8. *Ibid.* pp. 271-275.
9. Toland, John. *Vindicious Liberius: Or, M. Toland's Defence of himself.* Bernard Lintott. 1702. 166 pp.
10. Hanson, Laurence. *Op. cit.* p. 90.
11. Herd, Harold. *The March of Journalism.* George Allen and Unwin. 1952. p. 32.
12. Hanson, Laurence. *Op. cit.* p. 40.
13. Siebert, Frederick Seaton. *Op. cit.* p. 278.
14. Gillett, Charles Ripley. *Op. cit.* Volume II. p. 599.
15. Herd, Harold. *Op. cit.* pp. 47, 56.
16. Fuller, William. *Tryal of W. Fuller.* I. Cleave. 1702. 13 pp.
17. Gillett, Charles Ripley. *Op. cit.* Volume II. p. 588.
18. Herd, Harold. *Op. cit.* p. 47.
19. Siebert, Frederick Seaton. *Op. cit.* p. 278.

20. Burn. John S. "Books Burned by the Common Hangman." *Notes and Queries* October, 1953. pp. 346-348.
21. Siebert, Frederick Seaton. *Op. cit.* p. 17.
22. Herd, Harold. *Op. cit.* p. 49.
23. *Ibid.* p. 47.
24. *Ibid.* pp. 32, 33.
25. Gillett, Charles Ripley. *Op. cit.* Volume II. pp. 624, 625.
26. Herd, Harold. *Op. cit.* p.
27. Hanson, Laurence. *Op. cit.* p. 9.
28. *Ibid.* p. 3.
29. Salmon, Lucy Maynard. *Op. cit.* p. 48.
30. Gillett, Charles Ripley. *Op. cit.* Volume I. p 583.
31. Siebert, Frederick Seaton. *Op. cit.* p. 287.
32. Hanson, Laurence. *Op. cit.* pp. 1, 2.
33. *Ibid.* p. 10.
34. Siebert, Frederick Seaton. *Op. cit.* p. 249.
35. Gillett, Charles Ripley. *Op. cit.* Volume II. p. 559.
36. Tindal, Matthes. *A letter to a Friend.* London. 1708. 24 pp.
37. Siebert, Frederick Seaton. *Op. cit.* pp. 308, 309.
38. Gillett, Charles Ripley. *Op. cit.* Volume II. pp. 601, 602.
39. *Ibid.* Volume II. p. 540.
40. Siebert, Frederick Seaton. *Op. cit.* p. 225.
41. Gillett, Charles Ripley. *Op. cit.* Volume II. pp. 667-682.
42. Siebert, Frederick Seaton. *Op. cit.* p. 308
43. Gillett, Charles Ripley. *Op. cit.* Volume II. p. 617.
44. *Freedom Forum Calendar.* November 27, 1995.
45. Addison, Joseph. *The Thoughts of a Tory Writer, Concerning Press.* A. Baldwin. 1712. 33 pp.
46. Hanson, Laurence. *Op. cit.* p. 14.
47. Hohenberg, John. *Free Press/Free People.* The Free Press. 1973. pp. 26, 27.
48. Hanson, Laurence. *Op. cit.* p. 63.
49. Siebert, Frederick Seaton. *Op. cit.* pp. 308, 309
50. *Freedom Forum Calendar.* October 2, 1995.
51. Siebert, Frederick Seaton. *Op. cit.* pp. 4, 17.
52. Hanson, Laurence. *Op. cit.* p. 11.
53. Herd, Harold. *Op. cit.* pp. 43, 44.
54. Hanson, Laurence. *Op. cit.* p. 14.
55. Herd, Harold. *Op. cit.* p. 49.
56. Hanson, Laurence. *Op. cit.* p. 63.
57. Siebert, Frederick Seaton. *Op. cit.* p. 339.
58. Hanson, Laurence. *Op. cit.* p. 41.
59. *Ibid.* p. 64.
60. *Freedom Forum Calendar.* August 27, 1996.
61. Hanson, Laurence. *Op. cit.* p. 138.
62. Emlyn, Thomas. *A Collection of Tracts.* London. 1719.
63. Hanson, Laurence. *Op. cit.* p. 10.
64. Siebert, Frederick Seaton. *Op. cit.* p. 332.
65. *Ibid.* p. 339.
66. *Freedom Forum Calendar.* January 26, 1992.

67. Levy, Leonard William. *Freedom of the Press from Zenger to Jefferson*. Bobbs-Merrill Company. 1966. pp. 11-14.
68. Gillett, Charles Ripley. *Op. cit.* Volume II. p. 590.
69. Hanson, Laurence. *Op. cit.* p. 4.
70. *Ibid.* p. 66.
71. *Ibid.* p. 24.
72. Siebert, Frederick Seaton. *Op. cit.* p. 17.
73. Collins, Anthony. *A Discourse of the Grounds and Reasons of the Christian Religion*. London. 1724. 62 pp.
74. Salmon, Lucy Maynard. *Op. cit.* p. 392.
75. Siebert, Frederick Seaton. *Op. cit.* p. 370.
76. Curll, Edmund. *Trial for Publishing an Obscene Libel, 1727*. Howell's *State Trials*. Volume 17. 154 pp.
77. Siebert, Frederick Seaton. *Op. cit.* pp. 382, 383.
78. *Ibid.* p. 349.
79. *Ibid.* p. 382.
80. Wyckliffe, John. *Upon Two Late Presentments of the Grand Jury of the County of Middlesex*. A. Moore. 1729. 28 pp.
81. Woolston, Thomas. "Trial for Writing and Publishing Four Books on the Miracles, 1720." In Barrow's *Celebrated Trials*. Volume 3. pp. 432-39.
82. *State Law: On the Doctrine of Libels, Discussed and Examined*. Nutt and Gosling. 1730. 136 pp.
83. Herd, Harold. *Op. cit.* p. 51.
84. Hanson, Laurence. *Op. cit.* p. 69.
85. Siebert, Frederick Seaton. *Op. cit.* p. 382.
86. *Freedom Forum Calendar*. August 17, 1992.
87. Siebert, Frederick Seaton. *Op. cit.* p. 383.
88. Hanson, Laurence. *Op. cit.* p. 68.
89. Siebert, Frederick Seaton. *Op. cit.* p. 5.
90. Hanson, Laurence. *Op. cit.* p. 23.
91. *Ibid.* p. 112.
92. Herd, Harold. *Op. cit.* p. 64.
93. *Ibid.* p. 55.
94. Hanson, Laurence. *Op. cit.* p. 118.
95. *Ibid.* p. 140.
96. *Ibid.* p. 69.
97. Siebert, Frederick Seaton. *Op. cit.* p. 17.
98. Hanson, Laurence. *Op. cit.* p. 4.
99. Johnson, Samuel. *A Compleat Vindication of the Licensers of the Stage*. In his *Works* edited by Arthur Murphy. Harper. 1873. Volume 2. pp. 539-544.
100. *Ibid.* Volume 2. pp. 539-544.
101. Siebert, Frederick Seaton. *Op. cit.* p. 334.
102. Hume, David. "Of the Liberty of the Press." *Philosophical Works*. Little Brown. 1854. Volume 3. pp. 6-10.
103. Siebert, Frederick Seaton. *Op. cit.* p. 373.
104. Hanson, Laurence. *Op. cit.* pp. 69, 70.
105. *Ibid.* pp. 70, 71.
106. Siebert, Frederick Seaton. *Op. cit.* p. 342.
107. Herd, Harold. *Op. cit.* p. 56.

108. Hanson, Laurence. *Op. cit.* p. 146.
109. *Ibid.* p. 2.
110. Walpole, Horace. *A Second and Third Letter to the Whigs.* M. Cooper. 1748. 92 pp.
111. *Freedom Forum Calendar.* December 14, 1992.
112. Siebert, Frederick Seaton. *Op. cit.* p. 383.
113. *Freedom Forum Calendar.* April 9, 1995.
114. *Freedom Forum Calendar.* January 31, 1994.
115. Hayter, Thomas. *An Essay on the Liberty of the Press.* J. Raymond. 1775. 47 pp.
116. Siebert, Frederick Seaton. *Op. cit.* p. 17.
117. *Freedom Forum Calendar.* March 21, 1995.
118. Hanson, Laurence. *Op. cit.* p. 72.
119. Gillett, Charles Ripley. *Op. cit.* Volume II. pp. 685-702.

Chapter 7

1. Hohenberg, John. *Free Press/Free People.* The Free Press. 1973. p. 19.
2. *Ibid.* p. 19.
3. *Ibid.* p. 11.
4. *Ibid.* p. 94.
5. Gimlette, Thomas. "Books Burnt." *Notes and Queries.* July 14, 1855. p. 31.
6. Hohenberg, John. *Op. cit.* p. 19.
7. Wyckliffe, John. *Upon two late Presentments of the Grand Jury of the County of Middlesex.* A. Moore. 1729. 28 pp.
8. *Freedom Forum Calendar.* June 29, 1997.
9. Salmon, Lucy Maynard. *The Newspaper and Authority.* Oxford University Press. 1923. pp. 239, 240.
10. *Ibid.* p. 241.
11. Hohenberg, John. *Op. cit.* p. 151.
12. *Freedom Forum Calendar.* March 21, 1995.
13. *Freedom Forum Calendar.* April 21, 1994.
14. *Freedom Forum Calendar.* October 3, 1992.
15. Alter, Ann. "An Introduction to the Exhibit." *Censorship: 500 Years of Conflict.* New York Public Library. 1984. p. 15.
16. Black, Eugene C. "The Eighteenth Century: Control and Revolution." *Censorship: 500 Years of Conflict.* New York Public Library. 1984. p. 68.
17. *Ibid.* p. 68.
18. *Freedom Forum Calendar.* November 16, 1993.
19. *Freedom Forum Calendar.* November 23, 1996.
20. Hohenberg, John. *Op. cit.* p. 131.
21. *Ibid.* pp. 93, 94.
22. Salmon, Lucy Maynard. *Op. cit.* p. 250.
23. *Freedom Forum Calendar.* February 24, 1996.
24. *Freedom Forum Calendar.* April 17, 1993.
25. Salmon, Lucy Maynard. *Op. cit.* p. 242.
26. Hohenberg, John. *Op. cit.* p. 131.
27. Alter, Ann. *Op. cit.* p. 17.
28. Hohenberg, John. *Op. cit.* p. 131.
29. Black, Eugene C. *Op. cit.* p. 67.

30. Hohenberg, John. *Op. cit.* p. 73.
31. *Ibid.* p. 93.
32. *Freedom Forum Calendar.* November 16, 1996.
33. Salmon, Lucy Maynard. *Op. cit.* p. 53.
34. *Ibid.* p. 52.
35. *Ibid.* pp. 81, 82.
36. Black, Eugene C. *Op. cit.* p. 71.
37. *Freedom Forum Calendar.* May 6, 1995.
38. *Freedom Forum Calendar.* April 20, 1992.
39. Hohenberg, John. *Op. cit.* p. 131.
40. *Freedom Forum Calendar.* August 31, 1995.
41. Hohenberg, John. *Op. cit.* p. 75.
42. *Freedom Forum Calendar.* April 24, 1994.
43. *Freedom Forum Calendar.* November 27, 1995.

Chapter 8

1. Herd, Harold. *The March of Journalism.* George Allen and Unwin. 1952. p. 75.
2. Siebert, Frederick Seaton. *Freedom of the Press in England 1476-1776.* University of Illinois Press. 1952. p. 384.
3. Kidgell, John. *A Genuine and Succinct Narrative of a Scandalous Libel.* Robinson and Wilkie. 1763. 16 pp.
4. Herd, Harold. *Op. cit.* p. 97.
5. Schroeder, Theodore A. *Constitutional Free Speech Defined.* Free Speech League. 1919. 456 pp.
6. Herd, Harold. *Op. cit.* pp. 97-103.
7. Black, Eugene C. "The Eighteenth Century: Control and Revolution." *Censorship: 500 Years of Conflict.* New York Public Library. 1984. p. 65.
8. *Freedom Forum Calendar.* April 8, 1996.
9. Herd, Harold. *Op. cit.* p. 70.
10. *North Briton* Numbers 1 to 45. Two volumes. Bingley 1769.
11. Siebert, Frederick Seaton. *Op. cit.* p. 386.
12. Herd, Harold. *Op. cit.* pp. 97-101.
13. Almon, John. *The Trial of John Almon.* Miller. 1790. 65 Pp.
14. Bingley, William. *A Sketch of English Liberty.* Bingley. 1793.
15. Herd, Harold. *Op. cit.* pp. 70-76.
16. Siebert, Frederick Seaton. *Op. cit.* pp. 372, 377, 384.
17. *Freedom Forum Calendar.* October 8, 1994.
18. Siebert, Frederick Seaton. *Op. cit.* pp. 378, 379.
19. *Ibid.* p. 372.
20. *Ibid.* pp. 367, 373.
21. Herd, Harold. *The March of Journalism.* George Allen and Unwin. 1952. pp. 70-74.
22. *Freedom Forum Calendar.* November 1, 1994.
23. Siebert, Frederick Seaton. *Op. cit.* p. 386.
24. Herd, Harold. *Op. cit.* pp. 70-73.
25. Siebert, Frederick Seaton. *Op. cit.* p. 388.

26. Candor. *A Letter from Candor to the Public Advertiser*. J. Almon. 1773. Volume I. pp. 1-40.
27. Siebert, Frederick Seaton. *Op. cit.* p. 358.
28. Woodfall, Henry S. "Trial in London for Publishing Junius' Letter to the King, 1770." Howell *State Trials*. Volume 20. p. 895.
29. Rous, George. *A Letter to the Jurors of Great Britain*. G. Pearch. 1771. 67 pp.
30. *Freedom Forum Calendar*. December 12, 1994.
31. Woodfall, Henry S. "Trial in London for Publishing Junius' Letter to the King, 1770." Howell *State Trials*. Volume 20. p. 895.
32. *Freedom Forum Calendar*. December 1, 1994.
33. *Freedom Forum Calendar*. May 21, 1994.
34. Siebert, Frederick Seaton. *Op. cit.* pp. 4, 17.
35. *Ibid.* p. 387.
36. Sealy, George, and Joseph Hodson. *An Address to the Public*. London. Sealy and Hodson. 1774. 45 pp.
37. Siebert, Frederick Seaton. *Op. cit.* pp. 371, 372.
38. Hayter, Thomas. *An Essay on the Liberty of the Press*. J. Raymond. 1775. 47 pp.
39. Siebert, Frederick Seaton. *Op. cit.* p. 4.
40. Gillett, Charles Ripley. *Burned Books*. Columbia University Press. 1932. Volume II. p. 651-652.
41. Tooke, John Henry. *The Trial of John Horne for a Libel*. Tooke 1777. 69 pp.
42. Maseres, Francis. *An Enquiry Into the Extent of the Power of Juries*. D. Lynch. 1792. 48 pp.
43. Herd, Harold. *Op. cit.* p. 226.
44. Salmon, Lucy Maynard. *The Newspaper and Authority*. Oxford University Press. 1923. p. 251.
45. Winslow, John. *The Battle of Lexington*. New York Society of the Order of the Founders and Patriots of America. 1897. 39 pp.
46. Duffin, Patrick W. and Thomas Lloyd. *The Trial of P.W. Duffin*. D.J. Eaton. 1793. 46 pp.
47. Black, Eugene C. *Op. cit.* p. 73.
48. *Freedom Forum Calendar*. February 23, 1993.
49. Siebert, Frederick Seaton. *Op. cit.* p. 17.
50. Dawes, Manassah. *England's Alarm! On the Prevailing Doctrine of Libels*. London. 1785. 56 pp.
51. Hohenberg, John. *Free Press/Free People*. The Free Press. 1973. p. 83.
52. Society for the Suppression of Vice. *Reports*. The Society. 1803-1805 Annual.
53. *Freedom Forum Calendar*. October 25, 1992.
54. Withers, Philip. *Alfred*. Withers. 1789. 48 pp.
55. Magee, John. *The Trial of John Magee*. P.B. Yone. 1790. 68 pp.
56. Siebert, Frederick Seaton. *Op. cit.* p. 387.
57. Friends to the Liberty of the Press. *Proceedings 1792, 1793*. Committee Order. 1793. 22 pp.
58. Bowles, John. *Consideration on the Respective Rights of Judges and Jury*. 2nd Edition. London. 1791. 56 pp.
59. Salmon, Lucy Maynard. *Op. cit.* p. 244.
60. Siebert, Frederick Seaton. *Op. cit.* p. 391.
61. Kenyon, George T. *The Life of Lloyd, First Lord Kenyon, Lord Chief Justice of England*. Longmans Green. 1873. 403 pp.

62. Roberts, William. *The Whole Proceedings on the Trial of an Action.* Wheeler. 1791. 208 pp.
63. Stockdale, John. *The Whole Proceedings of the Trial Against John Stockdale.* Stockdale. 1790. 228 pp.
64. Paine, Thomas. *Letter Addressed to the Addressers.* Symonds and Rickman. 1792. 40pp.
65. Zeisel, William, ed. *Censorship: 500 Years of Conflict.* New York Public Library. 1984. Frontispiece.
66. Black, Eugene C. *Op. cit.* p. 75.
67. Herd, Harold. *Op. cit.* p. 87.
68. Friends to the Liberty of the Press. *Op. cit.*
69. Bowles, John. *Op. cit.*
70. Bruce, Archibald. *Reflections on Freedom of Writing.* W. Berry. 1794. 168 pp.
71. Salmon, Lucy Maynard. *Op. cit.* p. 285.
72. Frend, William. *An Account of the Proceedings in the University of Cambridge Against William Frend.* B. Flower. 1793. 262 pp.
73. Hall, Robert. *An Apology for the Freedom of the Press.* G.G.J. and J. Robinson. 1793. 103 pp.
74. Siebert, Frederick Seaton. *Op. cit.* p. 367.
75. Salmon, Lucy Maynard. *Op. cit.* p. 284.
76. Palmer, Thomas F. "The Case of Thomas Fyshe Palmer, September 1793." In Cockburn's *Examination of Trials for sedition in Scotland.* Volume I. pp. 184-220.
77. Herd, Harold. *Op. cit.* p. 90.
78. Towers, Joseph. *Remarks on the Conduct, Principles, and Publications of the Association for Preserving Liberty and Property Against Republicans and Levellers.* Cadell and Devies. 1796. pp. 247-298.
79. Hardy, Thomas. *The Trial of Thomas Hardy for High Treason.* Gurney. 1794-1795. Four volumes.
80. Rowan, Archibald. *Report of the Trial of Archibald Rowan.* Rowan and Bryne. 1794. 152 pp.
81. Montgomery, James. *The Trial of James Montgomery for a Libel on the War.* J. Montgomery. 1795. 94 pp.
82. Zall, Paul M. "Lord Eldon's Censorship." *PMLA.* June 1953. pp. 436-443.
83. Holcroft, Thomas. *Narrative of the Facts, relating to a Prosecution for High Treason.* Symonds. 1795. 215 pp.
84. Salmon, Lucy Maynard. *Op. cit.* p. 286.
85. Tooke, John Horne. *The Trial of John Horne Tooke for High Treason.* Crosby. 1795. 152 pp.
86. Black, Eugene C. *Op. cit.* p. 73.
87. Adair, James. *Discussion of the Law of Libel.* Cadell. 1785.
88. Smith, John. *Trial of John Smith, Bookseller.* Mrs. Smith. 1797. 35 pp.
89. Herd, Harold. *Op. cit.* pp. 110, 111.
90. Callender, James T. "Proceedings against James T. Callender, Walter Berry, and James Robertson." Howell's *State Trials.* Volume 23. p. 79.
91. Erskine, Thomas. *The King versus Thomas Williams.* Debrett. 1797. Volume 26. p. 653.
92. Curran, John P. "Speech at the Trial of Peter Finerty." *Speeches of the Right Honourable John Phillipe Curran.* Bohn. 1847. pp. 330-362.
93. Wakefield, Gilbert. "Trial for Publishing a Seditious Libel." 1799. Also see Howell's *State Trials.* Volume 27. p. 642.

94. Shipley, William D. *Proceedings in the Cause of the King Against the Dean of St. Asaph.* Goldney. 1784. 112 pp.

Chapter 9

1. Flower, Benjamin. *The Proceedings of the House of Lords in the Case of Benjamin Flower.* The author. 1800.
2. Siebert, Frederick Seaton. *Freedom of the Press in England 1476-1776.* University of Illinois Press. 1952. p. 374.
3. Salmon, Lucy Maynard. *The Newspaper and Authority.* Oxford University Press. 1923. p. 285.
4. Salmon, Lucy Maynard. *Op. cit.* p. 286.
5. *Freedom Forum Calendar.* July 4, 1994.
6. Society for the Suppression of Vice. *Reports.* The Society. 1803-1885. Annual.
7. *Freedom Forum Calendar.* February 8, 1993.
8. Salmon, Lucy Maynard. *Op. cit.* p. 281.
9. *Ibid.* p. 292.
10. New York Public Library. *Censorship: 500 Years of Conflict.* New York Public Library. 1984. p. 100.
11. Weiner, Joel. "Social Purity and Freedom of Expression." *Censorship: 500 Years of Conflict.* New York Public Library. 1984. p. 100.
12. "Whig Prosecutions of the Press." *Blackwell's Edinburgh Magazine.* March 1834. pp. 295-310.
13. Salmon, Lucy Maynard. *Op. cit.* p. 19.
14. Salmon, Lucy Maynard. *Op. cit.* p. 306.
15. Herd, Harold. *The March of Journalism.* George Allen and Unwin. 1952. pp. 103-121.
16. Finerty, Peter. *Trial of Mr. Peter Finerty.* Howell's *State Trials.* Volume 26. p. 901.
17. Herd, Harold. *Op. cit.* p. 118.
18. Philagatharches. "On the Liberty of the Press." *Hints on Toleration.* Cadell and Davis. 1810. pp. 257-330.
19. Herd, Harold. *Op. cit.* p. 17.
20. Salmon, Lucy Maynard. *Op. cit.* p. 285.
21. Herd, Harold. *Op. cit.* p. 117.
22. Starkie, Thomas. *A Treatise on the Law of Slander, Libel, Scandalum Magnatum, and fake Rumors.* G. Lamson. 1826. 616 pp.
23. Siebert, Frederick Seaton. *Op. cit.* p. 386.
24. Veeder, Van Vechten. "The Judicial History of Individual Liberty." *Green Bag.* January 1924 to November 1924.
25. Magee, John Jr. *Trial of John Magee.* J. Magee. 1813. 171 pp.
26. Bowdler, Thomas. *Liberty: Civil and Religious.* J. Hatchard. 1815. 73 pp.
27. Salmon, Lucy Maynard. *Op. cit.* p. 190.
28. Salmon, Lucy Maynard. *Op. cit.* p. 189.
29. Wiener, Joel H. *Op cit.* p. 96.
30. Herd, Harold. *Op. cit.* p. 113.
31. *Freedom Forum Calendar.* September 8, 1992.
32. Herd, Harold. *Op. cit.* p. 120, 121.

33. Forman, Harry Burton. *The Vicissitudes of Shelley's Queen Mab*. Richard Clay. 1887. 23 pp.
34. Sidmouth, Henry Addington. *Circular Letter*. House of Commons. 1817. 2 pp.
35. Society for the Suppression of Vice. *Reports*. 1819. Annual.
36. Wiener, Joel H. *Op cit*. p. 96.
37. Holt, Francis Ludlow. *Law of Libel*. Stephen Gould. 1818. 328 pp.
38. Herd, Harold. *Op. cit*. pp. 120, 121.
39. Tocker, Mary A. *The Trial of Miss Mary Ann Tocker*. William Cobbett. 1818. 48 pp.
40. Herd, Harold. *Op. cit*. pp. 120-123.
41. *Ibid*. p. 120.
42. Benbow, William. *The Trial of William Benbow for Publishing Certain Libels*. Wilson and Smith. 1822. 21 pp.
43. Herd, Harold. *Op. cit*. p. 124.
44. *Freedom Forum Calendar*. June 28, 1997.
45. Herd, Harold. *Op. cit*. p. 124. Also see *Freedom Forum Calendar*. October 1992.
46. Constitutional Association. "Address, April 17, 1821." Mence, *Law of Libel*. Volume I. p. 186.
47. *Dialogue between a Methodist Preacher and a Reformer*. John Marshall. 1819. 30 pp.
48. Dolby, Thomas. "Trial 1821. *Hansard's Parliamentary Debates*. June 6, 1821. p. 1114.
49. Flindell, Thomas. *The Trial, Defence, and sentence of Thomas Flindell*. T. Flindell. 1821. 28 pp.
50. Fox, W.J. *The Duties of Christians toward Deists*. George Smallfield. 1819. 48 pp.
51. Salmon, Lucy Maynard. *Op. cit*. p. .
52. Herd, Harold. *Op. cit*. pp. 116, 118.
53. Poynder, John. *Abstractions upon Sunday Newspapers*. London, not published. 1820.
54. Salmon, Lucy Maynard. *Op. cit*. p. 291.
55. *Ibid*. p. 211.
56. Herd, Harold. *Op. cit*. p. 120.
57. Wickwar, William H. *The Struggle for the Freedom of the Press*. G. Allen and Unwin. 1928. 325 pp.
58. Bailey, Samuel. *Essays on the Formation and Publication of Opinions*. R.W. Pomeroy. 1831. 240 pp.
59. Blacow, Richard. *Trial of the Rev. Richard Blacow*. T. Dolby. 1827. 16 pp.
60. Herd, Harold. *Op. cit*. pp. 60, 62.
61. *Ibid*. pp. 120-125.
62. *Ibid*. pp. 120-125.
63. *Ibid*. pp. 120-125.
64. Cleland, John. *Memoirs of a Woman of Pleasure*. Putnam. 1963. pp. xv-xxviii.
65. Hohenberg, John. *Free Press/Free People*. The Free Press. 1973. p. 87.
66. Davison, Thomas. *The Trial of Thomas Davison*. R. Helder. 1820. 58 pp.
67. Dolby, Thomas. *Op. cit*. p. 1114.
68. Hunt, John. *Report of the Trial of the King v. John Hunt*. William Hone. 1821. 40 pp.
69. Herd, Harold. *Op. cit*. p. 119.
70. Salmon, Lucy Maynard. *Op. cit*. p. 250.
71. Phocion. *Phocion in Reply to Cato*. By a Barrister. 1821. 17 pp.
72. Thelwell, John. *Trial of John Thelwell for Seditious Libel, 1821. Annual register*. 1822. p. 351.
73. *Freedom Forum Calendar*. September 5, 1955.
74. Salmon, Lucy Maynard. *Op. cit*. p. 285.

75. Bailey, Samuel. *Op. cit.* 240 pp.
76. Burdett, Sir Francis. "Trial of Sir Francis Burdett." Macdonnell's *Reports of State Trials.* Volume I. 1888. pp. 170.
77. Hohenberg, John. *Op. cit.* p. 93.
78. Herd, Harold. *Op. cit.* p. 124.
79. Mills, James. *Essays ... on the Liberty of the Press. Encyclopedia Britannica.* 1825 34 pp.
80. Barkley, John. *Report of the Trial of John Berkley.* Effingham Wilson. 1822 p. 20.
81. Boyle, Humphrey. *Trial of Humphrey Boyle.* Koran Society. 1822. 32 pp.
82. Herd, Harold. *Op. cit.* p. 123.
83. *Freedom Forum Calendar.* October 19, 997.
84. Waddington, Samuel. "Trial of Samuel Waddington for Publishing a Blasphemous Libel, 1822." Macdonnell's *Report of State Trials.* Volume I. pp 1339-1343.
85. Williams, John Ambrose. *Trial of John Ambrose Williams for a Libel on the Clergy.* Ridgway 1823. 63 pp.
86. Salmon, Lucy Maynard. *Op. cit.* p. 285.
87. Salmon, Lucy Maynard. *Op. cit.* p. 289.
88. Herd, Harold. *Op. cit.* p. 125.
89. Kimball, Edmund. *Reflections upon the Law of Libel.* Wells and Lilly. 1823. 55 pp.
90. Tunbridge, William. *A Report of the Proceedings against William Tunbridge.* R. Carlile. 1823. 160 pp.
91. Watson, James. *A Report on the Trial of James Watson.* R. Carlile. 1825 28 pp
92. Hunt, John. "Trial of John Hunt, 1824." Macdonnell's *Report of State Trials.* Volume 2. pp. 69-103.
93. Herd, Harold. *Op. cit.* pp. 116-118.
94. Hall, Robert. *An Apology for Freedom of the Press.* G.G.J. and J. Robinson. 1793. 103 pp.
95. Bentham, Jeremy. "Liberty and Licentiousness of the Press." *Book of Fallacies.* John Hunt. 1824.
96. Herd, Harold. *Op. cit.* p. 123.
97. *Freedom Forum Calendar.* December 17, 1992.
98. Alter, Ann I. "An Introduction." *Censorship: 500 Years of Conflict.* New York Public Library. 1984. p. 19.
99. Society for the Suppression of Vice. *Reports.* The Society. 1803-1805. Annual.
100. Cook, Samuel. *A Full Report of the Trial of Samuel Cook, Draper.* Samuel Cook. 1827. 72 pp.
101. *Freedom Forum Calendar.* December 30, 1992
102. Herd, Harold. *Op. cit.* p. 123.
103. *Ibid.* p. 116.
104. *Freedom Forum Calendar.* July 24, 1996.
105. Wiener, Joel H. *Op. cit.* p. 92.
106. Salmon, Lucy Maynard. *Op. cit.* p. 199.
107. Herd, Harold. *Op. cit.* p. 123.
108. Salmon, Lucy Maynard. *Op. cit.* p. 202.
109. Herd, Harold. *Op. cit.* pp. 126, 127.
110. Salmon, Lucy Maynard. *Op. cit.* p. 194.
111. *Freedom Forum Calendar.* August 3, 1992.
112. Phillips, Josiah. *The Trial of Josiah Phillips.* J. Hatchard. 1833. 131 pp.
113. Salmon, Lucy Maynard. *Op. cit.* p. 206.
114. Herd, Harold. *Op. cit.* pp. 147, 148.
115. Salmon, Lucy Maynard. *Op. cit.* pp. 198, 199.

116. Forster, Joseph. *The Rejected Address to the Editor of the Weekly Dispatch*. Howlett. 1835.

117. Herd, Harold. *Op. cit.* pp. 126, 127.

118. Salmon, Lucy Maynard. *Op. cit.* pp. 198, 199.

119. New York Public Library. *Censorship: 500 Years of Conflict*. New York Public Library. 1984. p. 94.

120. Salmon, Lucy Maynard. *Op. cit.* p. 195.

121. *Ibid.* p. 181.

122. *Ibid.* p. 306.

123. *Freedom Forum Calendar.* January 24, 1995.

124. *Freedom Forum Calendar.* June 2, 1992.

125. *Freedom Forum Calendar.* March 19, 1993.

126. Herd, Harold. *Op. cit.* p. 126.

127. Moxon, Edward. "The Trial of Edward Moxon." Macdonnell's *Report of State Trials*. Volume 3. pp. 693-722.

128. Southwell, Charles. *The Trial of Charles Southwell.* Hetherington. 1842. 104 pp.

129. Holyoake, George. *The History of the Last Trial by Jury for Atheism in England*. James Watson. 1851. 100 pp.

130. Salmon, Lucy Maynard. *Op. cit.* p. 281.

131. Macaulay, Thomas B. *Critical and Historical Essays*. Volume 3. 1943. p. 256.

132. Salmon, Lucy Maynard. *Op. cit.* pp. 407, 408.

133. Roalfe, Matilda. *Law Breaking Justified*. Matilda Roalfe and Company. 1844. 16 pp.

134. *Freedom Forum Calendar.* April 4, 1992.

135. Finerty, Peter. *Trial of Mr. Peter Finerty.* 1798. 62 pp.

136. Wiener, Joel H. *Op. cit.* p. 92.

137. *Ibid.* p. 97.

138. Gillett, Charles Ripley. *Burned Books*. Columbia University Press. 1932. Volume II. p. 591.

139. Collet, Collet Dobson. *History of the Taxes on Knowledge*. Unwin. 1899. Two volumes.

140. *Freedom Forum Calendar.* July 21, 1993.

141. Wiener, Joel H. *Op. cit.* p. 93.

142. Newman, John Henry. Achilli v. Newman. W. Strange. 1852. 65 pp.

143. *Freedom Forum Calendar.* July 9, 1993.

144. Salmon, Lucy Maynard. *Op. cit.* p. 207.

145. Hohenberg, John. *Op. cit.* p. 151.

146. Herd, Harold. *Op. cit.* p. 203.

147. Doyle, James. *A Special Report of the Trial of the Rev. Vladimir Petcherine*. James Duffy. 1856.

148. Hohenberg, John. *Op. cit.* pp. 130-133.

149. Wiener, Joel H. *Op. cit.* p. 94.

150. Schlesinger, Arthur, Jr. "Preface." *Censorship: 500 Years of Conflict.* New York Public Library. 1984. p. 7.

151. *Freedom Forum Calendar.* July 17, 1996.

152. New York Public Library. *Censorship: 500 Years of Conflict.* New York Public Library. 1984. p. 9.

153. Hohenberg, John. *Op. cit.* p. 127.

154. Siebert, Frederick Seaton. *Op. cit.* pp. 5-7.

155. Salmon, Lucy Maynard. *Op. cit.* pp. 197, 198.

156. Herd, Harold. *Op. cit.* p. 34.

157. Siebert, Frederick Seaton. *Op. cit.* p. 322.
158. Alter Ann I. *Op. cit.* p. 21.
159. Wiener, Joel H. *Op. cit.* p. 99.
160. *Freedom Forum Calendar.* July 16, 1993.
161. Herd, Harold. *Op. cit.* p. 170.
162. Sullivan, Alexander M. and Richard Piggott. *Report of the Trials of Alexander M. Sullivan and Richard Piggott.* Alexander Thom 1868. 286 pp.
163. Stephen, Sir James F. *Liberty, Equality, Fraternity.* Smith and Elder. 1873. 350 pp. (Chapter 2).
164. Wiener, Joel H. *Op. cit.* p. 101.
165. *Freedom Forum Calendar.* November 9, 1995.
166. Knowlton, Charles. *Fruits of Philosophy.* Freethought Publishing Company. 1876. pp. 2-3.
167. *Freedom Forum Calendar.* June 25, 1993.
168. Trulove, Edward. *The Queen v. Edward Trulove.* Edward Trulove. 1878. 125 pp.
169. Society for Suppression of Vice. *Seventy-Sixth Annual Report.* The Society. 1879. pp. 24.
170. *Freedom Forum Calendar.* August 9, 1992.
171. *Freedom Forum Calendar.* July 12, 1994.
172. Foote, George W. *Defence of Free Speech.* Progressive Publishing Company. 1889. 45 pp.
173. Stephen, Sir Leslie. "The Suppression of Poisonous Opinions." *Nineteenth Century.* March 1883. pp. 493-508.
174. Foote, George W., W.J. Ramsey, and H.A. Kemp. *Verbatim Report of the Two Trials for Blasphemous Libel in the Christmas Issue of the 'Freethinker.'* Progressive Publishing Company. 1883. 112 pp.
175. Spender, Stephen. "Thoughts on Censorship in the World of 1884." *Censorship. 500 Years of Conflict.* 1984. pp. 117, 118.
176. Coote, William A. *A Romance of Philanthropy.* National Vigilance Association. 1916. 235 pp.
177. Wiener. Joel H. *Op. cit.* p. 91.
178. Forman, Harry Burton. *Op. cit.* 23 pp.
179. Lilly, W.S. "The Ethics of Journalism." *Forum.* 1889. pp. 503-512.
180. Herd, Harold. *Op. cit.* p. 211.
181. *Freedom Forum Calendar.* March 2, 1994.
182. *Freedom Forum Calendar.* February 24, 1993.
183. *Freedom Forum Calendar.* September 11, 1993.
184. *Freedom Forum Calendar.* October 20, 1993.
185. Spencer, Herbert. "The Rights of Free Speech and Publication." *Principles of Ethics.* Appleton. 1893. pp. 141-147.
186. Salmon, Lucy Maynard. *Op. cit.* p. 1.
187. *Freedom Forum Calendar.* August 12, 1995.
188. Yevish, B.H. "Censorship: Public Libraries." *Censorship.* Winter 1967. pp. 20-27.
189. Bedborough, George. "Police and the Press: Scotland yard Censorship." *Review of Reviews.* August 15, 1899. p. 162.
190. *Freedom Forum Calendar.* April 6, 1993.

Chapter 10

1. Salmon, Lucy Maynard. *The Newspaper and Authority*. Oxford University Press. 1923. p. 15.
2. *Ibid.* p. 257.
3. *Freedom Forum Calendar*. June 4, 1995.
4. *Freedom Forum Calendar*. April 16, 1996.
5. Black, Eugene C. "The Eighteenth Century: Control and Revolution." *Censorship: 500 Years of Conflict*. New York Public Library. 1984. p. 71.
6. Salmon, Lucy Maynard. *Op. cit.* pp. 239, 240.
7. *Freedom Forum Calendar*. August 31, 1995.
8. Salmon, Lucy Maynard. *Op. cit.* p. 53.
9. Hohenberg, John. *Free Press/Free People*. The Free Press. 1973. p. 94.
10. *Freedom Forum Calendar*. January 9, 1995.
11. Salmon, Lucy Maynard. *Op. cit.* p. 59.
12. *Ibid.* p.
13. *Ibid.* p. 227.
14. *Ibid.* p. 287.
15. *Freedom Forum Calendar*. March 6, 1993.
16. Salmon, Lucy Maynard. *Op. cit.* p. 227.
17. New York Public Library. *Censorship: 500 Years of Conflict*. New York Public Library. 1984. pp. 19-23.
18. Hohenberg, John. *Op. cit.* pp. 106, 107.
19. *Ibid.* p. 92.
20. *Ibid.* pp. 93, 94.
21. Melot, Michel. "The Image in France." *Censorship: 500 Years of Conflict*. New York Public Library. 1984. p. 83.
22. Hohenberg, John. *Op. cit.* p. 90.
23. New York Public Library. *Op. cit.* p. 85.
24. Salmon, Lucy Maynard. *Op. cit.* pp. 84-87.
25. *Ibid.* p. 5.
26. Gerard (Grandville), Jean-Ignace Isidor. "The Decent on the Pressroom of Liberty of the Press." *Censorship: 500 Years of Conflict*. New York Public Library. 1984. End papers.
27. Salmon, Lucy Maynard. *Op. cit.* p. 296.
28. *Ibid.* p. 257.
29. *Ibid.* p. 18.
30. *Freedom Forum Calendar*. November 4, 1997.
31. *Freedom Forum Calendar*. March 23, 1996.
32. *Freedom Forum Calendar*. March 29, 1993.
33. Hohenberg, John. *Op. cit.* pp. 106, 107.
34. Salmon, Lucy Maynard. *Op. cit.* p. 257.
35. Hohenberg, John. *Op. cit.* p. 105.
36. *Freedom Forum Calendar*. May 6, 1995.
37. *Freedom Forum Calendar*. May 17, 1996.
38. Salmon, Lucy Maynard. *Op. cit.* p. 251.
39. Hohenberg, John. *Op. cit.* p. 109.
40. *Freedom Forum Calendar*. March 20, 1993.
41. *Freedom Forum Calendar*. December 5, 1995.
42. Salmon, Lucy Maynard. *Op. cit.* p. 59.
43. *Freedom Forum Calendar*. April 25, 1994.
44. *Freedom Forum Calendar*. August 6, 1993.

45. Hohenberg, John. *Op. cit.* pp. 102-103.
46. Salmon, Lucy Maynard. *Op. cit.* p. 67.
47. *Freedom Forum Calendar*. December 5, 1992.
48. *Freedom Forum Calendar*. February 9, 1993.
49. *Freedom Forum Calendar*. February 24, 1995.
50. Hohenberg, John. *Op. cit.* p. 142.
51. Salmon, Lucy Maynard. *Op. cit.* p. 140.
52. *Freedom Forum Calendar*. December 13, 1993.
53. Salmon, Lucy Maynard. *Op. cit.* p. 47.
54. Melot, Michel. *Op. cit.* p. 86.
55. Salmon, Lucy Maynard. *Op. cit.* p. 247.
56. *Ibid.* p. 256.
57. *Freedom Forum Calendar*. December 24, 1996.
58. Hohenberg, John. *Op. cit.* pp. 137-139.
59. *Freedom Forum Calendar*. March 18, 1993.
60. Salmon, Lucy Maynard. *Op. cit.* p. 225.
61. *Freedom Forum Calendar*. May 29, 1993.
62. Melot, Michel. *Op. cit.* pp. 88, 89.
63. *Freedom Forum Calendar*. March 29, 1995.
64. Hohenberg, John. *Op. cit.* p. 135.
65. *Freedom Forum Calendar*. March 10, 1996.
66. *Freedom Forum Calendar*. August 17, 1997.
67. Hohenberg, John. *Op. cit.* p. 214.
68. Salmon, Lucy Maynard. *Op. cit.* pp. 233, 234.
69. *Freedom Forum Calendar*. August 26, 1993
70. Hohenberg, John. *Op. cit.* p. 214.
71. *Freedom Forum Calendar*. May 8, 1992.
72. Wiener, Joel H. *Op. cit.* p. 99.
73. Salmon, Lucy Maynard. *Op. cit* p. 248.
74. Alter, Ann I. *Op. cit.* p. 22.
75. *Freedom Forum Calendar*. September 3, 1993
76. *Freedom Forum Calendar*. January 12, 1996.

Chapter 11

1. Salmon, Lucy Maynard. *The Newspaper and Authority*. Oxford University Press. 1923. p. 13.
2. *Freedom Forum Calendar*. September 26, 1995.
3. Council for Civil Liberties. *Six Arts Against Civil Liberties*. The Council. 1937. 27 pp.
4. *Freedom Forum Calendar*. April 16, 1992.
5. Salmon, Lucy Maynard. *Op. cit.* pp. 266, 267.
6. *Freedom Forum Calendar*. December 21, 1993.
7. Hohenberg, John. *Free Press/Free People*. The Free Press. 1973. p. 154.
8. *Ibid.* p. 154.
9. Russell, Sir Edward. *A Report of the Trial of Sir Edward Russell*. Liverpool Daily Post and Mercury. 1905. 251 pp.
10. *Freedom Forum Calendar*. July 19, 1996.
11. Salmon, Lucy Maynard. *Op. cit.* p. 13.

12. *Freedom Forum Calendar*. June 27, 1994.

13. Salmon, Lucy Maynard. *Op. cit.* p. 73.

14. *Freedom Forum Calendar*. March 27, 1992.

15. *Freedom Forum Calendar*. November 21, 1996.

16. *Freedom Forum Calendar*. July 25, 1994.

17. Hohenberg, John. *Op. cit.* p. 155.

18. Horn. K.A.R. "The Censorship of Indecent Publications in New Zealand." *New Zealand Libraries. March* 1949. pp. 25-29.

19. Salmon, Lucy Maynard. *Op. cit.* p. 80.

20. Allen, Carleton K. "Movies and Morals." *Quarterly Review.* July 1925. pp. 313-330.

21. "D_____." *Librarian.* March 1913. pp. 281-283.

22. *Freedom Forum* Calendar. May 30, 1992.

23. *Freedom Forum* Calendar. August 14, 1996.

24. Salmon, Lucy Maynard. *Op. cit.* p. 168.

25. *Ibid.* p. 110.

26. Herd, Harold. *The March of Journalism.* George Allen and Unwin. 1952. p. 258.

27. Salmon, Lucy Maynard. *Op. cit.* p. 12.

28. *Ibid.* p. 74.

29. "Gagging the Press in China." *The Literary Digest.* January 24, 1948. p. 152.

30. Salmon, Lucy Maynard. *Op. cit.* p. 44.

31. *Ibid.* pp. 57, 58.

32. *Ibid.* p. 248.

33. *Ibid.* p. 99.

34. *Ibid.* p. 105.

35. *Ibid.* p. 99.

36. *Ibid.* p. 267.

37. *Ibid.* pp. 248, 249.

38. Herd, Harold. *Op. cit.* pp. 242-244.

39. Salmon, Lucy Maynard. *Op. cit.* p. 384.

40. *Freedom Forum Calendar.* January 24, 1995

41. Salmon, Lucy Maynard. *Op. cit.* p. 90.

42. *Ibid.* p. 94.

43. *Ibid.* p. 13.

44. *Ibid.* p. 109.

45. *Ibid.* p. 12.

46. *Ibid.* pp. 101, 102.

47. *Ibid.* p. 169.

48. *Ibid.* p. 89.

49. O'Leary, Jeremiah A. *Awake! Awake! The Constitution Attacked.* American Truth Society. 1917. 8 pp.

50. Salmon, Lucy Maynard. *Op. cit.* p. 90.

51. *Ibid.* p. 45.

52. *Ibid.* p. 60.

53. *Ibid.* p. 100.

54. *Ibid.* pp. 99, 100.

55. "The Press and the Censorship in England and France." *Nation.* September 13, 1947. pp. 282-289.

56. Salmon, Lucy Maynard. *Op. cit.* p. 12.

57. *Ibid.* p. 101.

58. Lenin. U.S. "On the Freedom of the Press " *Laboer Monthly*. January 1925. pp. 35-37.
59. Salmon, Lucy Maynard. *Op. cit.* p. 72.
60. *Ibid*. p. 39.
61. *Freedom Forum Calendar*. March 3, 1997.
62. Salmon, Lucy Maynard. *Op. cit.* p. 89.
63. Hohenberg, John. *Op. cit.* p. 181.
64. Salmon, Lucy Maynard. *Op. cit.* p. 102.
65. *Ibid*. p. 104.
66. *Ibid*. pp. 88, 89.
67. Hohenberg, John. *Op. cit.* p. 180.
68. Salmon, Lucy Maynard. *Op. cit.* p. 57.
69. *Ibid*. p. 106.
70. Hohenberg, John. *Op. cit.* p. 181.
71. *Ibid*. p. 215.
72. Salmon, Lucy Maynard. *Op. cit.* p. 109.
73. *Ibid*. p. 92.
74. The Literary Digest reported of January 19, 1918, as quoted by Lucy Maynard salmon in *The Newspaper and Authority*. Oxford University Press. 1923. p. 71.
75. Salmon, Lucy Maynard. *Op. cit.* p. 91.
76. *Ibid*. p. 103.
77. *Ibid*. p. 309.
78. *Ibid*. p. 88.
79. *Ibid*. p. 110.
80. *Freedom Forum Calendar*. September 16, 1993.
81. Salmon, Lucy Maynard. *Op. cit.* p. 13.
82. Rogers, Bruce. "In Alaska." *Liberator*. February 1919. pp. 45-46.
83. Salmon, Lucy Maynard. *Op. cit.* p. 13.
84. *Ibid*. p. 92.
85. *Freedom Forum Calendar*. April 20, 1993.
86. Salmon, Lucy Maynard. *Op. cit.* p. 33.
87. *Ibid*. p. 110.
88. Hohenberg, John. *Op. cit.* p. 221.
89. *Freedom Forum Calendar*. October 10, 1997.
90. *Freedom Forum Calendar*. July 29, 1996.
91. *Freedom Forum Calendar*. December 2, 1992.
92. *Freedom Forum Calendar*. July 8, 1993.
93. *Freedom Forum Calendar*. January 14, 1994.
94. Hohenberg, John. *Op. cit.* pp. 211, 212.
95. *Freedom Forum Calendar*. November 1, 1996.
96. League of Nations International Conference for the Suppression of the Circulation and of Traffic in Obscene Publications. *Final Act*. The League. 1923. 4 pp.
97. *Freedom Forum Calendar*. June 15, 1995.
98. *Freedom Forum Calendar*. February 17, 1993.
99. Salmon, Lucy Maynard. *Op. cit.* p. 114.
100. *Freedom Forum Calendar*. February 19, 1996.
101. *Freedom Forum Calendar*. November 4, 1993.
102. *Freedom Forum Calendar*. February 21, 1992.
103. *Freedom Forum Calendar*. May 26, 1993.
104. Salmon, Lucy Maynard. *Op. cit.* p. 114.

105. Wilkinson, Clennell. "The Cinema and the Puritan." *Outlook*. January 6, 1923. p. 13.

Chapter 12

1. Hohenberg, John. *Free Press/Free People*. The Free Press. 1973. p. .
2. *Freedom Forum Calendar*. April 7, 1992.
3. *Freedom Forum Calendar*. December 9, 1995.
4. Committee on Freedom of the Press. *Report of the Committee on Freedom of the Press*. Inter-American Press Association. 1962. (Paging varies).
5. Yeats, William Butler. "The Irish Censorship." *Spectator*. September 29, 1928. pp. 391, 392.
6. Spender, Stephen. "Thoughts on Censorship in the World of 1984." *Censorship: 500 Years of Conflict*. New York Public Library. 1984. p. 117.
7. *Freedom Forum Calendar*. February 13, 1993.
8. *Freedom Forum Calendar*. August 20, 1992.
9. *Freedom Forum Calendar*. August 9, 1994.
10. *Freedom Forum Calendar*. November 26, 1994.
11. *Freedom Forum Calendar*. April 13, 1992
12. Special Committee for Licensing. Censorship of Cinematograph Films. County Council. 1929. 8 pp.
13. *Freedom Forum Calendar*. December 5, 1997.
14. *Freedom Forum Calendar*. September 14, 1993.
15. Hohenberg, John. *Op. cit.* p. 225.
16. *Freedom Forum Calendar*. February 26, 1992.
17. *Freedom Forum Calendar*. July 22, 1995.
18. Lawrence, D.H. *Dirty Words*. 1931. 6 pp. (Warren Roberts, however, in his *Biography of D.H. Lawrence* doubts that the statement was made by Lawrence. p. 370.)
19. Spender, John A. "Liberty of the Press." *Spectator*. November 22, 1935. pp. 857, 858.
20. *Freedom Forum Calendar*. April 6, 1996.
21. "Publishers Protest Leipzig Congress." *Publishers Weekly*. January 15, 1938. pp. 211-213.
22. Hohenberg, John. *Op. cit.* p. 229.
23. *Freedom Forum Calendar*. April 21, 1992.
24. "Celluloid Censorship." *Time*. June 1, 1936. pp. 40-42.
25. Brown, S.J.M. "Note on Censorship of Literature." *Libraries and Literature from a Catholic Standpoint*. Browne and Nolan. 1937. pp. 293-304.
26. *Freedom Forum Calendar*. December 16, 1994.
27. *Freedom Forum Calendar*. July 5, 1994.
28. Hohenberg, John. *Op. cit.* pp. 220-226.
29. *Ibid*. p. 295.
30. *Freedom Forum Calendar*. February 17, 1994.
31. Ingle, Lorne. "Control of the Press." *Alberta Law Quarterly*. April 1939. pp. 127-130.
32. Hohenberg, John. *Op. cit.* p. 241.
33. *Freedom Forum Calendar*. January 3, 1992.
34. Walpole, Sir Hugh. *The Freedom of Books*. National Book Council. 1940. 4 pp.
35. *Freedom Forum Calendar*. October 29, 1996.
36. *Freedom Forum Calendar*. August 16, 1995.
37. *Freedom Forum Calendar*. September 29, 1995.

38. Stephens, Alfred G. "On Censorship." In Vance Palmer's *A.G. Stephens: His Life and Works*. Robertson and Mullens. 1941. pp 218-221.

39. *Freedom Forum Calendar*. April 14, 1992.

40. *Freedom Forum Calendar*. December 4, 1993.

41. *Freedom Forum Calendar*. February 1, 1997.

42. Orwell, George. "The Prevention of Literature." *Atlantic Monthly*. March 1947. pp. 115-119.

43. Department of Justice Censorship of Publications Board. *Register of Prohibited Publications*. Stationery Office. 1931 on. Revised periodically.

44. *Freedom Forum Calendar*. December 13, 1994.

45. *Freedom Forum Calendar*. May 6, 1992.

46. *Freedom Forum Calendar*. December 19, 1993.

47. Hohenberg, John. *Op. cit.* p. 304.

48. Herd, Harold. *The March of Journalism*. George Allen and Unwn. 1952. pp. 312-317.

49. *Ibid.* p. 322.

50. *Freedom Forum Calendar*. July 27, 1992.

51. *Freedom Forum Calendar*. January 3, 1992.

52. Hohenberg, John. *Op. cit.* p. 318.

53. *Ibid.* p. 299.

54. Kauffman, Stanley. *The Philanderer*. Secker and warburg. 1954. 300 pp.

55. *Freedom Forum Calendar*. February 21, 1992.

56. Hohenberg, John. *Op. cit.* p. 304.

57. *Ibid.* p. 330.

58. Campbell, Walter B. "Censorship of Literature in Queensland." *Queensland law Journal*. December 1958. pp. 244-257.

59. *Freedom Forum Calendar*. July 20, 1992.

60. Spender Stephen. "Thoughts on Censorship in the World of 1984." *Op. cit.* p. 119.

61. *Freedom Forum Calendar*. April 26, 1992.

62. *Freedom Forum Calendar*. October 13, 1993.

63. Hohenberg, John. *Op. cit.* p. 433.

64. *Freedom Forum Calendar*. September 17, 1993.

65. *Ibid.* p. 292.

66. *Freedom Forum Calendar*. November 11, 1994.

67. *Freedom Forum Calendar*. December 26, 1994.

68. *Freedom Forum Calendar*. August 15, 1993.

69. *Freedom Forum Calendar*. March 1, 1993.

70. *Freedom Forum Calendar*. May 26, 1992.

71. *Freedom Forum Calendar*. November 30, 1996.

72. *Freedom Forum Calendar*. October 10, 1995.

73. Hohenberg, John. *Op. cit.* pp. 330-331.

74. *Freedom Forum Calendar*. May 19, 1995.

75. *Freedom Forum Calendar*. March 31, 1993.

76. *Freedom Forum Calendar*. September 25, 1993.

77. *Freedom Forum Calendar*. October 5, 1995.

78. *Freedom Forum Calendar*. February 28, 1992.

79. *Freedom Forum Calendar*. June 8, 1996.

Chapter 13

1. *Freedom Forum Calendar.* January 16, 1996.
2. *Freedom Forum Calendar.* March 10, 1993.
3. Byrnes, J.V. "Our First Book Trial and Conviction of Dr. William Bland." *Biblionews and Australian Notes and Queries.* August 1962. pp. 22, 23.
4. *Freedom Forum Calendar.* January 26, 1996.
5. *Freedom Forum Calendar.* January 13, 1997.
6. *Freedom Forum Calendar.* November 30, 1996.
7. *Freedom Forum Calendar.* May 4, 1992.
8. "*Lady Chatterley*: Turn up for the Book." *Economist.* November 5, 1960. p. 536.
9. Girodias, Maurice. "Confessions of a Booklegger's Son." *Censorship.* Summer 1965. pp. 2-16.
10. *Freedom Forum Calendar.* July 11, 1996.
11. *Freedom Forum Calendar.* April 11, 1996.
12. *Freedom Forum Calendar.* December 21, 1996.
13. *Freedom Forum Calendar.* January 1, 1995.
14. Harley, John E. "Some Case Studies of Official National Censorship of Motion Pictures." *World Affairs Interpreter.* January 1951. pp. 428-433.
15. *Freedom Forum Calendar.* June 18, 1995.
16. *Freedom Forum Calendar.* December 6, 1992.
17. *Freedom Forum Calendar.* November 24, 1992.
18. *Freedom Forum Calendar.* December 8, 1992.
19. *Freedom Forum Calendar.* November 7, 1997.
20. *Freedom Forum Calendar.* November 29, 1994.
21. *Freedom Forum Calendar.* March 28, 1994.
22. "Bow Street and After." *Bookseller.* February 22, 1964. pp. 1074-1076.
23. Girodias, Maurice. "The Arrest of Maurice; Literary Censorship in France." *City Lights Journal.* 1964. pp. 7-13.
24. *Freedom Forum Calendar.* August 14, 1992.
25. *Freedom Forum Calendar.* January 11, 1993.
26. *Freedom Forum Calendar.* January 24, 1997.
27. "Indecent Publications Tribunal: The First Decision." *New Zealand Libraries.* April 1964. pp. 62, 63.
28. Fryer, Peter. *Mrs. Grundy, Studies in English Prudery.* House and Maxwell. 1964. p. 368.
29. Hohenberg, John. *Free Press/Free People.* The Free Press. 1973. p. 373.
30. *Freedom Forum Calendar.* June 4, 1992.
31. Hohenberg, John. *Op. cit.* p. 363.
32. *Freedom Forum Calendar.* March 23, 1993.
33. Hohenberg, John. *Op. cit.* p. 409.
34. Comyn, Andrew F. "Censorship in Ireland." *Studies.* Spring 1969. pp. 42-50.
35. Hohenberg, John. *Op. cit.* p. 407.
36. *Freedom Forum Calendar.* November 19, 1994.
37. "'Last Exit' Conviction Quashed." *Bookseller.* August 3, 1968. pp. 358-362.
38. Hohenberg, John. *Op. cit.* p. 362.
39. *Ibid.* p. 355.
40. *Freedom Forum Calendar.* June 1, 1992.
41. Orchard William H. "Censorship: A Psychiatrist's View." *Meanjin Quarterly.* Spring 1969. 28:385-390.
42. Hohenberg, John. *Op. cit.* p. 364.

43. *Freedom Forum Calendar*. April 5, 1994.
44. Hohenberg, John. *Op. cit.* p. 399.
45. *Ibid.* p. 402.
46. *Freedom Forum Calendar*. January 23, 1996.
47. Hohenberg, John. *Op. cit.* p. 399.
48. *Ibid.* p. 399.
49. *Ibid.* p. 402.
50. *Freedom Forum Calendar*. September 19, 1996.
51. *Freedom Forum Calendar*. December 20, 1994.
52. *Freedom Forum Calendar*. December 4, 1997.
53. Whitehouse, Mary. "Freedom or License?" *Books*. Summer 1972. pp. 16-19
54. Hohenberg, John. *Op. cit.* p. 365.
55. *Ibid.* p. 511.
56. *Freedom Forum Calendar*. February 25, 1993.
57. *Freedom Forum Calendar*. June 12, 1994.
58. *Freedom Forum Calendar*. August 20, 1995.
59. *Freedom Forum Calendar*. May 13, 1994.
60. *Freedom Forum Calendar*. March 12, 1994.
61. *Freedom Forum Calendar*. February 27, 1995.
62. *Freedom Forum Calendar*. April 17, 1994.
63. *Freedom Forum Calendar*. August 2, 1994.

Chapter 14

1. *Freedom Forum Calendar*. March 21, 1996.
2. *Freedom Forum Calendar*. December 27, 1994.
3. *Freedom Forum Calendar*. September 19, 1995.
4. *Freedom Forum Calendar*. March 19, 1997.
5. *Freedom Forum Calendar*. February 27, 1993.
6. *Freedom Forum Calendar*. May 28, 1992.
7. *Freedom Forum Calendar*. August 10, 1997.
8. *Freedom Forum Calendar*. June 2, 1997.
9. *Freedom Forum Calendar*. July 23, 1996.
10. *Freedom Forum Calendar*. September 1995.
11. *Freedom Forum Calendar*. December 19, 1995.
12. *Freedom Forum Calendar*. September 25, 1993.
13. *Freedom Forum Calendar*. February 28, 1992.
14. Russell, Bertrand. *Wisdom of the West*. Rathbone. 1959.
15. *Freedom Forum Calendar*. January 7, 1997.
16. *Freedom Forum Calendar*. July 7, 1993.
17. *Freedom Forum Calendar*. December 15, 1994.
18. *Freedom Forum Calendar*. May 7, 1994.
19. *Freedom Forum Calendar*. October 26, 1993.
20. *Freedom Forum Calendar*. March 16, 1994.
21. *Freedom Forum Calendar*. March 29, 1996.
22. *Freedom Forum Calendar*. September 23, 1993.
23. *Freedom Forum Calendar*. January 3, 1993.
24. *Freedom Forum Calendar*. November 17, 1992.

25. *Freedom Forum Calendar*. March 14, 1992.
26. *Freedom Forum Calendar*. September 22, 1992.
27. *Freedom Forum Calendar*. November 1, 1992.
28. *Freedom Forum Calendar*. February 16, 1992.
29. *Freedom Forum Calendar*. February 19, 1992.
30. *Freedom Forum Calendar*. November 18, 1992.
31. *Freedom Forum Calendar*. February 8, 1992.
32. *Freedom Forum Calendar*. August 28, 1992.
33. *Freedom Forum Calendar*. July 15, 1992.
34. *Freedom Forum Calendar*. November 17, 1993.
35. *Freedom Forum Calendar*. July 3, 1992.
36. *Freedom Forum Calendar*. January 17, 1992.
37. *Freedom Forum Calendar*. February 24, 1992.
38. *Freedom Forum Calendar*. January 10, 1992.
39. *Freedom Forum Calendar*. December 24, 1992.
40. *Freedom Forum Calendar*. January 5, 1993.
41. *Freedom Forum Calendar*. August 20, 1993.
42. *Freedom Forum Calendar*. August 19, 1993.
43. *Freedom Forum Calendar*. August 3, 1993.
44. *Freedom Forum Calendar*. July 18, 1993.
45. *Freedom Forum Calendar*. June 22, 1994.
46. *Freedom Forum Calendar*. October 3, 1993.
47. *Freedom Forum Calendar*. August 21, 1993.
48. *Freedom Forum Calendar*. November 9, 1992.
49. *Freedom Forum Calendar*. December 3, 1993.
50. *Freedom Forum Calendar*. December 27, 1993.
51. *Freedom Forum Calendar*. January 16, 1992.
52. *Freedom Forum Calendar*. April 5, 1993.
53. *Freedom Forum Calendar*. April 22, 1995.
54. *Freedom Forum Calendar*. December 28, 1993.
55. *Freedom Forum Calendar*. September 28, 1993.
56. *Freedom Forum Calendar*. November 1, 1993.
57. *Freedom Forum Calendar*. February 21, 1993.
58. *Freedom Forum Calendar*. June 7, 1993.
59. *Freedom Forum Calendar*. August 28, 1994.
60. *Freedom Forum Calendar*. February 8, 1994.
61. *Freedom Forum Calendar*. December 28, 1994.
62. *Freedom Forum Calendar*. October 18, 1995.
63. *Freedom Forum Calendar*. February 24, 1994.
64. *Freedom Forum Calendar*. December 11, 1994.
65. *Freedom Forum Calendar*. May 11, 1997.
66.. *Freedom Forum Calendar*. August 29, 1996.
67. *Freedom Forum Calendar*. June 26, 1995.
68. *Freedom Forum Calendar*. January 22, 1996.
69. *Freedom Forum Calendar*. November 8, 1997.
70. *Freedom Forum Calendar*. July 24, 1995.
71. *Freedom Forum Calendar*. February 7, 1997.

72. *Freedom Forum Calendar*. March 14, 1997.

Chapter 15

1. *Freedom Forum Calendar*. May 17, 1996.
2. *Freedom Forum Calendar*. July 13, 1996.
3. *Freedom Forum Calendar*. August 25, 1996.
4. *Freedom Forum Calendar*. January 30, 1996.
5. *Freedom Forum Calendar*. June 26, 1997.
6. *Freedom Forum Calendar*. April 3, 1995.
7. *Freedom Forum Calendar*. August 24, 1995.
8. *Freedom Forum Calendar*. August 10, 1995.
9. *Freedom Forum Calendar*. October 9, 1996.
10. *Freedom Forum Calendar*. March 17, 1996.
11. *Freedom Forum Calendar*. September 25, 1996.
12. *Freedom Forum Calendar*. August 8, 1996.
13. *Freedom Forum Calendar*. May 1, 1995.
14. *Freedom Forum Calendar*. May 21, 1996.
15. *Freedom Forum Calendar*. March 8, 1996.
16. *Freedom Forum Calendar*. November 20, 1995.
17. *Freedom Forum Calendar*. December 24, 1997.
18. *Freedom Forum Calendar*. February 27, 1996.
19. *Freedom Forum Calendar*. January 11, 1996.
20. *Freedom Forum Calendar*. May 4, 1995.
21. *Freedom Forum Calendar*. May 5, 1995.
22. *Freedom Forum Calendar*. August 12, 1996.
23. *Freedom Forum Calendar*. December 2, 1995.
24. *Freedom Forum Calendar*. November 13, 1995.
25. *Freedom Forum Calendar*. October 11, 1996.
26. *Freedom Forum Calendar*. October 28, 1995.
27. *Freedom Forum Calendar*. June 8, 1995.
28. *Freedom Forum Calendar*. June 6, 1996.
29. *"Index* Index." *Index on Censorship*. No. 5. 1995. p. 169.
30. *"Index* Index." *Op. cit.* No. 5. p. 169.
31. *"Index* Index." *Op. cit.* No. 4. 1995. p. 169.
32. *"Index* Index." *Op. cit.* No. 1. 1996. p. 169.
33. *"Index* Index." *Op. cit.* No. 2. 1995. p. 168.
34. *"Index* Index." *Op. cit.* No. 4. 1995. p. 169.
35. *"Index* Index." *Op. cit.* No. 6. 1995. p. 167.
36. *"Index* Index." *Op. cit.* No. 2. 1995. p. 168.
37. *"Index* Index." *Op. cit.* No. 2. 1995. p. 169.
38. *"Index* Index." *Op. cit.* No. 2. 1995. p. 169.
39. *"Index* Index." *Op. cit.* No. 4. 1995. p. 170.
40. *"Index* Index." *Op. cit.* No. 2. 1995. p. 169.
41. *"Index* Index." *Op. cit.* No. 5. 1995. p. 170.
42. *"Index* Index." *Op. cit.* No. 3. 1995. p. 168.
43. *"Index* Index." *Op. cit.* No. 2. 1995. p. 170.
44. *"Index* Index." *Op. cit.* No. 4. 1995. p. 170.

45. *"Index* Index." *Op. cit.* No. 5. 1995. p. 170.
46. *"Index* Index." *Op. cit.* No. 4. 1995. p. 171.
47. *"Index* Index." *Op. cit.* No. 5. 1995. p. 171.
48. *"Index* Index." *Op. cit.* No. 6. 1995. p. 169.
49. *"Index* Index." *Op. cit.* No. 4. 1995. p. 171.
50. *"Index* Index." *Op. cit.* No. 3. 1995. p. 171.
51. *"Index* Index." *Op. cit.* No. 2. 1995. p. 171.
52. *"Index* Index." *Op. cit.* No. 5. 1995. p. 173.
53. *"Index* Index." *Op. cit.* No. 2. 1995. p. 172.
54. *"Index* Index." *Op. cit.* No. 4. 1995. p. 172.
55. *"Index* Index." *Op. cit.* No. 6. 1995. p. 170.
56. *"Index* Index." *Op. cit.* No. 6. 1995. p. 174.
57. *"Index* Index." *Op. cit.* No. 6. 1995. p. 172.
58. *"Index* Index." *Op. cit.* No. 2. 1995. p. 172.
59. *"Index* Index." *Op. cit.* No. 2. 1995. p. 172.
60. *"Index* Index." *Op. cit.* No. 3. 1995. p. 172.
61. *"Index* Index." *Op. cit.* No. 3. 1995. p. 172.
62. *"Index* Index." *Op. cit.* No. 3. 1995. p. 172.
63. *"Index* Index." *Op. cit.* No. 4. 1995. p. 173.
64. *"Index* Index." *Op. cit.* No. 5. 1995. p. 174.
65. *"Index* Index." *Op. cit.* No. 1. 1996. p. 174.
66. *"Index* Index." *Op. cit.* No. 3. 1995. p. 173.
67. *"Index* Index." *Op. cit.* No. 4. 1995. p. 173.
68. *"Index* Index." *Op. cit.* No. 5. 1995. p. 175.
69. *"Index* Index." *Op. cit.* No. 1. 1996. p. 174.
70. *"Index* Index." *Op. cit.* No. 4. 1995. p. 174.
71. *"Index* Index." *Op. cit.* No. 4. 1995. p. 174.
72. *"Index* Index." *Op. cit.* No. 2. 1995. p. 172.
73. *"Index* Index." *Op. cit.* No. 4. 1995. p. 174.
74. *"Index* Index." *Op. cit.* No. 2. 1995. p. 173.
75. *"Index* Index." *Op. cit.* No. 2. 1995. p. 173.
76. *"Index* Index." *Op. cit.* No. 2. 1995. p. 174.
77. *"Index* Index." *Op. cit.* No. 4. 1995. p. 175.
78. *"Index* Index." *Op. cit.* No. 2. 1995. p. 175.
79. *"Index* Index." *Op. cit.* No. 1. 1996. p. 175.
80. *"Index* Index." *Op. cit.* No. 4. 1995. p. 176.
81. *"Index* Index." *Op. cit.* No. 3. 1995. p. 174.
82. *"Index* Index." *Op. cit.* No. 2. 1995. p. 174.
83. *"Index* Index." *Op. cit.* No. 4. 1995. p. 176.
84. *"Index* Index." *Op. cit.* No. 3. 1995. p. 176.
85. *"Index* Index." *Op. cit.* No. 2. 1995. p. 177.
86. *"Index* Index." *Op. cit.* No. 3. 1995. p. 177.
87. *"Index* Index." *Op. cit.* No. 4. 1995. p. 178.
88. *"Index* Index." *Op. cit.* No. 5. 1995. p. 179.
89. *"Index* Index." *Op. cit.* No. 2. 1995. p. 177.
90. *"Index* Index." *Op. cit.* No. 3. 1995. p. 178.
91. *"Index* Index." *Op. cit.* No. 5. 1995. p. 180.
92. *"Index* Index." *Op. cit.* No. 5. 1995. p. 180.
93. *"Index* Index." *Op. cit.* No. 5. 1995. p. 180.

94. *"Index* Index." *Op. cit.* No. 3. 1995. p. 178.
95. *"Index* Index." *Op. cit.* No. 5. 1995. p 180.
96. *"Index* Index." *Op. cit.* No. 3. 1995. p. 179.
97. *"Index* Index." *Op. cit.* No. 2. 1995. p. 179.
98. *"Index* Index." *Op. cit.* No. 2. 1995. p. 179.
99. *"Index* Index." *Op. cit.* No. 4. 1995. p. 180.
100. *"Index* Index." *Op. cit.* No. 2. 1995. p. 179.
101. *"Index* Index." *Op. cit.* No. 2. 1995. p. 181.
102. *"Index* Index." *Op. cit.* No. 2. 1995. p. 180.
103. *"Index* Index." *Op. cit.* No. 2. 1995. p. 180.
104. *"Index* Index." *Op. cit.* No. 2. 1995. p. 181.
105. *"Index* Index." *Op. cit.* No. 3. 1995. p. 182.
106. *"Index* Index." *Op. cit.* No. 2. 1995. p. 182.
107. *"Index* Index." *Op. cit.* No. 4. 1995. p. 183.
108. *"Index* Index." *Op. cit.* No. 4. 1995. p. 183.
109. *"Index* Index." *Op. cit.* No. 2. 1995. p. 183
110. *"Index* Index." *Op. cit.* No. 3. 1995. p. 184.
111. *"Index* Index." *Op. cit.* No. 4. 1995. p. 184.
112. *"Index* Index." *Op. cit.* No. 2. 1995. p. 184.
113. *"Index* Index." *Op. cit.* No. 4. 1995. p. 184.
114. *"Index* Index." *Op. cit.* No. 4. 1995. p. 185.
115. *"Index* Index." *Op. cit.* No. 2. 1995. p. 186.
116. *"Index* Index." *Op. cit.* No. 3. 1995. p. 186.
117. *"Index* Index." *Op. cit.* No. 4. 1995. p. 186.
118. *"Index* Index." *Op. cit.* No. 3. 1995. p. 186.
119. *"Index* Index." *Op. cit.* No. 3. 1995. p. 186.
120. *"Index* Index." *Op. cit.* No. 2. 1995. p. 187.
121. *"Index* Index." *Op. cit.* No. 2. 1995. p. 187.
122. *"Index* Index." *Op. cit.* No. 3. 1995. p. 186.
123. *"Index* Index." *Op. cit.* No. 4. 1995. p. 187.
124. *"Index* Index." *Op. cit.* No. 5. 1995. p. 188.
125. *"Index* Index." *Op cit.* No. 1. 1995. p. 250.
126. *"Index* Index." *Op. cit.* No. 4. 1995. p. 187.
127. *"Index* Index." *Op. cit.* No. 2. 1995. p. 187.
128. *"Index* Index." *Op. cit.* No. 2. 1995. p. 187.
129. *"Index* Index." *Op. cit.* No. 3. 1995. p. 187.
130. *"Index* Index." *Op. cit.* No. 3. 1995. p. 188.
131. *"Index* Index." *Op. cit.* No. 2. 1995. p. 187.
132. *"Index* Index." *Op. cit.* No. 3. 1995. p. 188.
133. *"Index* Index." *Op. cit.* No. 3. 1995. p. 188.
134. *"Index* Index." *Op. cit.* No. 4. 1995. p. 189.
135. *"Index* Index." *Op. cit.* No. 4. 1995. p. 189.
136. *"Index* Index." *Op. cit.* No. 2. 1995. p. 189.
137. *"Index* Index." *Op. cit.* No. 2. 1995. p. 179.
138. *"Index* Index." *Op. cit.* No. 4. 1995. p. 188.
139. *"Index* Index." *Op. cit.* No. 5. 1995. p. 190.
140. *"Index* Index." *Op. cit.* No. 6. 1995. p. 188.
141. *"Index* Index." *Op. cit.* No. 4. 1995. p. 198.
142. *"Index* Index." *Op. cit.* No. 4. 1995. p. 192.

143. *"Index* Index." *Op. cit.* No. 1. 1996. p. 192.
144. *"Index* Index." *Op. cit.* No. 2. 1995. p. 191.
145. *"Index* Index." *Op. cit.* No. 5. 1995. p. 192.
146. *Freedom Forum Calendar.* April 12, 1998.
147. *Freedom Forum Calendar.* June 15, 1998.
148. *Freedom Forum Calendar.* July 15, 1998.
149. *Freedom Forum Calendar.* January 28, 1998.
150. *Freedom Forum Calendar.* June 26, 1998.
151. *Freedom Forum Calendar.* February 5, 1998.
152. *Freedom Forum Calendar.* January 8, 1998.
153. *Freedom Forum Calendar.* September 7, 1998.
154. *Freedom Forum Calendar.* March 9, 1998.
155. *Freedom Forum Calendar.* April 17, 1998.
156. *Freedom Forum Calendar.* March 6, 1998.
157. *Freedom Forum Calendar.* September 2, 1998.
158. *Freedom Forum Calendar.* May 31, 1998.
159. *Freedom Forum Calendar.* August 7, 1998.
160. *Freedom Forum Calendar.* April 25, 1998.
161. *Freedom Forum Calendar.* November 18, 1998.
162. *Freedom Forum Calendar.* June 11, 1998.
163. *Freedom Forum Calendar.* June 8, 1998.
164. *Freedom Forum Calendar.* November 9, 1998.
165. *Freedom Forum Calendar.* May 7, 1998.
166. *Freedom Forum Calendar.* April 29, 1998.
167. *Freedom Forum Calendar.* December 4, 1998.
168. *Associated Press Report.* February 15, 1998.
169. Cate, Fred H. *The Internet and the First Amendment.* Phi Delta Kappa Foundation. 1998. p. 31.

Chapter 16

1. Hohenberg, John. *Free Press/Free People.* The Free Press. 1973. p. 228.
2. Conference of Press Experts. *Final Report.* The League. 1927. 32 pp.
3. American Society of Newspaper Editors. "Report of the Committee on World Freedom of Information." *Editor and Publisher.* June 16, 1945. p. 5.
4. Schlesinger, Arthur, Jr. "Preface." *Censorship: 500 Years of Conflict.* New York Public Library. 1984. p. 7.
5. Hohenberg, John *Op. cit.* p. 400.
6. *Ibid.* p. 404.
7. Geyer, Georgie Anne. "Who Killed the Foreign Correspondent?" Red Smith Lecture in Journalism. University of American Studies. April 1996. p. 7.
8. *Freedom Forum Calendar.* January 6, 1996.
9. Associated Press Report of May 4, 1996.
10. Associated Press News Report.
11. Associated Press Report of May 19, 1996.
12. Orme, William. *Survey of World Press Freedoms.* Committee to Protect Journalists. C-Span. March 27, 1998.

SELECTED BIBLIOGRAPHY

Ambler, Effie. *Russian Journalism and Politics 1861-1881*. Detroit: Wayne State University Press, 1972.

Bennett, H.S. *English Books and Readers (1475-1640)*. Three volumes. Cambridge, MA: Cambridge University Press, 1965-1970.

Clyde, William M. *The Struggle for the Freedom of the Press from Caxton to Cromwell*. New York: Burt Franklin Reprinting, 1974.

Cranfield, G.A. *The Press and Society: From Caxton to Northcliffe*. London: Longman, 1978.

Dahl, Svend. *History of the Book*. Metuchen, NJ: Scarecrow Press, 1968.

Davis, G.R.C. *Magna Carta*. London: The British Library, 1877, pp. 9, 10.

L'Estrange, Roger. *Freedom of the Press, 1560-1681*. New York: Garland (Reprinting), 1974.

Febvre, Lucien, and Henri-Jean Martin. *The Coming of the Book: The Impact of Printing 1450-1800*. London: NLB, 1976.

Fisher, Desmond. *The Rights to Communicate*. Paris: UNESCO, 1982.

Fliess, Peter J. *Freedom of the Press in the German Republic 1918-1933*. Baton Rouge, LA: Louisiana State University Press, 1955.

Frank, Joseph. *The Beginning of the English Newspaper*. Cambridge, MA: Harvard University Press, 1961.

Freedom Forum Calendar. Arlington, VA: Freedom Forum, 1992-1997.

Garrison, Bruce, and Mildred B. Salwen. *Latin American Journalism*. Chicago: Erlbaum (LEA Communication Series), 1991.

Gillett, Charles R. *Burned Books*. Westport, CT: Greenwood Press, 1974 reprint.

Hachten, William, and Harva Hachten. *The Growth of Media in the Third World*. Ames, IA: Iowa State University Press, 1993.

Hachten, William A. *Muffled Drums: The News Media in Africa*. Ames, IA: Iowa State University Press, 1971.

Haight, Anne Lyon. *Banned Books, 387 B.C. to 1978*. New York: Bowker, 1978.

Hansen, Laurence William. *Government and the Press, 1695-1763*. Oxford, England:

Clarendon Press, 1936.

Hanson, Jarice, and Uma Narula. *New Communication Techniques in Developing Countries*. Chicago: Erlbaum, 1990.

Herd, Harold. *The March of Journalism: The Story of the British Press from 1622 to the Present Day*. London: Allen and Unwin, 1952.

Higman, Francis M. *Censorship and the Sorbonne*. Geneva: Librarie Droz, S.A., 1979.

Hohenberg, John. *Free Press, Free People: The Best Cause*. New York: The Free Press, 1973.

Inglis, Brian. *Freedom of the Press in Ireland, 1784-1841*. Westport, CT: Greenwood Press, 1985.

Kesterton, Wilfred H. *A History of Journalism in Canada*. Toronto: McClelland and Stewart, 1967.

Locke, John. *The Workes of John Locke*. (Nine volumes) London: C. and J. Rivington, 1824.

Milton, John. *Areopagitica* and *Of Education*. Oxford, England: Clarendon Press, 1973.

Myers, Robin. *The British Book Trade from Caxton to the Present Day*. London: National Book League, 1973.

Natarajan, Swaminath. *A History of the Press in India*. New York: Asia Publishing House, 1962.

Nordenstreng, Knark. *Mass Media Declaration of UNESCO*. Norwood, NJ: Ablex, 1984.

Papmehe, K.A. *Freedom of Expression in 18th Century Russia*. The Hague: Njhoff, 1971.

Parks, Stephen. *The English Book Trade, 1660-1853*. London: Garland Publishing, Inc., 1974.

Potter, Elaine. *The Press as Opposition: The Political Role of South African Newspapers*. London: Chatto and Windus, 1975.

Salmon, Lucy Maynard. *The Newspaper and Authority*. New York: Oxford University Press, 1923.

Schulte, Henry F. *The Spanish Press 1470-1966*. Urbana, IL: University of Illinois Press, 1968.

Shaabar, Matthias A. *Some Forerunners of the Newspaper in England, 1478-1622*. Philadelphia: University of Pennsylvania Press, 1922.

Siebert, Frederick S. *Freedom of the Press in England, 1476-1776*. Urbana, IL: University of Illinois Press, 1952.

Smith, Anthony. *The Newspaper: An International History*. London: Thames and Hudson, 1979.

Steinberg, S.H. *Five Hundred Years of Printing*. London: Faber, 1959.

Sullivan, Alvin, ed. British Literary Magazines. (Three volumes). Westport, CT: Greenwood Press, 1983.

Symonds, R.V. *The Rise of English Journalism*. Exeter, England: A. Wheaton and Company, Ltd., 1952.

Todorov, Dafin. *Freedom Press*. Prague: International Organization of Journalists, 1978.

Weiner, Joel H. *Radicalism and Free Thought in Nineteenth Century Britain. The Life of Richard Carlile*. Westport, CT: Greenwood Press, 1983.

Wickwar, William Hardy. *The Struggle for the Freedom of the Press, 1819-1832*. London: George Allen and Unwin, Ltd., 1928.

Writers and Scholars International. *Index on Censorship*. London: Volume 25 published in 1995. Previous volumes available.

Zeisel, William, ed. *Censorship: 500 Years of Conflict*. New York City Library, 1984.

INDEX OF PERSONS

INDEX OF SUBJECTS

About the Compiler

LOUIS EDWARD INGELHART is Professor Emeritus of Journalism at Ball State University and has been a champion of press freedom for at least fifty years. His most recent book is *Press and Speech Freedoms in America, 1619–1995: A Chronology* (Greenwood, 1997).

ISBN 0-313-30851-9

HARDCOVER BAR CODE